PORTAGE

Also by Sue Leaf
Published by the University of Minnesota Press

....

The Bullhead Queen: A Year on Pioneer Lake
A Love Affair with Birds: The Life of Thomas Sadler Roberts

A FAMILY, A CANOE, AND THE

PORTAGE

SEARCH FOR THE GOOD LIFE

SUE LEAF

UNIVERSITY OF MINNESOTA PRESS
MINNEAPOLIS · LONDON

Published by the University of Minnesota Press
111 Third Avenue South, Suite 290
Minneapolis, MN 55401-2520
http://www.upress.umn.edu

A Cataloging-in-Publication record for this book is available from the Library of Congress.

ISBN 978-0-8166-9854-7 (pb)

Printed in the United States of America on acid-free paper

The University of Minnesota is an equal-opportunity educator and employer.

20 19 18 17 16 15   10 9 8 7 6 5 4 3 2 1

For Tom, who reads the maps, carries the canoe,
and runs the rapids with me

How much more I notice the touch of things! The smooth paddle in my hand, the shock of cold water on my face, the texture of rough sticks and pine cones.

—Florence Jaques, *Canoe Country*

Contents

Prologue

IN THE BEGINNING, A SILVER STREAK

....

IN THE DAPPLED SUNLIGHT UNDER THE WHITE PINE, I LAY gazing over the surface of Lake Alexander, a sandy-bottomed lake in central Minnesota. The summer sun had bleached the colors of the afternoon. The water appeared metallic, the opposite shore a dusty green. Waves lapped docilely against the dock extending from the shoreline. The world was drowsy. It was mid-August, a good time to daydream, book in hand. I was ten years old.

As my eyelids were beginning to droop, I heard voices wafting up from the water, and I looked down at a sleek boat moving swiftly, heading west toward the bay. It seemed to glide effortlessly, the gentle wash of the water offering no resistance to its prow. There were two people, each with a paddle, one in the bow, the other in the stern. They chatted with low voices. I could hear laughter rising.

I was mesmerized by the ease at which the slender craft slid forward with each stroke. At ten, I had begun to row our old aluminum rowboat up and down the shore in front of the cabin. My mother sat in the stern as I placed my skinny frame between the oarlocks and took up the wooden oars. Rowing was not as easy as it looked. The oars had to be moved synchronously and pulled on with the same intensity or the boat would veer left or right. It was not immediately intuitive which oar to employ to move the boat back into alignment. The rower sat facing the stern and had to keep peering over a shoulder to gauge progress. It seemed hit or miss at first whether I would truly end up where I intended to go. The oarlocks creaked with each pull, and if I hauled them into the boat, they banged on the bottom with a thunderous clatter.

But I loved the sense of buoyancy, the opportunity to be on the water, away from the land, to smell the lakey fragrance of fresh water and green plants. I loved the autonomy, somewhat akin to that of pedaling a bicycle. I had a new Schwinn that summer, and it gave me the same feeling of adventure and exploration that I had with the rowboat. My world was widening.

I recognized the sleek gunmetal boat as a canoe, of course I did. Most schoolchildren, especially Minnesota schoolchildren, knew about canoes, the craft the Native Americans once employed to skim across the water. Native Americans made their canoes of birch bark. I had pondered this as I peeled thin white strips from the birch trees that grew near the cabin. So light, so papery—the wispy bark seemed impossible material to form a boat that could carry people. I tried my hand at fashioning a miniature canoe from bigger pieces of bark, cutting canoe shapes and lashing them together with needle and sturdy thread.

I hadn't ever seen a canoe in action before. Never on Lake Alexander. It slipped so silently through the water. If I sat in that canoe, I thought, I could look into the interior of the lake. Lake Alec's water was crystal clear. At the drop-off in the bay, you could see a long way down. It would be so quiet that the sunfish and minnows would not flee. I could watch them, admire the yellow bellies of the pumpkinseeds, catch the cyanic flanks of the bluegills. With a canoe, I thought, I could become one with the water.

At the end of the bay, there was a culvert leading to a winding channel that connected Lake Alexander with Fish Trap Lake. Through the culvert's aperture, I could see flowers blooming amid cattails, white blooms with pointed green leaves, pink domes with feathery edges. I wanted to see them up close, to be in the midst of them. The rowboat was too wide and too clunky to navigate the culvert. A canoe would slip right through and carry me into that marshy world.

I began pestering my parents for a canoe.

. . . .

My parents didn't get me a canoe. They didn't seem to have the need to interact with the lake. My dad, not a skilled angler, spent early mornings before breakfast fishing for panfish in certain holes in the lake. We owned a small Evinrude motor that was adequate to propel the rowboat across the water when he didn't feel like rowing. My mother seldom went in the boat. She was fine with supervising my rowing sessions, but she donned a bathing suit only on the warmest days. She was actually afraid of the water, I think. Afraid of having her face submerged.

Earlier that summer, our family had driven to the Colorado Rockies. My parents wanted their children to see the mountains. The alpine wildflowers spread profusely on either side of the highway as our Chevy Bel Air labored over the mountain pass. I wanted desperately to get out of the car and examine the tiny, colorful flowers up close, but we had not stopped. Neither would we, on a later trip, hike into the Grand Canyon. We would remain on the rim, a safe distance from the edge, and peer into its depths. We were always spectators—of the lake, of the mountains, of the canyon—and did not participate in scenes I found beautiful.

After enduring endless hours of swimming lessons at home in suburban Roseville, Minnesota, shivering in the shallows of McCarron's Lake and Lake Owasso, I taught myself to swim one summer by borrowing a library book and taking it down to our dock on Lake Alexander. Splaying out the pages, I read how to coordinate the front crawl and practiced until I got it. I went on to the back crawl, the breaststroke, the sidestroke. I swam up and down the shore. I swam out as far as I dared and back. I made my parents nervous with my increasing skill.

Friends at the east end of Alexander had a small Sunfish sailboat. I donned a life jacket and went sailing with the kids. (I'm not sure my mother knew this.) I was fascinated by the sensation of being propelled by the wind, the quiet speed, how the shoreline raced by. A fast crowd sailed those Sunfishes. The son of a local judge lived next door, and he sometimes joined us. The impression was enforced by the fact that my mother considered the father of these kids to have been "fast" in high school. So there was a certain ca-chet to sailing. Now I wanted a canoe *and* a sailboat.

When I was fourteen, in what I thought was an extraordinarily unfair turn of events, our neighbors down the street, kids who had been my friends since we were toddlers, got a canoe. They didn't even have a cabin and a lake on which to paddle it. They had to tie the canoe to the roof of their old, green Chevy station wagon and haul it to one of the city lakes to use it. True, this might have been the rationale for getting a canoe in the first place: they had no cabin. Also true, they had been to the YMCA's Camp Widjiwagan and learned how to handle a canoe, all the strokes: the J stroke, the draw, the cross-bow rudder. Bobby, my age, might even have been able to flip it and carry it on his shoulders.

The Itos' canoe was Minnesota-made, a shiny Alumacraft. It had a triangular orange-and-blue patterned stripe decorating its length, running under the gunwale. I thought it was beautiful. As far as I could tell, it was perfect. It was a canoe!

One Saturday in July, as the hot air shimmered off the pave-ment, the Itos organized an outing and invited me along. They were headed for Lake of the Isles in Minneapolis. We would be gone all afternoon. Mr. Ito had packed a book and a lawn chair and would spend the time on shore, but Bob and Joanne and I could paddle about to our heart's delight. I rushed home to change into my swimsuit and get permission.

I can still hear my father's voice. "Oh, I don't know, Susan Jean. That sounds like not a good idea. Too dangerous. Those canoes are tippy. What if you capsized?"

"I can swim," I pointed out. "I'd wear a life jacket. The Itos have life jackets. They're required by law."

"Yes, you can swim," he countered. "But can you swim in deep water? No, no, you can't go. It's just too dangerous."

My temper flared. This made no sense! The Itos weren't fool-ish. They were very smart, in fact. All sorts of people paddled ca-noes without fear, without endangerment. I was not going to lose this opportunity. "Well, I don't care. I'm going," I declared. I walked from the living room through the kitchen and out the back door, the screen door banging behind me.

As I walked the block to the Itos', I had passing trepidation. I had never done anything like that in my fourteen years. I had defied my father in all sorts of small ways, chafed under his protectiveness, questioned the rules. Always, there had been consequences and rather quickly at that. I had never just walked out before. But I knew what I knew: that I had the skill to be on the water, that normal people went out in canoes every day, that risk was involved in everything one does. I didn't want to be a spectator to my life.

What amazes me even now is that this time there were no consequences. No one yelled when I got home. No one clobbered me. I wasn't grounded. I lost no privileges. My parents and I must have reached a kind of détente that day, an unspoken agreement that they were going to let me live my life on my own terms—or at least that they realized they were limited in controlling me.

Looking back, I now see that the initiatory paddle on Lake of the Isles had been my entry into a new way of living. No longer would I be a spectator from the backseat of a car or the front porch of a cabin. With a canoe, I would immerse myself in nature, in the glories of the world. Years later, I would seek a mate who also wanted to live this way, and we would experience the world together. We would teach our children to be fully present in life, to not just watch.

How fortunate we sometimes are, the blind and naive young who operate without the benefit of experience. I realize now that I myself had been a canoe that day, cutting with ease through the water, swiftly gliding into my future.

The Pictographs on Lac La Croix

INTO THE BOUNDARY WATERS, 1979

....

"I'LL ALWAYS TURN TO THE NORTH!"
That first line of Florence Jaques's book *Canoe Country* intoxicated me at age twenty-six. I agreed wholeheartedly. My definition of "North" was expanding. Until my late teens, North had been my family's cabin on Lake Alexander in central Minnesota, nestled under towering white pines. The pines were few, though. Most had been cut in the great deforestation that took place in Minnesota in the nineteenth century. The second-growth woods surrounding the cabin were mixed deciduous forest, with plenty of red oak and ash. Yet it was woodsy, and there were loons, and it was north of the Twin Cities.

But then, when I was eighteen, my boyfriend introduced me to the Boundary Waters. The lakes on the border of Minnesota and Canada were bottomless, their waters stained mahogany with tannins. Balsam fir needles, crushed underfoot, scented the cool air. There were high cliffs, and there were diminutive plants on the forest floor. I learned about bunchberries, with scarlet clusters of fruit; tiny pink twinflowers, which also grew in Sweden and were beloved of Linnaeus, the famous botanist; and wintergreen, whose fragrance wafted clean and minty when you scraped the leaves with a fingernail. Loons on the border seemed wilder than those of my childhood. Their thin wails careened in the black nights.

There was a fight about whether powerboats, providing ease of travel, should be allowed in a wilderness area. Angry meetings, wilderness advocates hung in effigy, and demonstrations filled the evening news. Residents of Ely, Minnesota, thought outsiders had no business setting regulations on lakes that their parents and grandparents had fished. Wilderness advocates recalled John Muir and Aldo Leopold and saw this struggle in the light of past debates. In several senses of the word, the Boundary Waters were unsettled.

The boyfriend had a family cabin on Fall Lake, at the edge of the Boundary Waters, and we employed a canoe to enter the alluring wilderness at Pipestone Bay of Basswood Lake. In a few years, I joined a group of professors and fellow students from college in weeklong camping trips on big lakes near Grand Marais, and since then I had visited what I now considered the "true North" every year. In the same way I had once thought that a two-week vacation at our family cabin kept me sane, I now considered the Boundary Waters my sanctuary. The spires of black spruce, the wintergreen underfoot, the Canadian Shield were all keepers of my serenity.

At twenty-six I was newly married, not to the boyfriend with the Fall Lake cabin. One of the unspoken requirements I had had in a husband was that he share with me an inclination to true North, the boreal forest. Also, that when he went canoeing or camping, he would take me along. I wasn't interested in a marriage where I would sit home while my husband went out to the woods with his buddies and had fun.

When we were still dating, my "pre-husband" and I had taken a short trip into Henson Lake, a small cruciform body of water off the Gunflint Trail. I had viewed the jaunt as a trial of sorts: could I live for four days in a tent with this guy? My only memory of the trip was waking in the middle of the night to the sound of a banjo being loudly plunked very close at hand. "Go back to sleep," the pre-husband, Tom, groggily instructed. "It's just a turtle." I later discovered it was not a reptile at all but a green frog, *Rana clamitans,* which courts prospective mates in July with the enticing call.

Herpetological knowledge aside, my man passed the test. He could flip a canoe and carry it on his shoulders over mile-long portages. He owned a tent, and his father owned a canoe. We had at our disposal several sturdy canvas Duluth packs, looking identical to the pack Lee Jaques had sketched on page 20 of Florence's *Canoe Country.* Furthermore, our cook kettle, a wedding present, looked like their cook kettle, sitting next to the pack on page 20. These resemblances thrilled me. Tom and I were of substantial means, I thought. We never rented anything from an outfitter. And I, not a buddy, was the paddler in the canoe's bow.

We threw ourselves into the fight to preserve the wilderness quality of the Boundary Waters. Our guru, Sigurd Olson of Ely, had craftily enlisted young people in the effort, speaking on college campuses and visiting environmental learning centers. I had met the guru one winter term and had been mesmerized by him. We cheered when, in the first year of our marriage, legislation was passed by Congress that crafted a compromise that limited the use of motors to certain lakes. We would have preferred that the wilderness area be treated like every other wilderness area in America—no motors at all—but given the resistance of the northern communities, this seemed the best we could hope for.

At twenty-six, the irony of the situation was lost on me: that a place so soothing, so healing, could be the cause of so much turbulence. I didn't realize then that the furor sprang from the same well—a passion for what people on both sides saw as holy ground. But I got the reality. We joined the Sierra Club reflexively after the wilderness legislation was passed, in reaction to a primary election that a cynical businessman won on antiwilderness rhetoric. We didn't put a bumper sticker on our car, though. Bad things happened to cars trumpeting those kinds of sentiments.

....

"I'll always turn to the North!" When Florence wrote those words, she, too, had come under the spell of the Boundary Waters. She and her artist-husband, Lee, had spent three magical weeks on the boundary lakes Crooked and Lac La Croix. They were very big lakes, with more exciting attractions than lesser trips. Crooked Lake had Curtain and Rebecca Falls, two well-known waterfalls, and both lakes claimed pictographs on shoreline cliffs. Pictographs, not uncommon in the Boundary Waters, are aboriginal paintings of animals and of human hands, often telling a story.

The Jaqueses had made their trip in 1936, during the Great

Depression. They had taken a train from Duluth to the town of Winton on Fall Lake, and had paddled from there. They started out on August 25, after organizing their packs in Duluth, where it had been so cold that Florence, a Manhattanite, wore her fur coat. The Boundary Waters had not been formally designated a wilderness area in 1936, but it was more wild then than at present, and it was already under threat of development: schemes to run a road through its heart, to allow Model Ts access; plans to dam the border lakes for hydroelectric power.

I wanted to do the Jaqueses' trip with my husband! Having a husband was still a novelty to me. But I knew what it was like to paddle with a partner, a romantic partner, a life partner in the stern; to take the portage paths, working together as a team; to feel the solitude with a lover by your side.

The trip we planned in 1979 was not our first that summer. In late May before the leaves came out, we had taken a quick trip with Tom's brother and father and a Swedish friend who had not experienced a wilderness before. We had paddled into Caribou Lake off the Sawbill Trail and set up camp for several days. It had been short and oddly bright without leaves on aspen and birch. The men had gone fishing.

This trip would be different. We planned ten days in mid-July. The flies might be bad—would be bad—but Tom had vacation time he needed to take before the end of the month. We couldn't wait until August. It was not by chance that the Jaqueses made their trip at the end of the summer: the bugs are gone by August, and the water is still warm enough for swimming. Lee Jaques knew these things.

....

I kept a journal during that trip, like Florence, both of us being incurable scribblers. When I think back on those ten days now, I remember it as a time of summer warmth, skinny bodies, little clothing, and no sunscreen, of course. Our twenty-six-year-old skin would never wrinkle or develop cancers. In 1979, you could drink the water straight from the lakes without filtering or purification—there was no risk of giardia—and we did. We brought along Wyler's powdered lemonade to mask a supposed "lakey" taste, and Tang, used by U.S. astronauts, for breakfast.

Florence included a list of provisions that she and Lee had taken on their 1936 trip, and lemonade powder was on it (but not Tang). The list intrigued me, because it seemed so elemental: four pounds of dried beans, three pounds of apricots, three pounds of prunes, ten pounds of flour, for starters. Unlike Tom and me, who were barred by federal law from carrying any throwaway containers into the wilderness area, the Jaqueses could take cans, and so their list included three cans of Crisco, one can of veal loaf, and one can of corned beef. There were no plastic bags in 1936, and they packed each item into a little cloth bag.

We, on the other hand, brought along boxed meals like macaroni and cheese, instant potatoes, and Rice-A-Roni. Sausage keeps without refrigeration, so we included hot dogs and ring bologna. We also packed in fresh oranges, apples, carrots, and celery.

Our food pack did not become appreciatively lighter as the trip went on, though. July 1979 was so hot we ate very little after a long day in the sun. Instead, we drank copious amounts of water from our canteens, lay on our sleeping bags in the tent, and nursed sunburns and shoulder muscles sore from long days of paddling. The tent's screen protected us from mosquitoes, which whined loudly on the other side, sounding like an orchestral string section. Big blackflies "were horrendous," I wrote. "They swarmed about, as many as fifty at one time on one pack, or on our backs." We chose campsites on points that jutted out into the water, hoping the distance from land would help us catch a breeze and reduce the flies and mosquitoes. Sometimes it did.

Crooked Lake is a pleasing lake to paddle. It is long and narrow with a succession of bays, each one named for a day of the week: Thursday Bay, Friday Bay, Saturday Bay. We paddled the entire length of the huge lake on a hot, steamy day with scarcely a breeze. When we looked over the water from the canoe, the shoreline appeared hazy. We kept metal cups out of our packs by our seats in the canoe and dipped them into the lake from time to time to keep hydrated. When we arrived at Saturday Bay, we found an island campsite and decided to set up camp. Out in the middle of the lake, we would enjoy any breeze there might be.

Florence recounted acquiring a penchant for island campsites on their trip after encountering a fellow canoeist on a portage trail who told her that islands were safe from wolves. Up to this point, Florence hadn't worried about wolves, but now she did. On past trips, I hadn't gravitated toward islands, either, but now Florence whispered in my ear as we set up the tent on the island on Crooked Lake: no worry of wolves on islands! In 1979, I did not worry about wolves. There weren't many around. In fact, I'd have loved to have seen one. But I was concerned about black bears. Every night we strung up our food pack high in a tree, to thwart the bruins from raiding our food cache. But maybe we would not have to do so on an island, I mused, as I set up the tent.

With that thought, I looked up and discovered, to my amazement, a small black bear twenty feet from me, edging her way over to our number two Duluth pack, the one with the cheese and sausage and peanut butter. I yelled and ran over to Tom, reconsidered and ran to the equipment pack, pulling out the fry pan. Using a tent stake I still clutched in my hand, I beat a loud tattoo on its underside and screamed directions at the bear: Go! Shoo! Get out of here!

The bear peered at me uncertainly, crept back into the woods behind the campsite, and disappeared. Tom and I studied each other's faces wordlessly, then pulled down the tent, piled it in the canoe without packing it, buckled our packs, and loaded up. We realized that campsite was already taken. Thirty-five years later, I think of the bear on Saturday Bay whenever I fry eggs on a camping trip and see the sharp indentations left by a tent stake on the bottom of the pan.

We came to Curtain Falls the next day. It is one of two waterfalls demarcating Crooked Lake from Lac La Croix. Its bountiful waters spill over a rock ledge in a silky, broad stream, hence the name. It is a notably good place to fish, and we encountered a score of anglers, all men, dropping lines below the falls. I was acutely aware that I was the only woman on the portage. I didn't stop to reflect that it was a consequence of wanting to be the paddler in the bow when my husband went on canoe trips. We moved on up the portage and arrived at Rebecca Falls, a more narrow but no less lovely cascade. There was no one there, so we pulled out our trail lunch, which was the same every day: cheese, sausage and crackers, a handful of gorp (raisins, peanuts, and M&Ms), and Wyler's lemonade.

At Rebecca Falls, a family of some type of weasels were swimming. They looked too mean to be otters, and I studied them through my binoculars. They were clearly babies, bobbing about in the water, clambering onto adjacent rocks, watching us curiously and hissing. They all had buffy patches of fur on their chests, and we decided they must be martens, which we had never seen before.

The portage around Curtain and Rebecca Falls led us into Lac La Croix, another large border lake. The eastern shore of La Croix is Canadian land, and we stayed to the U.S. side, though in 1979, neither country was too concerned about casual visitors. It was another hot day, and we decided to lay over when we reached La Croix. We both suspected we had suffered heat exhaustion the day before, nursing queasy stomachs and slight headaches. We drank quart after quart of water from our canteens.

We had arrived late to Lac La Croix, but the next day, we lounged about, doing camp chores and swimming, jumping off massive rocks into clear, reddish water. We had not worn our suits for swimming up to this point in the trip. Even camped on La Croix, a major route, skinny-dipping was the order of the day. Naked as jaybirds, we leapt from rock ledges into the water and marveled at how the tannins turned our pale northern European skin the color of ripe apricots. The campsites were secluded, and we saw no one. Had the Jaqueses gone skinny-dipping on their trip, or were they too modest and proper? Florence didn't say.

We went fishing close to suppertime, and I caught a two-foot northern pike, the biggest fish I had ever landed in my abbreviated, modest experience as an angler. After that triumph, I learned that my spouse, my woodsman spouse, was not sure how to fillet it, nor did he want to.

We had seen Crooked Lake's pictographs, and I had been entranced by a cunning little heron painted on the imposing cliff rising high over the water. Lee Jaques had immortalized this cliff in several paintings: one set in summer, with canoes passing underneath the pictographs; one wintery, with snow blowing across the face of the rock, as a line of caribou saunters by. Lac La Croix also has pictographs, very human ones. Hundreds of year ago, men dipped their hands in some kind of red umber dye, some compound containing iron, and splattered their handprints about the wall. I could imagine doing the same thing myself, and the recognition made me laugh out loud. I raised my hand and splayed my fingers—the hands were about the size of mine. La Croix also had a small geometric man and several moose with perfect little rumps, painted skillfully by someone with a good eye.

The Jaqueses had picked blueberries in early September, the last of the summer's, when the leaves were already flamed with scarlet. On our July trip, Lac La Croix gave us the season's first blueberries. We crawled out of our sleeping bags at dawn to gather enough for blueberry pancakes—we must have packed buttermilk powder along, as well as dried milk. The thought almost makes me nostalgic now. These days, Tom and I seldom fuss over pancakes, especially while canoeing. We eat a no-nonsense bowl of oatmeal and consider it a frugal feast.

Our last days of the trip were spent paddling through Lake Agnes and Nina Moose Lake, past the Little Sioux burn of 1971. Tom and I were very interested in the aftereffects of the burn. We clearly remembered the fire that occurred the summer after our high school graduation. Our last campsite was in the burn itself. A few pines that had escaped the fire's fury edged the site, but behind it, blackened skeletal trees towered, the remains of old white pines that had perished. I called it "a graveyard of one of the loveliest organisms on earth."

Federal wilderness status for the Boundary Waters meant that fires were allowed to burn without hindrance. The area is prone to fires. In fact, years ago, a forest ecologist with the University of Minnesota, Myron Heinselman, studied the forest's proclivity to fire and determined that the ecosystem was "edaphic," that is, dependent on fire for its unique plant and animal community. Tom and

I understood this and fundamentally agreed with the "let it burn" philosophy, but the desolate, blackened hills of Nina Moose—eight years after the fire—made the camp a somber one. Nevertheless, as I bent over the Coleman stove that night, checking on the evening's stew, I looked up to see a slender doe stroll casually past our tent, nibbling on grass and little aspen seedlings that had sprouted after the fire. The deer was living proof that the aftermath of forest fires attracts wildlife.

"A happy, happy time," I wrote in my journal when we got home. "We were together and away from everyone else. We missed Skylab [which fell to earth when we were on the trail] and forgot about the Energy Crisis and the price of gasoline."

We made other trips into Minnesota's Boundary Waters in the years that followed. We wedged in short trips between rotations of Tom's medical residency program, or when I was off of school, without research to do or labs to teach. We went in the fall, when the nights were long and we crawled into our sleeping bags before eight o'clock. We went in the winter, when we skied on frozen lakes and untracked portage trails. We never found the time to take another extended trip, though. Ten days off never came again. We referred to our memorable paddle along the border lakes as the Grand Tour of the Boundary Waters, taking in all the classic sights.

Each time we returned to the wilderness area, we found the sanctuary we sought. Nights were black, unlike nights on Selby Avenue in St. Paul, which were continually lit with a pinkish glow. The air was cool and smelled like pines. Quiet reigned. We could hear ourselves think and were aware of our beating hearts. Above all, we experienced solitude, that delicious sense of being only two in the world, a primal man and woman together, Adam and Eve.

There may have been discussion in those days of what defines a wilderness, but we didn't think too hard about definitions. If asked, we probably would have said it is a place that is devoid of civilization and doesn't have a lot of people, where there were dark nights, quiet days, and clean air and water. No hand of man marring the beauty.

But then, in our early thirties, we had children, and we didn't visit the Boundary Waters for ten years.

Locked In

....

ON A HAZY, HUMID SUNDAY AFTERNOON IN JULY, WE CROSS the suspension bridge and pull on to Nicollet Island above St. Anthony Falls in the heart of Minneapolis. The summer so far has been rainy. Thunder and lightning rend the nights. From the look of the sky, things could be revving up again.

But Tom and I are buoyant, optimistic twenty-eight-year-olds. Violent weather won't happen this afternoon. Storms will hold off long enough for us to spend a few hours on the river, enjoying the summer heat and its lushness. We revel in nature where we can find it these days: along East River Road as we pedal to the university or in our tiny backyard behind our apartment building in a St. Paul neighborhood.

Tom and I have not been out on the water as much as we would have liked. He is a second-year resident at Fairview Hospital on Riverside Avenue and seldom gets time off. This July, he is on an obstetrics rotation, on call every third night, and asleep, dead to the world, every night after. Following a call night spent at the hospital, and a full day in clinic, he staggers home, eats supper, and falls into bed. Every third evening, he leads a normal life.

I am a graduate student launching a research project and fretting over methods, money, and job prospects once I finish. I also do all the household chores.

Nonetheless, we are young and full of energy. Tom plans diversions for his precious hours off. Unable to head out of town for an idyllic trip, we have decided to explore the river in our own backyard: the Mississippi River through Minneapolis. Our drop-in point is Nicollet Island, once verdant with sugar maples.

Sugar maples are tidy, restrained trees, not graceful like white pines, but beautiful in their own right. I try to imagine what a sugar bush on Nicollet Island would look like, but alas, the island's maple grove is long gone. When it flourished, it attracted a specific bird community. Yellow-and-black Evening Grosbeaks feasted through the winter on dried maple seeds. Bohemian Waxwings and Yellow-bellied Sapsuckers took in the sweet sap when it ran in the spring. Yellow-rumped Warblers gathered in great numbers, perhaps attracted to the insects that swarmed in April around fuzzy maple flowers.

The maples were cut early and gave way to swanky houses in the 1870s. The island became home to some of Minneapolis's elite. Over time, the neighborhood became poorer. As a teen, I recall Nicollet Island harboring a hippie enclave. The faded elegance of the frame houses lent a kind of luster to well-tended gardens, shabby fences, even a little pet donkey, staked in a side yard.

Today we will put in on the south end in the island's former business district. A sash-and-door company once flourished here near sawmills that provided its raw material. It has recently been turned into a new, ritzy hotel and restaurant, the Nicollet Island Inn. There is a city park directly adjacent, from which we will launch.

We are paddling our trusty seventeen-foot Grumman aluminum canoe. Purchased secondhand from an outfitter in Ely for Boundary Waters trips, it is dented and ever so slightly leaky but utterly indestructible. And that is good, because our first hurdle of the afternoon will be St. Anthony Falls, the only waterfall on the entire length of the 2,320-mile river.

No, we are not going to shoot the white water—what an idea. Not even cheerful twenty-somethings would consider that. Nor will it be a portage. I can't even think exactly how that could be accomplished with the present-day banks of the river through downtown. We are going to be transported via Upper St. Anthony Falls Lock and Dam, an immense structure of concrete and steel that will lower us to Lower St. Anthony Falls Lock and Dam, and from there, we will make our way down a scenic urban river to Hidden Falls, on the St. Paul bank, where we will disembark.

Our short time on Nicollet Island is memorable. The river flowing past is swift and carrying debris from last night's storm. In particular, I distinctly see strands of toilet paper float past. It winds through the branches of broken tree limbs and flutters gently with the current. Although in the coming decades, the Twin Cities will invest a large amount of money to separate storm sewers from sanitary sewers, in 1981, storm sewers can swamp the sanitary sewage treatment ponds, causing raw sewage to enter the Mississippi after heavy rain.

We launch our canoe into the dark, dubious water.

It's a quick paddle to the lock. There's a thick, floating rope lining the way, a warning to boaters that there is danger beyond it. The lock, we have heard, will open for a lowly canoe. Owned by the federal government—us—it is utilized both by commercial traffic and recreational boaters. But we won't be the only ones today. As we approach, a speedboat with a big outboard motor roars up, carrying six people in sun hats and swimsuits enjoying a Sunday afternoon. The gates of the lock are open. A barge, also headed downriver, hugs its west side. We follow the motorboat in.

The interior of the lock is snug. The speedboat in front of us has about four or five feet of wiggle room, our sleeker canoe a little more. We nestle next to the gigantic barge, which rises a dozen feet or more above us. A worker on the barge drops us a heavy knotted rope to hang on to. This is perhaps a safety measure, but for the life of me, I can't see how it is protective. What if the barge shifts? *Would* a behemoth like that shift? And how sturdy would a Grumman canoe be if it became squeezed between a barge and a lock wall?

When we enter the lock, we are at river level. The structure seems something like a safe harbor, a place to park on the waterway. But then heavy steel gates clang shut behind us, and we immediately hear a mechanical grinding and a rushing of water. The sound is everywhere at once, in stereo. The walls of the lock seem to rise. Up and up they go, or rather, down, down, down we go, as we hear water pouring out from the lock. I feel smaller and smaller, like Alice, shrinking. The drop in all is forty-nine feet, 10 percent of the entire descent of the Mississippi from Minneapolis to St. Louis.

In hardly any time at all—the Army Corps of Engineers is as businesslike as you would expect—the towering steel gates in front of us begin to move, swinging inward. Beyond we see again the green banks of the river and the second lock we need to pass through to avoid St. Anthony Falls.

Upper St. Anthony Falls Lock and Dam was constructed in 1963 to enable barge traffic to proceed upriver from the falls. It has seen its commercial use decrease in recent years. Decades later, more goods are shipped by rail and truck than barge. But although its use is declining, I can't imagine the behemoth lock and dam being removed. The Minnesota Department of Natural Resources has considered taking down certain small dams on some Minnesota rivers, but the numerous locks and dams on the Mississippi have turned the powerful river into a series of managed pools. They created such irreversible devastation, it is hard to envision their dismantling.

It's not as if St. Anthony Falls—once revered by Native Americans for its beauty and spiritual significance—was pristine when the upper lock and dam went in. The desecration to this Native holy site began early in European settlement, with the first mills that built Minneapolis into a world breadbasket. It continued with an ill-conceived attempt to tunnel from Nicollet Island to the west bank under the falls, leading to near collapse of the bedrock in 1869. Numerous attempts to shore up the collapsing limestone over which the river spills involved the U.S. Army Corps of Engineers and various dam builders. Work continued through the 1870s to 1885 when a steel cap over the bedrock was completed. It remains in place to this day.

What we cannot know in 1981 as we experience the locks firsthand is that thirty-five years into the future, the upper lock will be seen as an ecosystem savior. In the early twenty-first century, the mighty Mississippi will be threatened by an aggressive set of invasive species known collectively as Asian carp. The carp, escapees from fish farm operations in the southern United States, will successfully make their way upriver to St. Paul, threatening native fish populations and even jeopardizing the pleasure of a simple boating trip. The fish (it is hard to imagine this, but try) spring with force from the water when disturbed, and people have been injured by flying fish. They also voraciously outcompete native fish for food. To prevent them from invading northern Minnesota via the Mississippi, Upper St. Anthony Falls Lock and Dam will be permanently closed—the barrier to further invasion will clang shut.

Below the two locks and dams, the urban river is astonishingly scenic. The limestone-capped gorge of the Mississippi is wooded and untouched, save for the paths carved by a century and a half of human feet. Green parkways top the bluffs of both Minneapolis and St. Paul.

That Tom and I and all river users see trees and shrubs and not mansions on those bluffs is due to the vision of early movers and shakers of both cities. Chicago landscape architect Horace Cleveland spent intermittent time in the Twin Cities beginning in 1872, when he delivered a speech in Minneapolis on the importance of green space in urban areas. People were so enthused by his ideas that he repeated the talk in St. Paul two days later. Cleveland's relationship with the Twin Cities stretched over decades, as he prepared a park plan that encompassed the Minneapolis lakes, and recommended that Lake Como be made into a St. Paul city park. It was Cleveland who drew the attention of urbanites to the Mississippi River. He considered it a "jewel" and saw its valley as a way to ventilate the polluted air of the growing industrial city. The steep-sided channel would be the lungs, providing fresh air and health to city residents.

After an hour's paddle and one last lock at the Ford Dam, we beach the canoe at Hidden Falls, another city park, which is described as having "wilderness quality" with a "primitive" area. Lovers of Minnesota's northland may scoff, but it is amazing that those are words that can even be considered in conjunction with a park less than five miles from either downtown.

Our urban paddle is at an end, a brief escape into nature. How odd to see it that way, when we have experienced the industrial prowess—the massive concrete of locks and dams—with which it coexists. We felt that prowess personally in our vulnerable, unprotected bodies, when we edged our canoe into those locks.

Yet the green world has a force of its own, exactly represented as a grass shoot sprouting through a sidewalk crack. It calls to us, this verdant mother earth, and we hear it, we are hungry for it, beleaguered as we are by the demands of our schooling. Our vacation time will be one short week in August. If we need restoration at other times, we will have to seek it in abbreviated whiffs.

Canoeing the Spirit River

THE RUM, 1986

....

THE RUM RIVER WANDERS THROUGH THE ANOKA SAND-
plain of east-central Minnesota, sand deposited as outwash from
a melting glacier. Expansive Lake Mille Lacs, a remnant that lingers after the melting of the last glacier, is its shimmering source.
Leaving the big lake, the modest waterway runs 151 miles back and
forth through riverbanks edging farmland and remnant oak savannah before emptying into the Mississippi River at Anoka.

The name "Rum River" conjures up rowdy drunkenness, or at
least, a river running dark with tannins. The clear stream is badly
misrepresented by the appellation. The Mdewakanton Sioux considered both the river and Mille Lacs a sacred presence, a mystical
spirit. In a profane mistranslation, this view became an early fur
trader's idea of a spirit: distilled alcohol. How different would our
view of Lake Mille Lacs and its walleye population be today if we regarded that big blue lake as sacred, rather than a "natural resource,"
something to be used? Instead, we wrangle over how many fish and
of what size can be taken in a summer, always with an eye to consumption, not reverence.

The Rum River, though, is not a site of contention. Devoid of
rapids because it flows over sandy, flat topography, the Rum is surprisingly wild in appearance, running past banks lush with deciduous
shrubs and trees. Wildlife thrives. We have encountered river otters
in family groups and dozens of birds during summer floats down
the gentle Rum. Here and there the tall silhouette of a white pine
emerges from the canopy, a reminder of other ravages of east-central
Minnesota. White pines thrive in sandy soil and were thought to be
limitless. Most were cut a century ago and have not regenerated.

From the family photo files, I pull out classic Kodachrome slides labeled "Canoeing the Rum, Oct. 1986." Tom has captured on film a large outing we made one Sunday in autumn. Fifteen people are assembled in one photograph, two holding wooden paddles, smiling at the camera. They are our nearest and dearest—Tom's parents, in their sixties, our siblings and their spouses (or lack thereof, some not having yet entered the family fold). My girlfriend Paula with a halo of 1980s hair; Tom's swimming friend Gary with the young woman who is not yet his wife. And the V.I.P. guests of the expedition, our college professor Vic Gustafson and his wife, Betty, who had driven 120 miles to join us. Another photo with nearly as many people shows the Gusties—Gustavus Adolphus graduates—and I note at least two generations represented and possibly three if one considers a very young Vic teaching Tom's mother in 1948 the first generation. My mother-in-law is canoeing on this day with her former college professor.

In the years after the Boundary Waters trip on the border lakes, Tom and I finished our educations, started work, and began a family. We have two children. Andy and Katie are ages four and two and are at home with a babysitter. I am barely pregnant with our third child. In the photo, I am smiling but feel sicker than a dog.

We are incredibly young. We look impossibly thin. The women have perms, the men have hair, and in every picture, everyone is smiling.

It is hard to remember the days in which we plied the waters in large, moving groups. Tom and I began our canoeing life traveling in great assemblages like this one. It is how we learned to canoe and camp. Vic Gustafson, an outdoor education teacher at Gustavus Adolphus College, taught canoeing and camping courses—for which we got a physical education credit, good toward a baccalaureate degree—and led Gustie canoe trips into the Boundary Waters after graduation each May. I first met Vic on a January term course where thirty students camped in the Sonoran Desert for two weeks. Tom's acquaintance with Vic began in the swimming pool, with Vic as his coach. Vic accompanied the dozen or so swimmers on training trips to Florida. We of the baby boom generation came of age traveling en masse.

Vic and Betty were immensely good company and always up for a canoe trip. We felt honored that they made an effort to join us on the Rum, arriving with their Grumman canoe, christened the "Grandma II," on top of the car. In 1986, both were in their seventies. Eventually, they would relinquish canoes. Vic would later complain of being too arthritic to sit very long in one place. But in the photo taken on a sunny, cool fall day, they still appear vigorous. Betty has on hiking boots; Vic is wearing camping khakis. Staring at the photos, I can imagine him bustling about a Boundary Waters campsite, quick and squirrel-like, burrowing through Duluth packs, clanging the cook kettle, putting the percolator on to boil after revving up the Coleman stove—as if Vic needed caffeine.

Tom had planned this trip on the Rum, a short two-hour paddle from a landing near Cambridge to a take-out point at Isanti, both communities in Isanti County. The stretch is only seven and a half miles, but it was a complicated trip to organize. We needed canoes, paddles, and life jackets for fifteen people. We had to figure out how to shuttle cars, how to fit everyone into the least number of vehicles. Some, like Vic and Betty, had their own canoe and perhaps even a spare to offer. Others rented or borrowed craft. All this had been worked out in advance.

We had had a stretch of rainy weather that fall, so we were pleased to have Sunday dawn clear and bright. Duck hunters were out on the Rum. They did not pose a threat—seven floating canoes do not look anything like mallards—although the hunters in their camouflaged duck boats were probably not excited to see (and hear) our approach. The hunters had placed decoys on the water, anchored in place so they didn't move downstream. To my birding eye, the sight of these dummies afloat, nicely painted but without the glint of life, was bizarre. They reminded me of department store mannequins, only more disconcertedly lifelike. The hunters waved good-naturedly at us as we paddled past.

Three of the fifteen paddlers on the Rum River that day are now dead. Vic died just a few years ago at age ninety-four. The rest of us have matured nearly past recognition. Our children are the ages that we were when we congregated for the camera that preserved the image on Kodachrome. But the spirit of the Rum River, the mystical communion that we have with the departed, comes to me anew in the reds and blues of the jackets and jeans, the scarves and sweatshirts of the long-ago paddlers. The colors are vivid and bright. I can almost hear Vic twang in the early dawn, "All right you campers! Arise and shine!"

Missouri Breaks

THE UPPER MISSOURI RIVER, 1993

....

THE DRIVE ACROSS MONTANA HAD BEEN STORMY. PERIODIC rains lashed the car. We were happy we did not have our canoe strapped to the top. Tom had located an outfitter in Big Sandy, Montana, a few miles from the Missouri River, who agreed to rent a canoe and shuttle us to and from the waterway. The gas mileage on our little Honda Civic plummeted when we carried a canoe, and rental seemed a way to save money.

We planned to paddle a section of the river called the Missouri Breaks. This area of central Montana is still pristine short-grass prairie. It was mid-June, and the grasses would be new and green. We anticipated a somewhat exotic trip in an unfamiliar landscape, a landscape we had seen only from an automobile. We had never canoed a western river before.

For the first time in a long while, we were traveling sans children. In fact, Tom and I had not taken a canoe/camping trip in a decade. It seemed like we had been immersed in the care and feeding of babies and small children forever. But our fifteenth wedding anniversary was later in the month, and we had decided to celebrate it with a short, three-day trip on this magnificent river. We had left our four kids, ages three through ten, at home with their grandparents. Everyone was well pleased with this arrangement.

The year 1993 marked the 190th anniversary of the start of the Lewis and Clark expedition. They called themselves the Corps of Discovery, charged by President Jefferson to explore the land the United States had recently acquired in the Louisiana Purchase. Starting in St. Louis, the corps had ascended the Missouri River, poling laboriously against the current, before crossing the Rockies and heading for the West Coast.

To jog our memory about Lewis and Clark, we brought a copy of the journals they kept during the long expedition, and read them out loud as we drove west. Meriwether Lewis had been very moved by the beauty of the Missouri Breaks, which we would soon paddle through. The high, white cliffs of the Breaks lined the river, descending to a broad, grassy floodplain on which grew tall cottonwoods. Gleaming like alabaster in the sunlight, the rock had been eroded into fantastical shapes that reminded Lewis of ancient ruins. " As we passed on," he noted in his journal entry of May 31, 1805, "it seemed as if those scenes of visionary enchantment would never have an end."

We arrived at Virgelle, a tiny town marked by a single building, the two-storied Virgelle Mercantile, in late afternoon of the second day. It was as close to a ghost town as one could find and still be inhabited. This was to be our drop-in point.

The sun had not appeared once all day, and rain seemed imminent. No one at the outfitters nor the mercantile had mentioned a weather forecast. We had hoped for a sign, some word, on whether to begin a trip when the likelihood we would get wet was high, but the oracle—and the Montanans—was silent.

Since our time on the Missouri River was limited, we thought it best to get under way. We could sit out a night of rain. Our trustworthy tent didn't leak. And so, under leaden skies and a howling tailwind, we launched our canoe into the swift waters of the longest river in North America.

The first hour on the Missouri *was* a scene of visionary enchantment. Although the river was broad and steely under the dark sky, the birdlife we saw was breathtaking. The Charles M. Russell National Wildlife Refuge protects the area, keeping it as remote and untouched by the hand of man as it was in the time of the Corps of Discovery. Our canoe approached pair after nesting pair of White Pelicans, snowy against the gunmetal water. Western Grebes, long necks arched, swam past in pairs. They seemed delicate compared to the more common Canada Geese. We seldom saw any grebes up close, and this species was particularly graceful. Dozens of swallows swooped overhead, skimming the water for insects.

There was a fine mist in the air. It came on gradually. A gray sky seemed to slowly metamorphose into water droplets. At first we were too engrossed in the birds and the river to take much notice. The current of the Missouri was very fast. It was the swiftest river we had ever been on, and we felt we had to pay attention. The banks slipped quickly past us. We seemed to be making uncommonly good time.

When I noticed that my bangs were wet, I reached for my poncho and put it on, the loose folds flapping noisily in the wind. Tom donned his too, a blue one he had owned since college. It was getting old, and now on the Missouri, he discovered it leaked. He wore a hooded sweatshirt underneath it for warmth, and water found its way in through the leaky seams. Tom was usually fussy about waterproof seams—he fastidiously tended the tent—so it was odd that he had not considered the poncho.

It commenced raining in earnest, and we began to comment on the wind. Had it picked up, or had we just not paid attention? A stiff breeze blew from behind, shoving the canoe ever more quickly downriver. At times the wind came in gusts, and then the aluminum craft felt buffeted about and very fragile.

At some point, we asked ourselves what we were doing. From the look of the sky, this was not a passing shower. It was time to stop, set up the tent, and make camp. We suddenly felt a sense of urgency, cast about for an appropriate site, and chose a grassy spot at hand, taking care to steer clear of cottonwood trees. We had been warned that in high winds the brittle boughs of cottonwoods snap off and cause terrible damage.

Beaching the canoe on the grassy bank, we unloaded the packs and dug about for the tent and the ground cloth, which would keep the floor from getting damp. Then we set about staking the tent floor. To our consternation, this proved a difficult task. Our fingers had become so stiff from cold that they wouldn't take orders from our brains. Laboriously, we laid the ground cloth and staked the four corners anchoring the tent. Next, our clumsy digits tried to make sense out of the aluminum poles that provided the framework. The cold metal bled away whatever heat remained in our fingers. The wind, at high gale, whipped the tent fabric as we tried to grasp the hooks that would connect the poles to the nylon.

So slow, so slow. Tasks that normally took seconds unfurled into minutes. Which way did the arrows point on the plastic tubes fastening the ridgeline pole? If we got this wrong, the frame wouldn't fit together. Why didn't the elastic cords slip easily over the poles? Had we misread the arrows?

We shouted instructions to each other.

"I can't get the band to slip over the tube!" I yelled to Tom.

"Do first one, then the other! OK, now grab the fly!" he yelled back, as he attempted to lob the protective shield to me.

The wind blew our voices faint. Now the tent was erect, but the driving rain was soaking it. We needed to get the waterproof fly on in double time. Our hands worked at a snail's pace. The fly snapped smartly as we strove to hang on to it.

"Clip it!" Tom mimed, pointing to a hook and its anchoring point.

"Done!" I replied back. There! It was fastened to the ridgepole, and we bent over to secure it to the frame, and then to stake it taut.

Shivering and rattled, we grabbed sleeping bags from the packs and threw them into the tent, and tucked the remaining gear under a tarp outside. Tom turned the canoe over, making sure it would be out of the way of a rising river, and then we both crawled into shelter.

In the dim light of the tent's interior, we saw that another disaster awaited us. It had taken so long to attach the fly that rain had puddled onto the floor of the tent, and the sleeping bags were now partially wet. I was shaking from the cold, but I could see that Tom was shivering more violently. His sweatshirt was sodden. I was wearing a ratty old rag sweater that, being wool, afforded me some warmth. When the worst of my shaking subsided and we had caught our breath, I ventured outside again to paw through the packs for a towel and for some food.

Once more in the tent, I mopped up the water; we unzipped

the bags and crawled in together. Tom's inability to stop shivering alarmed me. I was, in truth, terrified. We had never been in such dire straits before, and I wondered how we had let ourselves get into such a state. We had four children at home! Neither of us was hungry, but we forced ourselves to eat. We tore off chunks of sourdough bread, cut pieces of cheddar cheese, and took great handfuls of granola.

Long ago in a college physical education course, we had watched a film on hypothermia. Up until that time, I had never thought much about it, or had cause to. Our prof, Vic Gustafson, had shown the film to all his camping and canoeing classes to prepare his students for a time when they would be in a situation just like the one we were now in. In the film, hikers were caught in the rain, its effects intensified by a wind. The hikers modeled what to do: find a place of shelter, don dry clothes, and crawl into a sleeping bag with another person. And eat—high-calorie foods, like cheese or peanuts or chocolate.

All of which we did. Tom got rid of the wet sweatshirt and T-shirt under it, found some wool to put on. Though the bags were wet, they weren't soaked all over, and we were able to avoid the wettest spots. Our efforts at recovery took an hour, two hours. I have no recollection of looking at a watch. Time was irrelevant.

Outside, the storm did not abate but seemed rather to worsen. The wind screamed from four directions, and the walls of the tent were sucked in and out, as if at any moment it would be lifted off and borne away on some wild gale. There was no possibility of a formal supper. We were hoping only to survive the night.

Once the specter of death by hypothermia seemed past us, we two sat wordlessly in the gathering dusk, listening to the ferocity of the storm and mentally planning the next step if the shivering returned or if the tent went down. I thought about how I would locate a flashlight, put on my boots, and don my sodden poncho, which was wadded up in a ball in a corner of the tent. I thought the shivering probably wouldn't return unless we exposed wet skin to the wind again. I intended to be very protective of my core.

Sometime before midnight, I fished out the flashlight, wiggled into my poncho, and went out to relieve myself. The white cliffs could not be seen in the stormy dark. I heard the cottonwoods creak and groan off in the distance, but other sound was lost to the shrieking of the wind.

Sometime even later, we fell asleep listening to the wind and the tent buckling and rebounding under its fury. When we woke, the storm had passed, and the sun was shining.

I blinked in the bright light of morning as I crawled from the tent. Off to the east, striations of storm clouds hugged the horizon. Looking about, I could see we had pitched the tent about five hundred feet from the base of the white rocks. They rose up eroded and craggy, every bit as impressive as Meriwether Lewis had described them. A line of cottonwoods grew on a ridge between the tent and the cliffs; clumps of sage clustered on the ridge as well. The tent itself was on flat, grassy terrain, which must flood annually, discouraging the grow of woody plants.

The wind still blew, and we took advantage of it and the sunshine to dry out our wet gear. Tom strung up a clothesline between two cottonwoods to hang up ponchos, wet pants, socks, shirts, jackets, and pack liners. Across the overturned canoe we draped the tarp, sleeping bags, and Duluth packs and set out damp boots, the lantern, and everything else.

Sunshine makes all the difference! I set up the stove amid the prairie grass and prepared breakfast, the fare we had not had the night before: lentil and rice soup . . . and rhubarb sauce and cocoa. Tom fished out the maps and figured out that we were camped directly across the river from Lewis and Clark's campsite of May 31, 1805. The party had taken its boats out at this point, the Missouri's confluence with Eagle Creek, after a day spent struggling upriver in cold water up to their armpits, towing their craft. Lewis remarked on the many sharp submerged rocks that cut the crew's feet, the slippery mud, the breaking of a towrope—their best rope, of hemp— and the near loss of gear. The two captains had rewarded their men, who "bear it without a murmur" (Lewis wrote) with a dram of whiskey as a reward, "which they received with much cheerfulness."

We received *our* reward—lentil soup—with much cheerfulness, too. Sitting on the grassy riverbank, I spooned in the thick, nourishing soup, intent on refueling. It was a novel breakfast menu but savory and hearty. I ate, feeling driven to prepare for whatever lay ahead. Now that we knew what this remote region of Montana was capable of, I remained on edge and anxiously scanned the blue morning sky for any hint of bad weather. In the short time since we had emerged from the tent, rain clouds had crept up out of the west.

As I enjoyed the unconventional breakfast, I reflected on what had saved us from the storm. In large part, it was good planning and common sense. We always use plastic liners in our Duluth packs, so the gear remained dry. I am mindful to wear wool for warmth (or today, polar fleece) because it keeps the body warm even when wet. We made sure the tent didn't leak before we started out, and Tom had the experience and skill to anchor that tent in any storm against any wind. And we always pack a ground cloth to prevent the floor from getting soaked. Lastly, we plan high-calorie meals, some of which can be eaten without additional preparation in a pinch, and we are aware of keeping the body core dry to retain heat.

We had gone wrong, I decided, by underestimating the cooling effect of a Great Plains wind. This trip was our first beyond the northern woods of Minnesota. There, trees ameliorate much of the force of the wind. We had never lived through anything like that fierce storm. We had read a pamphlet titled *Some Hazards on the Upper Missouri National Wild and Scenic River* that the Bureau of Land Management had sent us when we planned the trip, which mentioned violent thunderstorms and hypothermia. But being from Minnesota, a severe weather state, we found it hard not to just say, "yeah, yeah, yeah." We really had to experience it for ourselves.

We were both enthused by the location of our campsite. We had hoped to camp at some of Lewis and Clark's original sites. Historians long ago identified all of them and marked them on maps. In 1805, the party was working its way slowly upriver, preparing to portage around the great falls and then to traverse the challenging Rockies before winter. We weren't exactly at the site—in our haste to get out of the storm, we didn't take that into consideration—but we could see the site across the river.

Tom and I both love American history, especially that little-studied aspect American natural history. We constantly try to imagine the North American continent before Europeans began altering it in massive ways. This intrigued Thomas Jefferson, too. He designed Lewis and Clark's military expedition—chiefly, an undertaking to further commerce—to be many things: to explore the Missouri and other major waterways with an eye to making a link between it and the Pacific Ocean; to make usable maps of the unexplored region; and to become acquainted with the American Indian tribes that called the area home, detailing their lives and possible avenues of trade with them.

Beyond that, Jefferson was exceptionally interested in natural history. He wanted to know about plants and animals, fossils and volcanoes, soil types and land formations. Before the expedition, he sent Lewis to Philadelphia to study under the foremost botanist in the United States, to learn how to preserve biological specimens and to label and describe them. He also spent time there with the country's authority on fossils, who had discussed the possibility with Jefferson that the expedition might encounter mastodons on the prairie. Lewis himself had prior knowledge of natural history. His mother had been an herbalist, and Lewis had gleaned from her a fair understanding of native plants and their medicinal value.

One of the pleasures of reading the journals written by Lewis and Clark, and several of their men, is to find out what they thought was novel, beautiful, or fearsome. At the Eagle Creek campsite on May 31, 1805, Lewis encountered "the most beautiful fox in the world," "a fine orange, yellow white and black." He thought it might be a different species than the red fox he was familiar with. The party saw bighorn sheep in this area and described them for Western science for the first time. They also had recently encountered the fabled grizzly bear for the first time and taunted it. The bear's response subdued any further interest in engaging grizzlies.

The storm had postponed our plans to be aware of the Corps of Discovery as we passed by landmarks of their trip. We had taken a little detour into survival, but now, in the sunshine, we recalled our initial interest, with a greater appreciation of the rigors the valiant party endured.

Despite the sunshine and our enthusiasm for Lewis and Clark, the storm had unnerved us. Mindful of those four young children back in Minnesota, we decided that the Missouri wilderness was not a good place for parents. We agreed to end the trip. Tom unfolded the Bureau of Land Management map that we were using to navigate, and we searched for a suitable take-out point near us. How could we best get off this river? We scrutinized the map. The answer was, we couldn't. There appeared not to be a road, a ranch, or a take-out of any kind along this stretch of the Missouri. Our previously planned end point, the Judith River, was the only way out. We were committed to the adventure.

....

Clouds that raced across its face, driven by the unrelenting wind, soon obscured the rising sun that had so cheered us. Shadows shot across the alabaster cliffs that towered high on either side. It was still a tailwind, however, and the canoe fairly flew down the Missouri. As paddlers, we felt superfluous—the canoe would reach our destination whether or not we dipped a paddle. Lewis and Clark had also felt the effects of the wind along this stretch, although for them it was a hindrance, since they were trudging upriver. "The wind was hard against us," Lewis noted in his journal on May 30, 1805. Rain showered them in spurts that day, and they detected snow mixed in at higher elevations.

I kept glancing over my shoulder at the point in the sky where the weather came from, but the rain held off. We chose a broad, gravelly bank for lunch, just below the Pablo Rapids. From the red Coleman cooler, which served as a lunch table, we pulled cans of Coors beer, originally intended for last night's supper, to enhance a simple trail lunch of Thuringer, cheese and crackers, and apples. Tom later wandered off to take pictures, and I sat back to enjoy the view. There was a bend in the river, and arid, denuded hills rose all around. The white rocks were a distinctive, textured band through the high banks. There were no trees save for the magnificent cottonwoods growing at the foot of the cliffs, near the Missouri.

Despite persistent anxiety over another storm, I birded all the way down the river, binoculars slung around my neck. The speed of the canoe at five miles per hour (we estimated the river flow at that) made it hard to focus on anything long enough. At one junction, though, the identification was clear: an unmistakable Golden Eagle soared high above, circling a formation our map called Eagle Rock. Knowing the Golden's fidelity to its nest site, I wondered if it were possible that this particular bird was a descendent of the eagle that gave the promontory its name.

Our luck held. No rain fell, and we stopped for the evening at the Slaughter River campsite where Lewis and Clark rested on May 29, 1805, and where Lewis also returned on his trip home, July 29, 1806. The gruesome name derived from the pile of rotting buffalo carcasses that the men had passed immediately downriver from the camp. Clark estimated the number of dead animals to be about a hundred. Lewis was more explicit in his account, describing the "mangled carcasses" and an "immense pile of slaughter" that created "a most horrid stench." He thought the destruction was a result of an American Indian hunt that used a man as a decoy to lure a herd over the cliff in order to gain fresh meat. In this manner, he noted, "the Indians of the Missouri destroy vast herd of buffaloes at a stroke."

It is true that Plains Indians did conduct hunts this way, particularly before they obtained horses, guns, and metal arrowheads, though at this site, the country atop the bluff was not conducive to a buffalo stampede. Scholars now think that the animals drowned in the Missouri upriver and floated to this point. The slaughter, of course, was not near the same magnitude of the millions killed by American market hunters just a few decades later.

The corps observed scavengers hanging around the mound of decay. Clark wrote of a "great number of wolves . . . about this place and very gentle." He killed one with his spear.

The day in 1805 had, in fact, been filled with bison encounters. The two captains both noted that the night before, a large buffalo had crossed the river and charged through their campsite "with great force," its deadly hooves coming within a few inches of the sleeping men's heads. The burning campfire had not deterred it;

the animal seemed to become more agitated as it swerved from one obstacle to another. It had all happened so quickly, the sentry did not have time to give an alarm. Lewis's dog "flew out" and barked madly, causing the beast to veer away, leaving the men "all in an uproar with our guns in our hands," as Lewis wrote later. The only casualty was a rifle carelessly left outside. Lewis was relieved the damage had not been greater.

We found the campsite was lush and grassy with beautiful cottonwoods and long-dead driftwood to use as benches. Overhead flew Bullock's Orioles, the western counterpart to eastern Baltimore Orioles, no doubt nesting in the high boughs. Wild roses grew in waist-high thickets near our tent. As I bustled about starting dinner, I heard an unfamiliar, garrulous bird chattering from the interior of the thicket. It proved to be a Yellow-breasted Chat, a bird I had long pondered but never seen. It displayed a great repertoire of utterances, singing high, singing low, a maniacal Robin Williams of a bird.

As I performed the homey domestic kitchen chores, chopping broccoli and setting instant rice to boil, the sun came out, flooding the world with cheery light. Serenity settled around the camp like a silky shawl. What a stark contrast to the terror a mere twenty-four hours before.

The white rocks section of the Missouri River, the "Missouri Breaks," is still among the most remote anywhere in the western United States. We had seen no evidence of any human being since leaving Virgelle, no one on the water and not a trace on the uplands, no roads, no cattle—although cattle do graze here—no fences, no structures. I imagined it had not changed much in the almost two hundred years since Lewis and Clark passed through.

The awareness of isolation such as we were experiencing remained a constant presence. In the golden light of sunset, amid the sweet scent of wild roses and the melodious call of birds, it seemed a secret pleasure: we were all by ourselves!

But in the tumult of the storm, as lightning flashed and the wind tossed the cottonwood boughs, shrieking with intensity, it inspired stark fear: we were all by ourselves!

What isolation really did is to pull back the curtain of protection that the presence of other people seemed to afford us, and it showed us that we are, in truth, actually alone in this world. Even if we fool ourselves into thinking there is safety in numbers, in having people around, the idea is illusory. There is no guarantee that they would be there when needed, or that they would know what to do, or that they would even come to our aid.

This was a reality that the men in the Corps of Discovery lived with every day. There was no one "out there" to rescue them from bad decisions. They had many life-and-death moments, and it is those that readers of their journals remember best: the first, unwise encounter with a grizzly bear; the equally unwise skirmish with Blackfeet Indians on the way home. Every day they must have felt both the unease and the pleasure of being wholly on their own.

This was not an experience we had hoped to capture in planning our short time on the Missouri, and yet, there we were, life pared to its essence in two short days.

. . . .

The next morning we arose and prepared to break camp. We had arranged to meet the outfitter at noon at the mouth of the Judith River. There was a boat landing there and a road running down to the water's edge. The road would take us back to Virgelle, our car, and the sparse settlement of central Montana.

I was interested in seeing the Judith. It marked another campsite of the explorers. They came upon this tributary in late May. They noted honeysuckle bushes in bloom and bighorn sheep accompanied by half-grown lambs—"fauns," as Clark would have it. Clark had walked up the river along the banks when the corps first encountered it and named it "Judith" after a young woman back home, whom he would marry in 1808.

The outfitter was chatty when he arrived.

"That was quite a storm we had the other night," he observed, making conversation. "Where'd you guys hole up?"

When we told him, his eyes widened. "You were out in it?" Silence, then.

We hauled the canoe out of the river and on to the outfitter's truck. As he strapped the canoe to the roof, the outfitter spoke again. "I can't believe you guys were out in the storm!" We left the Missouri's valley and gray skies. The ever-present wind hinted that rain might blow in later.

Breaking in the New Canoe

THE KETTLE RIVER, 1994

....

LET ME ADMIT UP FRONT THAT ANY RIVER THAT HAS A stretch known as Hell's Gate will not be my first choice of waterways to paddle. This would also be true for those boasting of Devil's Cauldrons, Devil's Kettles, Devil's Tracks, or even a Dragon's Tooth. In the same way that it does not matter to me whether a snake in the vicinity is poisonous or nonpoisonous, any river that has an inclination to white water is suspect. So someone must have been talking pretty fast when I agreed to paddle the Kettle River one Sunday in July, taking along our four precious children, ages eleven, nine, seven, and four.

We took two canoes on this jaunt. The youngest was finally old enough to paddle, somewhat, and able to swim, somewhat. We now planned canoe outings with all four kids. We had bought a new, lighter-weight, seventeen-foot Old Town Penobscot canoe earlier in the summer. Made out of green high-tech Royalex, a type of plastic, it weighed only sixty-five pounds, a full ten pounds lighter than our aluminum Grumman, which was built like an airplane and was nearly as indestructible.

In June, we had launched the Old Town in the clear waters of the Big Fork River in northern Minnesota. The trip on this summer's afternoon would be our second time out with all six of us. I was still learning to handle the Old Town. It seemed to slip sleekly through the water, and I was still becoming accustomed to paddling in the stern, after a decade of being the bowman. I *knew* how to paddle in the stern. The paddler in the stern steers the canoe, and I knew all the strokes. I just wasn't used to being the one in charge.

On the Big Fork River and now on the Kettle, Tom took the tanklike Grumman with Katie, age nine, in the bow, and the two little ones sitting side by side amidships. Andy and I paddled the new Old Town. He was eleven and strong, and the Old Town, so the reasoning went, was maneuverable and slipped easily over submerged rocks, of which the Kettle has many. So the deficit of my being at the stern was equalized.

Canoeists consider the Kettle to be one of the prettiest rivers in Minnesota, a state that has many gorgeous little rivers. The source for the eighty-four-mile river is in the bog streams of Carlton County. As the waters collect, the river flows south through Pine County into the St. Croix River. It tumbles over rock ledges and around big boulders, rapids and riffles creating a delightful river to paddle in a canoe or kayak. Water levels can change dramatically, because it is mostly dependent on water from its tributaries, not from underground springs, so the challenge to paddlers changes, too. Sometimes rocks are exposed, sometimes the same ones are hidden, and in high water, those very rocks pose no threat at all.

The Hell's Gate section of the Kettle—a section that kayakers love for its thrills—was farther upstream from the stretch we intended to canoe. Our trip was on a fifteen-mile portion from Sandstone to Hinckley. We put the canoes in directly below an old dam erected across the river in 1908. A year after our trip, in 1995, the Minnesota Department of Natural Resources would remove this dam, and the entire length of the Kettle River would once again be free-flowing. (Give a little cheer here for the removal of dams!) But when we dropped our two canoes in, the dam was in place. Tom assured me the rapids we would encounter were all fairly tame. Furthermore, he would go first and show me the safe path through them.

We had not been on the river more than ten minutes when we came upon our first set of rapids. They looked intimidating to me, though they were categorized as a Class I, the easiest ones. Class I's do not have standing rocks, are simple to run, and as the guide book says, "The risk to swimmers is slight." But, of course, the class categorization changes with water level.

There were two ledges to this rapids. Andy and I watched Tom and crew hang up on the first ledge. Tom got out—the water was shallow—and steadied the canoe. His passengers, the midcanoe duffers, clutched the gunwales for dear life, their blond heads yellow in the sunlight. Katie waited expectantly in the bow, paddle in hand. Water thrashed and foamed all around them. Then Tom pushed the Grumman over the second ledge, which was a drop of a foot and a half, and everyone continued to the end of the white water, dry and exhilarated.

Now it was our turn. We knew that the aluminum Grumman tended to catch on submerged rocks where the plastic Old Town did not. So I thought perhaps we would have an easier time of it. Andy and I cleared the first ledge like pros (I thinking, Ha! Royalex!) and then, on the second ledge, we flipped. We flipped in less time than it would take to snap one's fingers. What I had thought was a chute had proven not a very good chute. The canoe veered to the left, Andy was tossed to the right, and I followed, with just enough time to grab my day pack, which held my binoculars and bird book. Hats and paddles headed off downstream.

We had life jackets on, of course, and tried to gain some footing, but the current was very swift. Andy, hanging on to the canoe, as he had been instructed, disappeared momentarily under its flank, and from my perspective, he seemed to be wedged underwater between the stern and the rock ledge. As we struggled, the power of the river roared about us, water rushing by, spraying high over standing rocks, a force that could not be denied.

I shoved the canoe to free Andy. My maternal alarm seemed to afford me ferocious strength. The Old Town slipped downstream a few yards away, lodging between two boulders. At least we would not have to chase it. We managed to plant our feet and stand upright, and think about what to do next. The tempestuous nature of white water doesn't lend itself to contemplation, but it is nice to have a plan.

Tom landed his canoe at the river's edge below the white water and waded back to aid in the rescue. The three children in the Grumman had watched in horror as their mother disappeared into the roiling river, and Tom later reported that Katie especially seemed traumatized. They then had great views as we pried the Old Town out of its trap, dumped out most of the water, clambered in and paddled about collecting the gear that still floated in the aftermath. It must have been quite a show.

Once on shore, we took stock of the damage. My binoculars were intact, but the bird book was soaked. I had two big welts and a gash to my leg; Andy suffered no injury, thank goodness, but of course, we were both drenched. We took off our T-shirts and shorts and wrung them out so they would dry faster. The July sun was warm, and we weren't cold.

Alas, the really wounded participant in the incident was our new Old Town canoe. Upon inspection, we saw that it now bore a deep crease in its port side, a scar that would be permanent. For the rest of its life, and perhaps for the rest of my life, there would be a lasting reminder of my ineptitude in running the rapids on the Kettle.

....

The younger children were not eager to go back on the river. They had nearly lost their mother! They had traveled in the Grumman as babies, wearing tiny life jackets, but we had taken them on calm lakes and never through rapids. True, they had shot the rapids with exhilaration, but Andy and I had not.

In many circumstances, though, it is impossible to abort a canoe trip, and this was one. The Rice Lake National Wildlife Refuge flanked the east side of the river; unbroken, privately owned woods bordered the left. We would have had a difficult time walking out, and we had canoes and gear to haul, as well. And then what? The car was over fifteen miles away.

So, we all collected our nerve and resumed paddling.

The Kettle continued its rough-and-tumble descent to the St. Croix. Soon we were upon the next set of rapids. Andy and I now shared a reluctance to have anything to do with rapids, but too bad! Down we plunged into them, the froth and the foam. Out we shot, safe on the other side, jubilant for having faced our fears and triumphed. We raised our paddles in the air, hooting in victory.

But when we eyed the third set of rapids, we were quite sure we did not want to tangle with them. They could be heard a long way off, a roar of power and substance. They were a Class II, but I was beginning to think the classification system was not very helpful.

These rapids were also in two parts. Tom and crew slipped through them with great skill. But despite the prior rapids, Andy and I had lost our confidence. There was a grassy side channel off to our right. We eased our canoe through it, and that took care of half the rapids. We then met Tom on the bank, who joined us and steered us through the second half. In a gesture of true devotion, he had landed his canoe and walked through a patch of poison ivy to meet us and pilot our canoe through. As it turned out, the last of these rapids looked more menacing than they really were. We could have run them ourselves and had a little thrill. As they say, no guts, no glory.

After this third set of rapids, the Kettle became quiet. We found a scenic picnic spot and realized that we were ravenous. No longer under pressure, I could appreciate the beauty of the few tall pines that remained along the river. The Kettle River runs through the heart of the virgin pinery that once grew in east-central Minnesota. I grow sad when I imagine what this pinery was like—two-hundred-foot white pines towering like royalty above the understory, if there was understory. In some areas, the pines were so thick that they cast intense shade. Little could grow in the half-light and thick pine needles that blanketed the forest floor. It has been said that a man could easily walk for miles without hindrance.

The mixed-woods forest that now shades its banks is second growth. After the pines were cut—and it was utter devastation, a clear-cut—loggers mounded slash of stray branches, extraneous saplings, and bark into huge piles. In September 1894, a dry fall, a roaring fire consumed the desiccated clear-cut and the slash. The towns of Hinckley and Partridge were incinerated, with scarcely a trace remaining. The heat was so intense it melted railway steel. Five hundred people died. Survivors along the river ran to the Kettle for protection. They submerged themselves as flames raced above them.

Sitting in the shade as we ate our picnic lunch, I told the kids the story of the fire, the roaring inferno that could be seen by townspeople from afar, how they raced to the river and used the hollow stalks of reeds as straws to breathe through. The tale was nearly incomprehensible to them and to me. Overhead, oaks and elms waved their broad, green leaves. How could there have been white pines here? How was it possible that they were then cut to mere stumpage, opening the land to sun and wind and ravaging by wildfire? And why did the people think of the river as a safe place? Wasn't the Kettle a scary river that just banged up our new canoe?

The story of the Hinckley fire would be a hundred years old in two short months. I anticipated a retelling of the heroism of the engineer who backed up the train into town and carried many to safety. Minnesotans would be reminded of the terror and the destruction of the heat and flames. But would the story include the human greed that destroyed magnificent trees, and the timidity of state government to rein it in? That's what I wanted my children to know.

"People make choices," I told the lunch eaters. "People make decisions, good or bad, and things happen. I made a bad decision at those first rapids. The river wouldn't have been scary had I done things differently."

The gash on the hull of the Old Town remains, reminding me to choose wisely.

But what remains after the Hinckley fire to remind Minnesotans of the importance of wise choices? Who remembers the pines and what happened to them?

Canoe Swarms

....

UNLIKE SOME OF OUR FRIENDS, WE DID NOT TAKE OUR children on overnight canoe trips when they were toddlers. We had a healthy respect for a wilderness area and worried about stumbling preschoolers. The kids learned to swim at an early age, but the images of those immense flat rocks at wilderness campsites, trailing off into unfathomable depths of water chilled me. I could too easily imagine an unguarded moment when the child was not in a life jacket and wandered off, hit a toe against a tree root, and fell noiselessly into the water, unnoticed. Or I thought about how cold northern lakes were, even in summer, and how quickly small bodies could cool off if they landed accidentally in the drink. Even a life jacket couldn't protect them from hypothermia.

For years, we vacationed with young children on sandy beaches on the south shore of Lake Superior. We bought a rough cabin on Superior's south shore, in cutover woods of aspen and birch. It wasn't boreal forest, though, and I continued to hear the echo of that first line from *Canoe Country*, "I'll always turn to the North!" in the recesses of my mind. When the kids could carry at least some items over a portage—the lantern, canoe paddles, the Coleman stove—we made plans to return to the Boundary Waters Canoe Area Wilderness. We took Grandpa Leaf, who could supervise fishing and help small campers set up a tent and organize gear. It had been fourteen years since we had made that idyllic trip down Crooked Lake and Lac La Croix.

Life for Tom and me had become complex to another order of magnitude in that decade and a half. On our first trip back, we took three grade-schoolers but left a younger, fourth child with

Grandma. Like Lee Jaques, Tom had very limited vacation time, but the Jaqueses didn't have children, so we had lost our 1930s mentors when we became parents. The children had camped and paddled a canoe before. We thought they could manage a simple, three-day trip into the Boundary Waters.

Tom studied our maps and planned an uncomplicated trip beginning on the South Kawishiwi River and involving a couple short portages, ending up at Lake Two. By going in August, we eliminated the worst of the biting flies and mosquitoes. We had seen the kids react to bites with big, puffy lesions, which they often scratched to the point of infection. We also hoped to tip the odds toward dry, sunny days.

The camping party set off in two canoes. Tom and I paddled with John, age six, as our duffer. Grandpa and Andy, ten, manned the other canoe, with Katie, age eight, sitting amidships. We used this arrangement for traversing the river, but once at the campsite, where the lake was calm, the kids went out together to explore. Both Andy and Katie had already been to summer camp, where they learned how to do a J stroke and canoeing skills.

We had to portage to get from Lake One to Lake Two, and as we approached the take-out, we saw a large number of canoes backed up, also trying to land and portage. The sight of multiple canoes swarming, as it were, around a landing gave Tom and me a moment's pause, but maybe this was to be expected in August on a popular route. We hadn't ever seen so many canoes together in one place in the Boundary Waters, but then it had been years since we had been there.

We were lucky to have perfect summer weather. All three kids wore life jackets when swimming—the water just offshore was way over their heads—and all three pursued casting fishing lines with gusto. We even enjoyed a fresh fish dinner one night, although this may have been due more to Grandpa's skill than anything else.

The trip was wildly successful. The kids loved camping, traveling by canoe, eating around a campfire, and sunning on the broad basalt rocks. There hadn't been any quarreling, as I feared there might be. Generally, everyone got along, but on occasion, a child could be grouchy and pick a fight with a sibling, or, conversely, two might play nicely together and leave the third one excluded and sobbing. The key to a pleasant trip, I think, was to keep them busy and tire them out.

Things went so well, in fact, that we planned another trip the following year. All the elements of what we had hoped the kids to experience had been present in the trip before: the sense of isolation, of wild beauty, of conviviality around a camp, playing cards, telling stories. The sense of northernness.

Once again, we felt we had to leave our youngest child with Grandma. She was only four, not yet a skilled swimmer, although she enjoyed day trips with us down the Brule River and the St. Croix. The older three were enthused about the trip: two short portages off the Gunflint Trail, with essentially three adults carrying gear for six people, into Caribou Lake for three nights.

Our plans changed as we picked up the permit to enter at the ranger station in Grand Marais: there was a nuisance bear in the Caribou Lake area, characterized by the ranger as "nasty." The animal knew the ins and outs of food packs and was not afraid of people. Clearly, this bear had seen a lot of humans. I thought back to our timid black bear on Saturday Bay in 1979 and our hasty retreat. A retreat with three children and a grandpa would not be hasty.

Our options to plan A were few, though. We had to enter at our assigned entry point because all fifty-some others were at capacity. So, studying the maps on the wall, we altered our route to avoid the bear and decided on one long portage into Crocodile Lake instead. Crocodile was a small, low-lying lake, a dead end to anywhere, but the attraction to it was the four campsites on its shores.

We were suddenly interested in the number of campsites because of the at-capacity crowd. We were amazed by this. The Boundary Waters plus the adjacent Quetico Provincial Park is a million-acre wilderness area. How could it be filled up? We had paddled through its heart, the most legendary lakes, fifteen years ago in the peak of the summer and hardly seen anyone. Where did all the people come from? How could so much change in fifteen years?

Then we recalled the canoe swarm at the portage from Lake One to Lake Two the year before.

The next day, we loaded up two canoes, assigning the youngest children as duffers, and set off for Crocodile Lake. We met a party at the portage trail, the only portage we would take. It was early in the morning, and they, too, were headed our direction, but they were intent on fishing and were aiming for the river at the far eastern end of the lake. We had more than idle interest in their activity and destination: they were possible competitors for a campsite on Crocodile Lake.

Confusion reigned at the portage, two sets of gear intermingling, try as both parties did to keep them separate. Tom and I anxiously kept track of our Duluth packs, the free-floating paddles, life jackets, stove and lantern, the kids' personal packs. Somehow, everything sorted itself out, and we reloaded and headed for our campsite.

By choosing a low-profile lake with no special claims to beauty (where in the Boundary Waters is it not beautiful?), no reputation as a muskie lake, and no waterfalls or pictographs, we were hoping for seclusion, to experience true wilderness with the kids once more. We wanted to see no mark of the hand of man. It was not starting out auspiciously, however. Frankly, the children saw fewer people at our cabin on Lake Superior.

We got lucky: there was a campsite for us on Crocodile. We had increased our odds for luck by reaching the site early, before noon. Later in the day, canoes would paddle past, looking for an open site, and there would be none. Had we arrived later, those unfortunate paddlers would have been us, and we would have had to retrace our steps over the portage and paddle on, in hopes of finding an unoccupied site on another lake.

The push to get off early distressed me. We couldn't dally on the portage, investigating the tiny forest plants, which I was sure would delight the children. We didn't have wiggle room to deal with a mishap, or to pursue something the kids found interesting. Somehow, there was an edge of pressure that I didn't like to have when on vacation. But perhaps there would have been pressure for me regardless. Just traveling with children, their needs often unpredictable, is stressful.

The children chortled at the Crocodile Lake campsite, and the boys immediately set about fishing, even though Grandpa advised them that midafternoon on a bright, sunny day was not the best time to catch fish. Katie was not interested in hauling in fish this trip, but took a puzzle to work on and joined them on the flat rock, to inspect the "pretty lures" and make small talk.

John, the younger son, was just learning how to cast, and I worried about a misguided hook landing in a sibling's eye. My brother-in-law, a surgeon, had recently told of encountering a camper in the Boundary Waters who had a fishhook impaled in his cheek. Luckily, the brother-in-law had tools in his tackle box to remove the hook.

I have good memories of the camping trip to Crocodile Lake. The first evening as we sat about a roaring campfire, we heard an odd little beeping coming from a spruce tree nearby. I got a flashlight and shone it into the sloping boughs. There, sitting close to the trunk, was a tiny Saw-whet Owl, bright-eyed and pert, blinking at the intense beam of the light. The kids were thrilled and so was I.

The next day, on a paddle to inspect the river, we witnessed a red squirrel hop into the water from a beaver dam and swim toward the shore. We watched, enchanted as the round furry head bobbed about in the water. Had we not actually seen the squirrel jump in, we would have passed it off as a young beaver. The squirrel worked its little paws in a dog paddle, holding its tail out of the water, possibly to prevent drag.

And the funniest incident I have ever experienced on any camping trip came one morning after a night of rain. I was presiding at the camp stove, scrambling eggs. The ground was damp with little bits of debris, spruce needles, twigs, and flakes of pinecones clinging to our shoes. Grandpa, dressed in his bright-yellow rain suit, was bustling about, fussing with coffee and eating utensils, somehow reminiscent of an oversized woodchuck. I handed him a plate of eggs, fried potatoes, and buttered bagel, and he sat down on an adjacent log to dig in. Alas, the log, slick from the rain, was not stable and slowly began to rotate in place. Grandpa tipped backward with it, his plate full of breakfast in one hand and a fork and cup of coffee in another. He could not put out a hand to act as a brake to stabilize the log, and he was loathe to ditch a hot breakfast, so he just rode that log all the way to the ground, until he rested supine with his legs in the air. He had kept the food on the plate, however, and the coffee in the cup—despite a howling audience that could not contain its mirth.

Even now, almost twenty years later, I can still smell the damp of the campsite, hear the comforting buzz of a working Coleman stove, and see my father-in-law reclining like a yellow marmot with that full plate of food. I get tears in my eyes from laughter even thinking about it.

The kids enjoyed the trip. Parents, hoping to give their children a significant experience, can never be sure exactly what their offspring will take away from the time. We had wished to give them the sense of a pristine wilderness, the blackness of the night, the silence of the woods, the feeling of isolation, smallness, and awe that people have when contemplating the universe and their miniscule place in it. Perhaps we prepared the ground in which a yearning for these things could flourish. The more immediate impressions, though, were of the little owl, detected by a flashlight, and of Grandpa in his bright-yellow rain suit. When I asked them recently about what they remembered, they pointed out that Grandpa also fell into the water from the canoe at the campsite.

Because they had no recollection of the Boundary Waters of twenty years before, the children were not disturbed by the filled-to-capacity wilderness. They didn't fret about whether we would find an open campsite on our destination lake. They weren't distressed by canoes off in the distance. They didn't see the deeply trampled portage paths and wonder how many boots had pressed down upon the soil, exposing the gnarled tree roots, and making the rocks seem to rise from below.

Tom and I, however, had felt all of these stresses. The image of the canoe swarm would linger in our memories for decades. We wondered how long the ancient portages, trails that had served the Ojibwe and voyageurs for centuries, could remain in use.

Kids Canoeing

....

IT LOOKED LIKE AN EXPEDITION ON PAR WITH LEWIS AND Clark. Our two canoes held two Eureka Timberline tents, six Duluth packs with six sleeping bags, pads, and clothing; also, a food box and equipment box with tarps, clothesline, tableware, matches, shovel, tub for washing dishes and two cook kits; assorted life jackets, seat cushions, cookstove, water jug, six paddles (two were spares), and four personal backpacks with amusements, one for each kid. We left the dog at home.

We would be gone for two nights.

Tom and I were embarking on what we hoped would become a tradition of family canoe trips. We had already taken three children on overnight trips. Now we would add the fourth, our family at full-strength until that time in what seemed like a distant future when the first one left home.

We had decided to launch on the placid Crow Wing River in central Minnesota. The Crow Wing was a perfect first river, Tom thought. It was without rapids, reliably navigable, and usually no more than three or four feet deep. There was a sandy riverbed and campgrounds maintained by Wadena County every five miles or so. We could stop and pitch a tent if rain threatened or the kids got cranky. The current was a calm three miles per hour. That meant that even if no one paddled, we would proceed downriver at that rate. The Minnesota Department of Natural Resources considers the Crow Wing to be one of the best rivers in the state for family canoeing and what they call a wilderness experience.

This tranquil waterway cuts through the heart of central Minnesota. It has its source in a unique chain of eleven lakes that act as natural impoundments that help to maintain the water level in the river. After leaving the lakes, the Crow Wing threads its way south through a sand plain past the town of Nimrod, and then east through Motley and Pillager before meeting up with the Mississippi River at Crow Wing Island near Brainerd. Ten thousand years ago, the newly formed river drained a retreating glacier. The sandy bottom is the remainder of Glacial Lake Wadena, pooled meltwater estimated to have once been 130 feet deep.

Much of the upper river winds through the Huntersville State Forest, so there is no development alongside the river, save county parks. I took in the vegetated riverbanks and was struck with nostalgia. Here were the woods of my childhood lake cabin—the rugged oaks, elm, and basswood, white pines rising above the deciduous canopy, and all of it coming out of a yellow sand substrate. That cabin was, in fact, only thirty miles away, as the crow flies.

And oh yes, there was poison ivy, just like at the cabin. Poison ivy thrives on sand. We would have to issue stern admonitions: "Leaves of three, let it be."

The four Leaflets were all grade-school age: Andy, twelve, would begin middle school that year. Katie was ten, in the prime of childhood. John was eight, fun-loving and ever in motion. Christina, five, would enter kindergarten in the fall. We paddled with two kids and one parent in each canoe, with various combinations. Sometimes the girls wanted to be together, but often the middles asked to team up. They were very close, often in their own little world, with maps, rules, and code words. When Christina was paired with her ancient older brother, she duffed in the middle and retreated into a book, while Andy and I carried on grown-up conversation.

Surveying our paddling team, I saw a motley crew. They were dressed in T-shirts, which in some cases hung to their thighs, jeans patched at the knee and gathered at the ankle (fashionable), and river sandals. Katie wore mauve pants, once haute couture in the elementary school, but she had shot up in the past few months, and the pants legs inched well above her ankles. The younger two had bowl cuts because their fine blond hair would not lie flat. Katie's yellow bangs were shaggy.

It was June, and the bugs might be swarming, but luckily as we started, it was cool enough to wear long pants and sweatshirts. I hoped it would warm up so that later in the day the kids could swim.

The Crow Wing River is named for the island at its juncture with the Mississippi on the east edge of what is now Camp Ripley. The Native Americans thought it resembled the shape of a raven's wing. This area was once a hotbed of activity. The Dakota, who had lived in the river's vicinity, were pushed farther west in the 1700s by Ojibwe, who were expanding out of their traditional grounds. The confluence of the two rivers saw many battles. My mother picnicked in the area as a child in the 1930s and recalled frequently finding arrowheads in the sandy soil.

In the 1800s, there were European trading posts along the Crow Wing and at its mouth. The multicultural Métis, arising out of French Canadian–Ojibwe marriages, passed by with their oxcarts on their biennial trips between St. Paul and the Red River valley. They trapped mammals for fur and hunted bison for hides in the summer and then carried the goods to market each fall.

The charismatic Ojibwe chief Bagone-giizhig, also known as Hole-in-the-Day the Younger, had a great deal of influence in the Crow Wing watershed in the mid-1800s. Claiming to be chief of all the Ojibwe in the state (other bands disagreed), he negotiated treaties with the United States and was instrumental in establishing the White Earth Reservation. He was murdered near the trading post at the confluence in 1868. The crime was a complicated murder-for-hire that was not fully understood for decades. When Hole-in-the-Day negotiated the reservation, he attempted to restrict the presence of Métis traders, fearing they would detract from Ojibwe business interests. These traders hired killers at $1,000 each to assassinate the chief, but since the hired guns were never paid, they eventually revealed who hired them.

Here, too, was another echo from my childhood. My mother, who had grown up in central Minnesota, had spoken of Hole-in-the-Day when we were kids. She referred to him as a known historical figure. It is quite likely that there were people alive in her hometown then who knew the influential chief. She told us that he had prophesied that her town, Little Falls, would be safe from tornadoes, protected by the Mississippi River, which flowed through town.

We had arrived at the Crow Wing River in midmorning and were under way shortly before noon. Before long the kids were chirping for lunch. One thing we learned early in parenthood was not to delay a meal. The consequences of waiting were crabbiness, fights with siblings, and a general souring of the bonhomie we were trying to promote. Luckily, lunch was at hand.

We brought the two canoes together, and many hands held them as I pulled out the floating lunch: cheese and crackers, apples, and gorp. I had mixed large quantities of lemonade in a jug, and Tom passed out Tupperware cups (much jockeying over who got what color; "plain old brown" always allotted to Dad, who didn't care) and juice. I sliced chunks of cheddar and handed them off. The duffers lined up tidy little rows along a thwart and doled them out as requested. We topped off the noon feast with big handfuls of gorp—raisins, peanuts, and M&Ms. Again, much discussion over what color was the best: red? yellow? green? Never plain old brown.

The happy paddlers resumed paddling, and when we came to an acceptable campsite, we quit the river and set up the tents. On this first trip, the three oldest children slept in one tent, and Tom and I took Christina into ours. Later, we would carry an extra backpacking tent for Andy, who needed some space as a teen. Tom also strung a tarp between four closely situated jack pines, for it looked like it might rain later in the evening. He added a couple clotheslines for towels and swimsuits.

"Go get your suits on," I told the kids. "This is a perfect place to swim." They needed no urging. We had beached the canoes on a riverbank of sand. The water sparkled in the afternoon sun. Its clarity revealed the amber substrate. We hustled them into life jackets—the current wasn't strong, but they were used to swimming in quieter lakes.

"Hey, Mom! Look at me!" John floated by, feet first, yellow head gleaming.

"Watch, Mom, watch!" Katie squealed. She paddled about, buoyed by her purple-and-blue vest.

Christina could barely touch bottom, but the life jacket held her up, and she splashed comfortably in the water, which was a lot warmer than Lake Superior, where she normally swam. Tom stayed out with the troops and regulated the horseplay.

Time for supper! Whenever we camped with the kids, I aimed for a one-pot meal, something simple. This night it was chili. We carried a cooler, so we had ground beef and milk. I included bread sticks—a novelty that the kids appreciated—and a tossed salad. And we always had dessert. Tom's sweet tooth would be indignant without it. Often dessert was as uncomplicated as instant Jell-O pudding. The kids made it. We used a Tupperware half-gallon pitcher. I measured out the milk, and the kids added the boxed pudding and shook, pouring it into tin Sierra cups to set.

Later that evening, before the bugs got too bad, we played games. Cards were a favorite—hearts or gin rummy—but dominoes were a close second, and they didn't blow away in a breeze. We might make a campfire but usually not—only when s'mores were on the menu. I was not fond of the pervasive scent of smoke on my clothes and in my hair. We never cooked over an open fire. It blackens the pots, and the soot then besmirches hands, towels, and often clothing for years after the fire that first laid down the soot. The college professor who taught us to camp had this ban, and we adhered to it. I loved my Coleman stove.

The campsites along the Crow Wing got mixed reviews from Tom and me. The first night's site was flat and grassy, with a cluster of spindly jack and white pines throwing shade and giving us a place to tie a tarp and clothesline. The kids ran barefoot over the sparse grass. This site had no road access. Campers could reach it only via the river, and it had no litter. It was very quiet. We were the only paddlers we saw on the Crow Wing.

The second site, however, was in a county park that had river access plus an unpaved sandy road leading to it. We camped there on a Saturday night and had rowdy neighbors blaring pickup truck radios. Beer was involved. We found pieces of brown broken glass everywhere, and the kids kept their sandals on.

The next morning when we crawled from the tents and I began

the Sunday breakfast of scrambled eggs and Swedish skorpa—a cinnamon hardtack—we found our neighbors had not pitched a tent, and we now had the campground to ourselves.

Our maiden voyage down the Crow Wing River convinced Tom and me that the six of us could have fun on Minnesota's many streams. Rivers were ideal since we wouldn't need to portage and clearly the kids would not be able to carry their full amount of gear until they were teens.

The kids chattered about the trip for days. Andy was anticipating a week at summer camp in July, and he would find he had acquired valuable canoe skills that would establish him as an expert in the eyes of his fellow campers. Everyone enjoyed making a home in a tent and under a tarp, and drinking hot cocoa at the morning breakfast table. Gorp became the epitome of a good snack.

Tom and I saw that this first trip with all four kids reinforced in our children less tangible ideas: that it's good to roll with the punches and learn how to execute plan B, for there is always a need for a plan B; that rain needn't ruin an outdoor adventure; and that a river is a fine place to swim.

This trip and the others to follow would also hand down to them all what Tom and I had learned as college-age students: how to pack for a camping trip, how to set up a tent, how to plan and prepare food, and how to handle rain. We hoped in the process they would learn to appreciate the darkness of night, the quiet of the woods, and the unexpected beauty of a rainbow after a rain shower.

Self-Reliance

....

DESPITE OUR UNHAPPY EXPERIENCES IN THE BOUNDARY Waters in recent years, we decided to plan another trip there. Like most lovers, we were unwilling to relinquish a failing romance. Vacation time allotment and kids' schedules forced us into an August visit, that unholy time in the wilderness area when an abundance of paddlers pack the eight hundred thousand acres of lakes and conifers, all with permits to enter, of course.

We planned too late and found we could not enter the wilderness area at our desired access point. We remembered the jockeying for campsites and the uncomfortable tension paddling into a new lake, wondering if there would be a place for us. After some discussion, we turned to plan B, a canoe trip on the upper Mississippi River. Tom had in his files a Department of Natural Resources map of the upper Mississippi, showing campsites, river miles, landings, and rapids. It was detailed and descriptive. We had never known anyone to paddle the upper Mississippi and thought there was a certain romance to it. Memories of Lake Itasca and the intimate beginnings of the great river flooded over us. We planned a midweek trip and thought we would experience solitude in an unrecognized wilderness and foster in our children an appreciation of discovery and history.

The search for the source of the magnificent Mississippi River is legendary. In 1805, only a year after Lewis and Clark set out for the Pacific Ocean, President Jefferson organized a delegation to explore the far reaches of the largest river in North America. He chose young Lieutenant Zebulon Pike to lead the party. Like Lewis and Clark, Pike set out from St. Louis with a keelboat, working his way upstream. The expedition had a late start, however, and was forced to pause at what is now Little Falls, Minnesota, and build a winter fort. When the river froze, they continued by sled, first to the North West Company's fur post at Sandy Lake and then onward to the fur post at Leech Lake. It was a typical Minnesota winter, which is to say that Pike had not experienced such low temperatures before. Arriving at Leech Lake half-frozen, he declared the lake the "main source of the Mississippi," and then upon further exploration, he confused the issue by claiming Upper Red Cedar Lake as the "upper source" of the river.

In 1820, Lewis Cass, who was the territorial governor of Michigan at the time, led an expedition of thirty-eight men into the Minnesota wilderness from Lake Superior. On this journey, the men in the party reached Upper Red Cedar Lake and changed the name to Cass Lake, to honor their leader. There is some discussion over whether this party thought Cass Lake was indeed the headwaters of the big river. Journals from the trip also mention Lac La Biche, which empties into Cass, as being a possible source. One of the members of the Cass party was Henry Schoolcraft, who wrote an unofficial account of the adventure. He was twenty-seven at the time.

Schoolcraft's published tale sold well and garnered him recognition. On Cass's recommendation, young Schoolcraft was appointed the Indian agent in charge of the tribes in the Lake Superior region. He headquartered at Sault Ste. Marie and soon married into the band centered on Chequamegon Bay of Lake Superior; his bride, Jane Johnston, was half Ojibwe. This marriage gave Schoolcraft a connection to Ojibwe culture, history, and language that was invaluable to him.

Schoolcraft's carefully drawn account of the Cass expedition was soon supplanted by a more flamboyant trip undertaken by an Italian who had fled his native country in distress over the death of a woman, one of the Medici family. Giacomo Beltrami arrived in the United States in early 1823, made his way west, seemingly without a plan, and became caught up in the romance of the elusive source of the Father of Waters. Without wilderness experience, he nonetheless convinced Major Stephen Long to include him on a U.S. military expedition to Lake Winnipeg, but before reaching that region, Beltrami cobbled together a party led by him to search for the Mississippi's headwaters. The venture was ill-fated. Perhaps disconcerted by the lack of preparedness, his Ojibwe guides abandoned him in the vicinity of the Red Lake River. Undaunted, Beltrami pushed forward until happening upon a heart-shaped lake between Red and Cass Lakes. This he named "Julia" for his deceased Medici friend (Giulia) and claimed it to be the true source of the Mississippi.

It wasn't until 1832 that Schoolcraft, led by Ojibwe guide Ozawindib (Yellow Head), discovered the real source of the mighty river to be the three-armed lake we now call Itasca. When the Schoolcraft party arrived at Star Island in Cass Lake on their push westward to the unknown beginnings of the Mississippi, they spent some time with the Native Americans living there, the band of Schoolcraft's original guide, Ozawindib, who led them to the village. There, Ozawindib further offered to take the party to the headwaters. He hunted in that region and knew it well. He then drew up maps and rounded up canoes and five men to serve as additional guides.

Even with Ozawindib's presence, it was not an easy task to discern the source. The river had many forks. The party ascended one major branch until they reached an impasse. Schoolcraft in his journal described the terrain as "a morass where it seemed equally impracticable to make land, or proceed far by water." Ozawindib found the portage leading away from the tributary, but it was not a path as we would normally understand it. Firm ground was lacking. This marsh-like quality is typical of the headwaters of rivers. The men waded through muck for a hundred yards before reaching terra firma.

The portage from this tributary to the true source of the river, the farthest point from the mouth of the Mississippi in the Gulf of Mexico, was about six miles. The path through the woods was deemed by Schoolcraft to be "rather blind and requires the precision of an Indian eye to detect it." The men, following the guide who bore one of the canoes, were cheerful and accustomed to the wilderness. Schoolcraft observed that with every step, "the ardor with which we were carried forward [increased.]" As they descended the last elevation, they beheld "the cheering sight of a transparent body of water." Schoolcraft described it as "beautiful."

The intrepid Leaf party of paddlers planning their trip on the upper Mississippi would have benefited from rereading the historical accounts of the discovery of the headwaters of the river. As it was, our source of information about the Mississippi came solely from a Minnesota DNR map of the river. The map turned out to be not as romantic as history, nor as useful.

Our trip began at Lake Itasca, Schoolcraft's "beautiful sheet of water," where the kids waded across the outlet—the nascent Mississippi—and where we packed the Duluth packs. We planned only a three-day trip, but with six people (kids ages fourteen, twelve, ten, and seven), the gear was impressive: we stuffed three number four Duluth packs with kids' clothes, sleeping bags (the gear also included a teddy bear and one stuffed dog, Zippety, which I did not know about until it was too late to leave them behind), tents, sleeping pads, cooking equipment, and the food box; a number three for Tom and me; and a number two for the oldest child, who preferred not to mingle with his peon siblings. We also took a cooler, and because the upper Mississippi is not a federally protected wilderness area, we were able to pack cans and glass containers. Our route had no portages marked on the map, so we anticipated merely a float trip.

We did not set out from Lake Itasca, however, even though that would be the romantic start. The clear, free-flowing stream that tourists see issuing from the lake is man-made. The true source bubbles up from the marsh just below the lake. We opted to drop in at Coffee Pot Landing, which our map designated the first landing downstream from Itasca. It had campsites and drinking water.

First, we had to shuttle cars, so that we would have a car waiting for us when we finished our trip. To do this, we dropped the canoes and packs off at the put-in point, Coffee Pot, and then drove to our take-out, Pine Point, where we would complete the trip. We left a car at this landing, then drove back to Coffee Pot to begin the trip.

Back at Coffee Pot, we were surprised to see another canoe laden for an overnight trip. It belonged to three Ojibwe young men, who told us they were headed farther downriver than we were planning to paddle. They were dressed in T-shirts and jeans and had several fishing poles jabbed between their gear. They looked like they were embarking on an angling expedition, and they certainly seemed like they knew what they were doing. Tom and I found this somewhat reassuring: we weren't the only ones to paddle the upper Mississippi. The young men pushed off as we were loading our canoes. We never saw them again.

We departed around noon, two canoes, each with two paddlers and a duffer. Tom paddled with the daughters, Katie and Christina, in our Old Town canoe of Royalex; I with the sons, Andy and John, the latter riding high over the water, using the cooler as a seat. The boys and I paddled our battered aluminum Grumman, a canoe that tracked well but had a slow leak—hence, the elevated cooler seat. The day was warm and breezy, and though we were hampered somewhat by thick vegetation that choked the channel, we were cheerful. The Mississippi was narrow, no more than twenty feet across, and it meandered back and forth between its banks. The banks themselves were marshy in nature, with cattails, bulrushes, and wild rice emerging from the clear water.

As fair weather clouds raced across the blue sky, the boys and I chatted about fishing, birds, and camping. Andy, verging on manhood at fourteen, over six feet tall and strong, was my bowman because of his strength—for which I was grateful, since the potamogeton and coontail, lanky submerged plants with small leaves, tended to wrap around the paddle's blade. They were making it difficult to get off a full stroke. Andy tended toward the sardonic and pessimistic, but this was offset by the sunny and incurably optimistic nature of his younger brother.

On either side of the river grew dark, tangled forest, a mixed woods of conifers and deciduous trees like ash and maple. It seemed very remote, and the fact that we had encountered natives plying the river's waters reinforced that sense.

The kids remained in good spirits as we made our way downstream. Once, when someone voiced a peep of displeasure, I reminded them of the three questions of wilderness camping: Are you warm? Are you dry? Are you well fed? If you can answer yes to all three, you are in very good shape. At one point on the paddle a fallen spruce blocked the passage, and we had to get out of the canoes and tug them over the tip of the tree. Andy and I stood in knee-deep water, struggling with the heavy Grumman, while John, the cheerful passenger, tried to remain upright on his cooler throne. The river's water was clear, we saw no leeches, and in the August sun, we soon dried out.

We came upon the Stumphges rapids late in the afternoon. They proved to be unimpressive, not really even riffles, and the Grumman glided over them with ease. The campsite that was situated next to the rapids was littered with broken glass and beer cans, so we paddled on to the next site at a landing just off the forest road to the rapids.

We were delighted with this campsite. It was on a hill, where a slight breeze promised to alleviate some of the mosquitoes. Three-foot-high big bluestem grass blanketed the site, incongruous with the tall red pines looming in the background. The prairie grass emphasized that this area is the pines-prairie border. The tent sites were fresh and untrampled, there was a picnic table and a fire grate, and we set about making camp.

As the kids put up the tents under Tom's direction, I produced a sloppy joe/baked bean hot dish (alas, the hamburger buns had been left in the car) and three-bean salad. Later, Andy built a roaring fire in the grate, which discouraged the mosquitoes. He had been unhappy with fishing on the river—the catch was small, five inches in length or less—and the scenery, he thought, was monotonous, but he told us the fire—that elemental magic—raised his spirits. The blazing light, the aroma of wood smoke, the crackle of resin in flame—does life get any better than this?

We awoke the next morning to a very gray sky. Tom wanted to take down the tents before it rained, so we got the troops up early, enticing them with scrambled eggs and bagels. Then we were off, dipping our paddles once more into the Father of Waters, with our two canoes, five Duluth packs, and one cooler, John atop.

In his account of the 1832 trip to the headwaters, Schoolcraft described the varied nature of the upper Mississippi. The river alternated between channels of riffles and strong current where the water descended in a stream, and what he termed "savannah valleys," plateaus where the water meandered to and fro, and where tall aquatic plants grew. We had taken note of this the day before without much reflection. On the second day, we again found ourselves in one of the marshy areas, the water winding back and forth between wild rice and cattails. The channel seemed to be deeper, however, and less choked with aquatic plants, so we could make good, solid strokes with the paddle. Andy and I discussed the likelihood that as the river collected water from the surrounding watershed and became a bigger river, the going would get easier. We were cheered by the thought.

A myriad of birds rose up before the canoes, flocks of ducks gathering for migration and stout-bodied, long-billed shorebirds that might have been snipe. Many kingfishers rattled overhead. Tom and the girls in the lead canoe spotted a seldom-seen rail slipping through the watery grasses. Cattails formed tall green curtains on either side of the channel and gently swayed to and fro, whispering. We had never paddled in such an environment, and Tom and I, at least, were intrigued. I imagined the Ojibwe harvesting wild rice in the fall under such conditions. I conjured up the intrepid Schoolcraft leading his expedition downstream to Fort Snelling, jubilant after finally reaching The Source.

We had paddled along, back and forth, back and forth, past the green curtains for about two hours, and were perhaps halfway through the marsh, when we suddenly came to the end of the channel. The river seemed to terminate. A solid wall of cattails rose up before us, waving cryptically. We were dumbfounded. There was nowhere to go. How had we lost the river?

We thought perhaps we, all six of us, had not been paying attention, so we paddled back a hundred yards to see if we had just missed a turn. But no, there was no clear channel. Off to the right, however, there appeared to be a narrow pathway through some tussocks that could lead to a channel, and it seemed possible that the grass stems were bent slightly. Perhaps someone—the Ojibwe trio?—had recently taken that route.

So we took it. Tom and the girls went first. The duffer had to get out, too, and all three stood knee-deep in the water on tussocks of cattails while they pushed, pulled, and cajoled the canoe through the curtain of green, over the lumpy tussocks, into the impassable passage. When it was our turn, Andy and I discovered that there was black muck beneath that clear water, and we sank up to our knees. The Grumman moved incrementally, and the boys and I felt we were at a disadvantage, because the aluminum Grumman did not slide as easily as the plastic Old Town.

Inch by inch, we urged the canoe downstream (we hoped) in the Mississippi. It was a struggle, hard and physical. I recognized the same helpless feeling I had had some years before in childbirth: of being faced with a nearly impossible situation, requiring physical strength I did not have, and yet having no option but to proceed.

Finally, we emerged through the tiny opening and lo! There was the channel. Or so we thought. Before us lay a clear riverine course. Beneath the water, the long leaves of submerged plants waved in the direction of the current. We celebrated by pulling out a bag of gorp and handing it around. We hadn't had lunch, but gorp served as a decent alternative. Apparently, this *was* the way—and we paddled on.

Until we once more fronted a wall of cattails and another dead end.

Again we hunted for the passage. How had the Ojibwe gone? I don't recall why we thought they had inside information about the river, but they seemed to have paddled it regularly. We assumed that they had proceeded downstream. Again we thought we saw a faintly marked way through and took it. This time, the technique we employed only involved poling. Standing up in the canoe—imagine! Standing up in the canoe! The bow and stern paddlers pushed off against tussocks, slowly easing the craft forward. Going ahead of us, Katie stood in the Old Town's bow and shoved hard, backward, as Tom counted, "One! Two! Three! Push!" She grinned with the challenge of doing something hard.

This second passage also led to an open channel and briefly renewed hope. It was only minutes, though, before we came to a point where we lost the current altogether. The waving fronds of the underwater plants had nothing to say to us. At this point, the words of Schoolcraft would have resonated: "We appeared to be in a morass . . . "

We estimated we were still halfway through the marsh and anticipated three more hours like the three we had already spent. Tom and I could not believe that there wasn't an actual route through. The map had mentioned nothing about this, and wasn't this the Mississippi River, now over twenty-five miles from its source? We kept thinking we must have messed up in some way, and we retraced our route, paddling back and forth, trying to figure out where we had gone wrong. We appeared to be lost, or rather, the river was lost. We knew where we were: we were immersed in a marsh we could not paddle through or see over. There were no people around—not a soul. No one knew where we were. But ironically, far off in the distance on a high riverbank were a scattering of houses that we could see, but from which, of course, we could not be seen. The cloudy day had turned sullen. The light darkened. It began to sprinkle and then to rain in earnest.

We were in an impossible situation, and I grew rather panicky because we had dragged our *children* into this silly and potentially dangerous position. I was especially concerned about the duffers, John and Christina, the ones with the smallest bodies, who were getting wet but were not able to keep warm by paddling. Hypothermia was a distinct possibility. The marsh was like a tremendous wild maze, and while we always knew the direction we had come from and the direction we were headed, we truly did not know the way. Now the three wilderness questions—Are you dry? Are you warm? Are you well fed?—could all be answered no.

After another hour of fruitless paddling, during which we had all donned rain gear, Tom said, "Well, as I see it, we have two options: we can go on, pulling the canoes over tussocks and hope that the Highway 5 bridge (marking "civilization") comes soon, or we can turn back and retrace our steps." We had pulled the two canoes together and hung onto the gunwales as we powwowed. The kids, their blond bangs plastered to their foreheads from the rain, had not complained at all. Not a peep about the outrageous conditions of this canoe trip. Now they looked at us with round eyes, wondering what would happen next.

We decided to vote on what to do. One by one we voiced our opinion, letting the children go first. It was unanimous, without hesitation: we should turn around. We were all aware that a retreat meant going back over that first horrendous "portage," shoving the laden canoes over the tussocks—if we could even find the opening again. It would mean the end of the trip. That would be OK.

After making the decision to retrace our paddle, the next order of business was to find a place to pee for the girls and me. We had been five hours in the canoes without dry land, and there was none to be found now. It was part of the impossible situation: the substrate was too watery to walk on but too vegetated to paddle. It took us twenty minutes of searching to find a very mucky point to clamber on to, but we were relieved to be relieved, and immediately our moods brightened.

Tom pawed under the protective tarp that was keeping the packs dry, unbuckled the food pack, and fished out a box of crackers to accompany the gorp. Andy and I shared an ample supply of Jolly Rancher hard candies to be doled out at intervals as enticements. Then, we commenced the retreat.

The marsh presented a gray and muted face as we made our way through the interminable green cattails, which waved gently under the steady beat of rain. The first "portage" we needed to make was the one we had poled through. I was sure I couldn't identify it. The vast stretches of cattails seemed without feature. We ended up stumbling upon it, with Andy and Katie, the two paddling in the bows, simultaneously recognizing the narrow passage. The second, awful "portage," the one we had stood knee-deep in muck for, we did find, but scouting about, we discovered an alternative route that required us only to pole through the cattail curtain.

Once we were through that, it was a matter of retracing our way upstream, against a very slow current, to the campsite we had vacated seven hours before. Tom and the girls took the lead. Songs from *The Lion King* wafted downriver, as Katie and Christina sang through a repertoire of music to make the hours pass more tolerably. In late afternoon, John let out a whoop as he spied the bridge marking our last night's campsite. It was a wonderful sound.

Tom strung up a tarp, and we hauled the packs out of the rain and under its protection. Tom then took off on an eight-mile run/walk to retrieve our car that was parked at Pine Point. I set up the stove and made cocoa for the kids. They stripped off their wet clothes and donned sweatshirts, jeans, and jackets. The raincoats were soaked. We got out a deck of cards and played hearts and munched on cheese and crackers, awaiting Tom's return.

He arrived around what would have been the dinner hour. We all piled in and drove to our first landing, where we had left the second car (How long ago! How naive we were!). We then returned to the tarp to load up the canoes, the sodden clothes, and all the packs. The rain had ceased, the sun shone brightly, its golden rays low on the horizon. It would have been a lovely evening at a campsite, sitting around a fire, eating food cooked on a Coleman stove. But we didn't rethink our decision. We were happy, so happy, to be out of the marsh.

The kids had been troopers throughout the whole ordeal. True, Andy had spoken, not helpfully, of all of us dying in the marsh, perhaps taking a cue from my worst apprehension, which I had not voiced. But he pushed on forcefully, with determination, when called upon. Katie had used her sharp memory and pluck, John had kept buoyant and humorous, and Christina, only seven, had been courageous and uncomplaining. We rewarded their grit with a night on the town in Bemidji.

We drove to a favorite motel right on Lake Bemidji—which is actually an out-pocket of the Mississippi—and secured a huge room in which we could dry out wet clothes, clean up, and shake off the memories of the day. Then we walked to a great restaurant that had tap root beer and told the kids they could order anything they wanted. Money meant nothing at that moment. That realization was one of the first fruits of our ordeal in the marsh. They ate monstrous meals, while Tom and I savored locally brewed beer and enjoyed hot, nourishing food as if we had expected never to experience such a delight again. It was late when we made it back to the motel. We fell into our beds. Were we warm? Were we dry? Were we well fed? Yes, happily, to all three.

Our two days on the little river that issues forth from Lake Itasca confirmed for us our belief that there are more wilderness areas in Minnesota than the Boundary Waters Canoe Area Wilderness. The 1964 federal Wilderness Act defines wilderness as "those areas . . . where the earth and its community of life are untrammeled by man, where man himself is a visitor who does not remain." Seen through this lens, the upper Mississippi River is actually more wild than the BWCAW, with its portage trails so heavily trodden by boots that they sink six inches down into the thin soil. People do not remain in the near watershed of the upper Mississippi, because it is a netherworld for a two-legged terrestrial mammal.

Why would Tom and I want to expose our children to such an unpopulated place, putting them at a special kind of risk unique to wild spaces? As young people, Tom and I had reveled in the natural beauty of the north country, in its silence, a quality that has almost vanished in today's everyday life. We had hoped to expose our kids to a grandeur that was bigger than the landscape of daily existence in their small town—the tidy lawns and gardens and well-worked farm fields. We hoped they would be amazed, which is to say, we wanted to inspire in them a sense of wonder. We had thought that maybe, paddling under their own steam, being outside day and night, without the distractions of the computer or television, they would glimpse an alternative way of living. We hoped they could become self-reliant, in the most fundamental meaning of the word. Most of all, Tom and I were looking for fun—a vacation is supposed to be fun! And part of the fun is meeting challenges and rising to the occasion.

So what we wanted—a changed sensibility in our children—doesn't require a landscape "untrammeled by man." Really, is there such a place? It seems to me that the reverence in which the Boundary Waters is held and the high demand to experience it is just a nonsense dream, pursued in the same way well-heeled people pursue a new craft beer or a trendy restaurant. We want to *feel* that sense of wonder—dare I say, "sacred wonder"—and the Boundary Waters is seen to be The Place, when in truth the sacred is all around us. Is there not something sacred in the miraculous germination of seeds and the explosive green growth of spring? Might there be a spark of divinity in the instant awareness of another's thoughts when two people make contact?

In this world, wilderness is a state of mind and can be found anywhere. In the marsh, where we found it, much of what we had hoped for on the trip came true. We needed, all of us, to rely on ourselves to extract ourselves from the impossible situation, and we did. We discovered hidden strengths that were there when we needed them. Tom and I realized that each child had valuable personality traits that augmented our family unit and made us a tougher whole. I, for one, have greater appreciation for the effort it took to understand and map the course of the Mississippi River and think now of it as a collaborative effort that extended over decades and across cultures, making known what was once unknown.

Tom, the planner and navigator of the trip, retains ill will toward the inadequate DNR map. "I learned never to trust them!" he told me when I asked him what he recalls now about that trip seventeen years ago. Today, one can access online the DNR map of the upper Mississippi River as it runs through Hubbard and Beltrami Counties. It resembles the map we had, but with far more detail. Of particular pertinence are points where there are gauges measuring water depth and warnings that below a certain depth, paddlers will find the river unnavigable. The description of each section is exact and designed to alleviate just the situation we found ourselves in. Today, we would also carry cell phones that could employ satellite transmission, technology that few had in 1997. We did not actually need outside help on the trip, but lurking on the edges was a skulking fear that it was a situation that could intensify and that we were wholly dependent only on ourselves.

Does this increase in knowledge—a more detailed map, more water level gauges, and the existence of cell phones—reduce the marsh's wildness? Does wilderness exist because we do not know everything, and if we did, would there be no wilderness? As we increase mastery of our world through the spread of technology, is there a corresponding loss of wilderness?

I think so. I think the wilderness is shrinking. But the wildness of the world—in which, Thoreau claimed, is its preservation—remains unchanged. People continue to surprise us, and themselves, with daring and creative acts. Seeds sprout under hostile conditions, storms rage, and winds carry unusual birds aloft. We cannot predict what will land at our doorstep. We are all just along for the ride, at the mercy of rivers that disappear, cattails that become impenetrable curtains, and a sun that clears the sky after a sobering rain.

Canoeing the Sandhills

THE NIOBRARA RIVER, 1998

....

WE ARE SAILING ON AN IMMENSE SEA OF GRASS, THE North American Great Plains, our small ship a red Honda Civic, our single sail an eighteen-foot green Old Town canoe. It is an insubstantial craft on such a vast sea, but the billowing road carries us forward, our bow dips and rises over the undulating hills, propelling us toward Valentine, Nebraska.

A fittingly named place in which to celebrate a wedding anniversary, Valentine. It will be our twentieth. Who could not see the symbolism of a canoe trip? A twosome launches and paddles in synchrony, facing the elements together. They work a rapids as a team to avoid a fate that would benefit neither: one misjudgment and a quick swamping, a soaking, and possible loss of gear.

The canoe we carry on top of the car is no longer new. There's a distinct gash in one side, a souvenir from the Kettle River, and countless scrapes from rocks in streams too numerous to remember. In arid South Dakota, though, a canoe on top of a car is a standout. We feel like we swagger. We're on an adventure.

As we leave the interstate and head south toward the Rosebud Indian Reservation, the swagger weakens, like a grin slowly fading. The strong west wind catches the canoe broadside, and the little Honda is led by the nose toward the centerline of the road time and again. Tom fights to keep the car in the right-hand lane. But when we see the bow of the canoe sliding left, Tom pulls over. The wind has loosened the ropes that keep the canoe fastened snugly to the roof. We both get out. Tom yanks on the ropes and reknots them. From the way he purses his lips and the authoritative jerk of his wrists, I know the canoe won't budge henceforth.

I throw my arms wide, twirl around, and let the wind snap my clothes and toss my hair. The air is sweet and smells like dry grass. The sky is wide, our view unobstructed. There is a raw freedom to the prairie wind. The thin, dulcet notes of a Western Meadowlark rise from a distance.

We are on our way to canoe the Niobrara River of northern Nebraska. The river flows nearly the length of the state, originating just beyond Nebraska's far western border and running 568 miles east to its confluence with the Missouri. It is the only surface water in northwestern Nebraska. It appears on a map as a thin blue line in an area with a paucity of roads, settlements, and significant geological features.

The land it drains is known as the Nebraska Sandhills, a region of mixed-grass prairie, the largest intact mixed-grass prairie of the Great Plains. As we approach Valentine, just over the northern border of the state, the undulating quality of the sandhills becomes apparent. In June, there is fresh green growth on the gently rolling hills, but also last year's grass stems, looking like ragged bits of fur, tufts here and there. Yellow puccoon, a sand-loving wildflower, grows in clumps in the swales.

The Niobrara is a canoeable river only in the early summer, when it still runs with the winter's snows. June is a good month to paddle it. Later in the summer, the water levels drop, and a canoe trip would be an exercise in frustration, as the canoe scrapes bottom time after time, and paddlers are forced to get out and push the craft along, floating on mere inches of water. Tom has read up on the vagaries of the river and consulted with the outfitters in Valentine, who will drive with us upriver to our drop-in place and then shuttle our car to our trip's endpoint.

We have planned a three-day trip, two days above Valentine, and one day below. That last day will be spent on the portion of the Niobrara that has been designated a federal Wild and Scenic River. We have heard that people take inner tubes down the federally protected section and that on hot summer weekends it teems with activity. There are twelve outfitters in Valentine that rent tubes and canoes to float down the Niobrara below Valentine. We chatted with one outfitter, who guessed there were about six hundred canoes available to paddlers.

So already this trip is riddled with paradox. We are paddling through a dry part of the state, and the least traveled section of the river does not have the federal Wild and Scenic designation.

Our desire to begin our trip on a section of river above Valentine puzzled the outfitters we called. The concept of a multiday canoe trip was new. No one had ever outfitted a party that wanted to put in west of town. Because there are few roads in the sandhills, access points to the river are limited, and apparently no one has considered paddling on a prairie river. We finally located an outfitter, Yucca Dune, that provides their clients a bit more in the way of adventure trips, and they agreed to the shuttle. We have brought all the gear we will need along with us from Minnesota. We don't need to rent equipment from them.

....

Valentine, Nebraska, is a working town. With a broad Main Street paved with aging concrete and lined with modest, two-storied brown brick businesses, the community is the only sizable settlement for miles. It is the Cherry County seat, with a courthouse to match the somber brown brick of its Main Street. It also boasts of a Penney's catalog store, a mercantile, a Coast to Coast, and a huge Western wear store. On the north end of Main, we come upon the Plains Trading Company Booksellers, a rare gem of an independent bookstore that carries a fine selection of books on Nebraska's history and books by local writers and others whose passion is Nebraska.

The Nebraska Sandhills has a native daughter, Mari Sandoz, who served as scribe to the settlers of western Nebraska. The story of Sandoz's life is as meager and scrappy as life in Valentine. Her father disapproved of her girlhood literary interests and kept her occupied with backbreaking farm work. With only an eighth-grade education, she became a country schoolteacher in the sandhills at age seventeen in 1913. She married young, to a harsh man. The marriage failed. She left home for Lincoln, where she worked odd jobs and submitted short stories for publication, all rejected.

At age thirty-four, though, she embarked on a new literary endeavor. Her dying father had made a startling request: that she write a biography of his life—his immigration to the sandhills, the pioneer life he endured to carve out a farm from the infertile land, his interactions with the native Oglala. The idea appealed to her, and after extensive work with historical accounts, she produced *Old Jules*. She received acclaim for the book before she turned forty, but only after every major publishing house in the country rejected it.

Other books followed, cementing her fame as a regional writer. Her first work, *Old Jules*, though, is the one Tom and I want. We often read to each other on drives, particularly on road trips, to settle ourselves into a mind-set to experience the land. Perhaps *Old Jules* would serve us as guide on our paddle down the Niobrara.

We hadn't chased down *Old Jules* before we left on our trip and are thrilled to find it on the shelf at the Plains Trading Company. We buy a copy and tuck in its leaves a souvenir bookmark from the store.

....

One of the piquant pleasures of travel is to realize that my Minnesota story, the immigrant story by which I frame my life, is not the same story everywhere. In *Old Jules,* the immigrants are Swiss; the outfitters taking us upriver at the start of our trip were also from mountainous central Europe, Austria. Our driver claims that his great-grandfather, the immigrant, didn't like the Iowa "mud" and moved west to the sand—not, I think to myself, the wisest move for farming. Unlike many who moved into western Nebraska, he brought a team of horses and a plow and was equipped to farm. When the hard, precarious undertaking caused his neighbors to give up and leave, the Austrian bought their claims.

Four generations later, the family prospers. Our driver owns the outfitting business. Three of his children are in medicine—two daughters as nurses, and a son who is a physician on the Rosebud Reservation and makes the one-hour commute from Valentine each day.

We had met his youngest child, Nora, at the shop in town. She was deeply immersed in repair of a bicycle when we arrived. Protected by a work apron, hands slick with dark grease, she greeted us and then cleaned up to go over river maps with us. She pointed to tributaries we would encounter to mark our progress, bridges spanning the river that would be our chief landmarks, and certain land formations. She cautioned us to beware of barbed wire strung out across the water and x-ed certain spots in which we might come across it. As we head out, these maps are in our pack, tucked into a plastic map case that Tom will keep with him in the stern, for reference.

We launch at midmorning outside of the town of Nenzel, population twenty. It is our only choice for drop-in, the only semi-major road crossing the river. The day is gloriously sunny with puffy white clouds drifting eastward across the sky under the prevailing wind. The Niobrara sparkles with a thousand tiny lights. The river is fairly narrow immediately below Nenzel, no more than two hundred feet, and is bordered by a lush floodplain in some stretches. As we paddle, we are close enough to identify some of the trees—a mixed woods of oak and cottonwood, willow, and hackberry. Juniper and ponderosa pine line the north bank of the river. We also note wild grapes draping over tree branches, and lush carpets of poison ivy, a sand-loving plant.

Beyond the green of the waterway, the nearly naked Nebraska Sandhills roll off into the distance. The tacit message is crystal clear: it is the water of the river that supports this riot of green. Away from the river is the arid West.

But inside the narrow corridor of running water, a finger of eastern forest pokes westward. We are surprised to find a variety of birds along the river that are generally considered eastern species. The clear carol of a Rose-breasted Grosbeak, the sweet warble of an Eastern Bluebird, and the harsh question of an Eastern Phoebe, asking, "Phoebe? Phoebe?" rise up at midday. At our lunch break on a flat, sandstone shelf, we spy a pair of Orchard Orioles, a new species for both of us, a bird to add to our life lists. Their brilliantly orange cousins, the Baltimores, are common here.

Pairs of Eastern Kingbirds, their white tail bands flashing, are numerous. It seems like nesting couples have staked out nearly every section of the river. They twitter aggressively as we pass, wheeling above the canoe.

The Niobrara cuts through thick layers of sand, and these are revealed at bends in the river. Dark, verdant forest tops the cut like frothy icing on a layer cake. The white sandstone, the cake itself, gleams under the harsh prairie sun. Both Tom and I wear broad-brimmed hats and lots of sunblock. We are northerners, used to sunlight filtered by maple leaves or pine boughs. We feel naked under the brightness of the sun. The river is undeniably scenic, though. Tom has been shooting photos since we dropped in.

We discover in our first hour of paddling that the Niobrara is not straightforward, neither in its course nor in the paddling technique one needs to traverse it. Overall, it is very shallow, just barely canoeable even in June. Many times we hang up on sandy ridges and get out to lead the canoe along. In the stern, Tom ponders the flow and improves his guessing at where the deepest water is. We head for the outside curves, especially where the river has carved out a vertical cliff. A large volume of water with force is needed to perform such a task. After this insight, we get hung up less often.

At midday, the clouds begin to thicken. Soon there are more clouds than sun. The river changes in character, too, becoming narrower and somewhat deeper. Landmarks on our map come more frequently, although we have yet to encounter a single person. We see a cable from some unknown structure and the remains of a footbridge. We pass a barbed-wire fence strung across the river that is particularly nasty. The mesh of the fence leading down the river's bank is obvious, but we can barely detect the single strand of wire with its dangerous spikes that hangs over the water at neck height. I think worried thoughts about decapitation. Luckily, Nora has marked this hazard on our map. We paddle over to the south bank and by ducking, slip beneath it.

The barbed wire is a pointed reminder of the Wild West mentality that embraces this river. Though rivers are public thoroughfares, the land on either side is privately owned by ranchers. The barbed wire is strung to prevent the wandering of cattle. Technically, I suppose it would be illegal to impede a public waterway—at least, I could imagine arguing that back home in Minnesota. In Nebraska, I will prudently keep my opinions to myself.

Shortly after the barbed wire, we come upon a stretch of rapids. It's a mild, two-foot drop, and Nora assured us we could run it—running is always preferable to the work of a portage, if it can be done safely—but when we get out on the south bank to survey the scene, Tom decides there is not enough water to carry the canoe over the drop. Instead, there is a smaller channel of the river to our right that has the drop in ledges, and Tom thinks we can line the canoe over this section without unloading it.

To line a canoe over rapids, ropes are tied to both bow and stern, and the paddlers simply guide the canoe, bow first, down the rushing water. We both wear water shoes, and the river is shallow, no more than shin deep. It seems like a good plan. It is only a short distance, the ledges are mere stairsteps, and water cascades over them in a thin, white curtain.

At first it goes well. Tom walks ahead with the bow; I feel competent and businesslike guiding the stern, and we march along. But as we approach the drop, it becomes harder to hold the canoe in place. The rushing water presses against the side of the canoe, and the craft swings outward, away from me. I don't *intend* to give it more line, but maybe I do. And the more perpendicular the canoe is to the flow of the water, the more pressure the water applies and the harder it is to pull it back in parallel.

Fighting with the suddenly beastly canoe, I slip on a submerged rock and go down. I scrape my knee and shin on other rocks and now am wet to the waist. Meanwhile, the canoe has swung even farther away from me, and Tom gets caught downstream with the canoe threatening to hit him broadside. The roar of the water—and really, it is a very modest rapids!—fills my ears. Maybe we are shouting to each other, I don't remember. Maybe Tom is telling me what I need to do. I think with vexation that once again, he has overestimated my strength. But I still hold the rope attached to the stern in my hand. We are about to lose the canoe, which will make life much more difficult, and so because there is no other option, I pull with all my might and bring that canoe back into line, and we proceed very properly, bow first, down the ledges and are on our way once more.

While we have been preoccupied with the rapids, we have failed to notice that a storm is approaching from the west. The sky is very dark blue, so dark that the white sand cliffs gleam like alabaster in what remains of the sun. Sitting through a storm on the water makes me nervous, and I keep glancing over my shoulder until my stern's man tells me to relax. He thinks we have about an hour before the storm breaks and that our campsite for the night should be just up ahead.

We need to camp on public land. This stretch of the Niobrara runs mainly through privately owned land and to camp on private land would be to trespass. In Sweden and other parts of Europe, there is a tradition called "everyman's right," a custom, formalized by law, that allows campers and hikers to utilize privately held land, as long as they don't defile it and stay a certain distance away from dwellings. That concept has yet to reach central Nebraska. We Americans need public land, and happily, it is nearby. The Anderson Bridge State Wildlife Management Area is accessible from this part of the river, and that is where we are headed.

We are looking for Anderson Bridge, which crosses the river and leads into the wildlife refuge, and we paddle and paddle. The eyes in the back of my head image the oncoming storm, which has now painted the river a darker blue. Finally, after a bend in the river that seems interminable, we spy the Anderson Bridge.

Nora's instructions are to disembark on the north bank of the river after the bridge, pull up the canoe there, then cross the bridge, and enter the refuge. We do as we are directed, but find with dismay that three rows of taut barbed wire stretch across the top of the bank to the bridge, preventing us access. There is no gate or other opening.

Thunder rumbles intermittently to our left. The wind has begun to rise. "All right," says Tom, "we'll go over it." While he turns over the canoe and secures it, I toss our several packs over the fence. Then he steps with his long legs over the barbed wire and holds it down for me. We trot across the bridge as the first drops of rain fall. We will put up the tent, tuck a tarp over the packs, and be snug during the worst of the storm. And we will admire the rainbow it leaves in its wake.

....

A full day on the Niobrara and we have yet to see a person. On our second day out, we paddle through water and sky, past sand and hills that seem as virginal as the birth of time in Eden. Save, of course, for the "wildlife": those sloe-eyed, dim-witted, white-faced cattle that ponder us dumbly from the banks or moo forlornly at a distance.

On one foray atop the banks, to stretch our legs, we come upon a bleached skull and assorted other bones. Tom examines with medical interest several vertebrae, identifies the axis, a scapula, a clavicle. Far lovelier is the profusion of prairie flowers that bloom amid the dried grasses from the previous year. Prairie grasses are slow to start. In June, the bluestem is only inches high, but the flowers are large and lush. Prickly pear is in bloom, with three-inch apricot flowers. We find waxy sego lilies, papery pink wild roses, and prickly poppy, with white petals and thistlelike leaves that clearly say, "Don't eat me." Spikes of yucca rise from gigantic pom-poms of daggerlike leaves. Plains larkspur, another spike, sport intricate pale-pink flowers reminiscent of the cultivated ones that bloom at home in my garden. We have always liked to wander on prairies. The flowers, which are subtle and showy at the same time, delight the eye.

Prairie birds are more evident as we poke about on top of the banks. We see Lark Sparrows and Western Kingbirds, Grasshopper Sparrows and Bobolinks. The unexpected mix of prairie and forest species will give us a list of well over eighty species by the end of the trip.

Back in the canoe, we paddle doggedly, with miles to go before the next parcel of publicly owned land and the night's campsite. We encounter a number of stretches with standing waves about a foot or two high. These don't seem to be rapids per se; there's not much of a drop, if any, although the farther east we go, the more we descend in elevation. Tom thinks the waves are created by a lot of water rushing through a narrowed channel. We take on a little water, which settles into the midsection of the canoe, but the standing waves give us no trouble, and we easily run them.

Ironically, we create the trouble ourselves.

Sometime in the afternoon, we take a break to swim. Tom hauls the canoe up, stern first, to secure it on the bank. We splash about in the cool water and the bright sun, the breeze from yesterday's storm brushing the surface of the river and frilling it.

While we frolic, the water that we took on runs into the bow, where my pack is stowed, soaking it and the bottommost items stowed inside. I am disheartened when I discover this. My journal! My bird guide! My binoculars!

Tom pushes the brim of his canvas hat back with two fingers and remarks, "Well, I sure hope *you* didn't get *my* new book that I just bought wet!" Then, "I *told* you that you should put your pack in a plastic bag! Packs should *always* be in a plastic bag!"

His book? *Old Jules* is not *his* book! I was the one who suggested we buy the book, thinking it would be a good one to read together. And who was it that tilted the canoe to make that water run into the bow? Not me! I was busy with something else when that move was made. The tilter didn't notice where the excess water was going, did he?

Old Jules is damp about the edges. The black-and-white portrait of the man on the cover appears morosely soggy. Tom takes the book from me, blots it carefully against his T-shirt, and places it in his own pack (encased in plastic), where it will be properly cared for.

Then we pick up our paddles, shove off from the sandy bank, and paddle on.

As I dip my paddle in and pull it back, I seethe silently. I think about men who blame others unfairly and don't apologize. I think about what I will write in my journal tonight. I think about sawing the canoe in half. I think about walking across the sandhills to the landing by myself. Do I think about stuffing my pack in a plastic bag? Somehow I don't think about that.

It takes forever to reach the Boardman Bridge, our next campsite. Apparently the land on either side of the bridge is public space, but it is a mess. Beer bottles and cans are scattered about, and on one side poison ivy spreads like shag carpet over every possible tent space. Furthermore, the bridge itself is old and made of steel. It bangs with metallic cacophony when a pickup rolls over it, which seems to be frequently. Tonight is Friday night, and we suspect that there will be a good share of traffic headed to town.

Suddenly, Eden seems less idyllic. Now that we've bitten that apple and quarreled, our eyes are open to litter and noise and other blights. Or maybe there's more intrusion into the landscape because we're closer to town. We don't analyze. We're tired from a very long day. The Fort Niobrara National Wildlife Refuge is reachable, but we just don't feel like trudging with our big Duluth packs down a sandy road to get there, making a double trip to haul all the gear. We are, in fact, deflated.

It's late, past six o'clock; we've paddled twenty-three miles; the banks at this point in the river are high and hard to surmount. We need an easy place to land, pull up the canoe, and set up the tent without poison ivy at every turn. We need to eat supper and find respite in the domestic routine of setting up camp, nurse our self-inflicted wounds, and right the keel. The only feasible campsite, it turns out, is on private land, just south of the wildlife refuge. We hope the owner won't mind. Surely, we will treat his land better than his cattle do. There is still poison ivy in abundance, but it has been kept at bay by the cattle, which apparently eat it. We find that the thickest stands are at the base of scruffy little green ash shrubs, where a grazer can't reach them.

At eight thirty, supper over and the dishes washed, the sun disappears behind a sandhill, the river darkens, and the shadows of oaks creep across the water. The breeze settles, and the last of the birds chatter off to roost. A great chorus of coyotes suddenly enlivens the growing calm. They yip and squeal and howl and yap. They are not as elegant as wolves. There appears to be no object to their outbursts. They bark, it seems, just to make noise.

. . . .

In the morning, we have only a short paddle until we reach the take-out and our brief trip down the Niobrara is over. We didn't plan it that way, but we paddled longer than we had thought we would yesterday, in search of a suitable campsite. But this may work in our favor. Nora, the outfitter, told us that the day-trippers floating down the Wild and Scenic portion of the river launch below Cornell Dam but generally not before ten o'clock. If we reach the dam earlier, we will avoid the crowds.

This is not true. On a hot summer Saturday, there are dozens and dozens of canoes launching below the dam as we portage the canoe along the grassy path skirting the cascading curtain of water. Tom has the canoe on his shoulders, and I am shouldering a heavy Duluth pack, but we suddenly realize that there is no longer any reason to hustle. We will be canoeing with hundreds for the last leg of the trip. What we see are only canoes. The float tubes and kayaks must put in at another access point.

The canoeists are mostly young and flaunt bare, pink skin, which causes me to wince as the sun beats down. Some have hooked several canoes together to raft downriver; one particularly oblivious pair has brought along a boom box, which thumps to a primal beat. We are so happy that we decided to start our trip several days away from the masses of humanity and the noise and other hallmarks of modern life. The unexpected solitude gave us a chance to appreciate the clear Niobrara and the rolling sandhills that it cuts through. For a brief moment of time, we could imagine the Oglala on their ponies, riding across the sweeping grasses, or the settlers with their wagons, struggling to put down roots in a land that did not nurture unrealistic dreams.

Our take-out point is at Smith Falls State Park. It is tiny by Minnesota standards and fairly new. It protects a lovely little waterfall on a tributary of the Niobrara. We received a park brochure describing the land. It was written in an apologetic tone, as if the state reluctantly bought the land from a private, albeit *willing* landowner, because there was no better way to protect the waterfall. We wonder if government-owned land is an unappealing concept, though judging from the many who are enjoying the federal Wild and Scenic River that hot day, there are mixed emotions toward it.

Our trip is at an end. In the quiet routine of camp life, in the necessity of paddling together to reach our destination, in the tether of twenty years that yoke us together as a team, Tom and I have regained our equilibrium. *Old Jules* is a slightly damp artifact from standing waves and will not become an icon of our paddle down the sparkling Niobrara.

In fact, we will bring the book home and stash it on our bookshelf and never read it. It will be years before I think to open it, in an attempt to bring back the sandy-bedded river as I recount our June journey. Then I will find that our copy of *Old Jules* is yet one more paradox. Ironically damaged by water, which is scarce in the sandhills, it is a tale of violence and vulgarity and desperation. There is little of the beauty, the expansiveness, and the limitless vision of central Nebraska and its river. These I will find in the photos Tom took, in the words that I penned in the journal that didn't get wet in my pack, in the memory of the twitter of courting kingbirds coming from the river's edge as we paddled along.

Loving It to Death

....

WE COULD NOT WEAN OURSELVES OFF BOUNDARY WATERS canoe trips. Despite experiencing the canoe swarm of 1993 and the "filled to capacity" trip of 1994, we remained enchanted with the wilderness area's narrow, pristine lakes, its high basalt cliffs, and its majestic white pines.

In summer 1997, we had planned a trip taking all four children. The kids eagerly promoted another canoe adventure. Tom, planning much farther ahead than he had ever done, applied in mid-July for a permit to enter a month later. He learned over the phone that we could not enter the Boundary Waters Canoe Area Wilderness at Little Gabbro Lake any time in August. There were three entry spots open (out of fifty) for August 14, when we had hoped to begin our trip—this was for the entire wilderness area—and for the day before, August 13, only one more canoe would be allowed to enter the BWCAW.

Confounded by those numbers, we had switched to plan B, a trip to north-central Minnesota on the upper Mississippi River, near the headwaters. On that venture, we discovered why most paddlers do not gravitate to that part of the state. We returned to the Boundary Waters the following year, 1998, despite misgivings. Gabbro Lake with its weird prehistoric rocks rising out of its waters still called to us. On this trip, the children would be fifteen, thirteen, eleven, and eight—all good paddlers, all competent swimmers. They had been stalwart on the upper Mississippi trip. We planned the trip with great enthusiasm, if apprehensive over the anticipated crowds.

Tom and I learned as young adults that if you want to avoid people in the Boundary Waters, you must take long portages—as long as a mile, if need be. Our trip began with a three-quarter-mile portage into Little Gabbro Lake from the entry-point parking lot. Andy carried one of the canoes, Tom, the other, and Katie and John each carried one of the heavy Duluth packs and were very pleased with themselves. Maybe there was something to the philosophy that wilderness trips build self-confidence by presenting physical challenges.

After a trail lunch on Gabbro of cheese and crackers, gorp, and oranges, we headed for the portage into Turtle Lake—181 rods, half a mile. It was rocky and hilly, and when we were over it, everyone was exhausted. We took the first campsite we saw, small but with huge, flat rocks for sitting on. The rocks would also serve as countertops in my outdoor kitchen. Domesticity at the campsite is one of my secret pleasures.

After a night at Turtle Lake, we kept moving. We paddled to Clearwater Lake the next day, where the water-filtering hand pump broke. It had been working hard to produce drinking water for six people. Tom was silently irked by the necessity to filter water, an imperative caused by the introduction of the intestinal parasite giardia into the Boundary Waters. The parasite had not been present in our youth, and we missed being able to drink directly from the lake, but we couldn't risk a giardia infection, especially in the children. After the pump broke, we boiled the drinking water and filled the water jug and canteens from the big cook kettle.

We were cheered to see the kids act as a team on the trip. They worked together on the portages, lifting packs on and off for each other, making sure the loads were fairly distributed. I never carried a canoe on any portage. Andy toiled like a draft horse, and he also took responsibility for the heavy equipment pack, the one with the tents and other gear. Even Christina, at eight, carried her share, wearing four life jackets over the portage and carrying the lantern. She told me after one portage that she needed a neck rub to ease the soreness from such a heavy load.

We returned to Gabbro Lake on the way out, planning to end the trip on a high note. But on the penultimate day, as we entered Gabbro, we learned that those initial two long portages had indeed insulated us from the crowds: the lake can be accessed many different ways, and it teemed with people. There are a lot of campsites on Gabbro, and we had felt confident of nabbing one. However, as we proceeded down the lake, with another canoe party on our tail, we began to wonder. Site after site had tents, clotheslines, stoves, and overturned canoes at the shoreline.

We finally did find an unoccupied site, perhaps the last one. It was high above the lake, with stunning views, a classic Boundary Waters scene. Alas, the site looked spent from heavy usage. The plot had no grass, only bare earth. The long roots of the pines that sheltered it lay exposed because of soil compaction. It was free of trash. The campers before us had been considerate, but I wondered if there had been a day all summer when this lovely site had not hosted a tent.

Our boys had entered the wilderness with hopes of catching lots of fish, but they had been skunked to this point. On the last night on Gabbro, Andy suggested that I take them out and paddle from the stern while they both cast off either side of the canoe. John had on his line a Rapala that he had found on a portage trail. He had lost two lures on Clearwater Lake, including a favorite that had cost a lot of money, a significant loss for an eleven-year-old, so he was protective of this lure and almost frantic when it occasionally snagged on submerged obstacles.

Andy, older and wealthier, had brought his tackle box and an arsenal of lures: a blue Dardevle, a Rattling Fat Rap, a Mepps squirrel tail, among others. Nothing appealed to the fish we knew were out there. After two frustrating hours, we gave up and went in. It was Kraft macaroni and cheese for dinner, the default in lieu of walleye or lake trout. The only consolation was, the kids *liked* mac and cheese, so there were murmurs of approval when I pulled out the box from the food pack.

The next morning, we were cleaning up from pancakes, and John was down at the water's edge, practicing casting—Andy had heavily criticized John's skill, or lack thereof, the night before— when suddenly the docile Rapala on his line took off, out of his control. He began hollering, and we all came running. Andy issued instructions: let out line . . . let him take it . . . wear him out . . . keep the tip of your rod up . . . keep it up, John!

When the fish finally surfaced, we saw that it was half as long as John was tall, a sleek northern pike. Tom and Katie ran for their cameras, and Andy managed to grab the fish behind the gills and lift it out of the water. Photographers snapped away as John posed beside the fish. We estimated it at six pounds, the biggest fish anyone in our family had ever caught.

A fish that large is old, a good reproducer, and the boys intended to work the lure free and release the pike back to the lake. But northern pike are slimy, and one snappy jerk of its tail set it free of Andy's grasp. It landed on the rocks, where it injured itself. Upon inspection, Andy thought it wouldn't survive, so now the capture became a kill. Andy fetched his fillet knife and, using the paddle as a cutting board, expertly filleted the great fish, all the while castigating himself: "My fault! All my fault! I should have kept it in the water!" John got the shovel, took the remains of the fish out in the woods, and buried them. Both of these acts assumed sacramental significance, the boys later told me. Andy said he always thanks a fish for giving its life before filleting it. John merely offered thanks to God for prayers answered—for only minutes before, he had been praying for a fish!

We had the northern pike for supper that night. It was a complex meal, laced with sorrow over the death of the fish, pleasure at its wonderful taste, and bewilderment at the ambivalence of our emotion. The fillets were nearly an inch thick, firm and white, wild and sweet. It fed the six of us.

The big fish was a gift to us from the Boundary Waters, the last one, as it turned out. For while we reveled in the pleasure we had taken from the clear waters and the magnificent bedrock of that unique wilderness area, we also retained our memories of paddling the length of Gabbro Lake, seeing every campsite occupied. The Boundary Waters was telling us something with its exhausted campsites, its compacted portage trails, its elaborate reservation system, and the lack of openings.

Long ago, a friend who had been raised Catholic told me of his philosophy of denying one's self something in order to more fully appreciate it. This idea confounded me, a Protestant lacking familiarity with priests, nuns, and monks. I still don't fully understand the idea. I am not alone. It is not the American way to deny one's self a pleasure. A century ago, when the stunning, exotic-looking Wood Duck suffered plummeting numbers and was headed for extinction, because of overhunting and habitat loss—but mostly because of overhunting—men nonetheless argued forcefully for a hunting season. The birds were tasty, fun to hunt, and beautiful. Shooting the birds allowed them in some way to participate in that beauty. The Wood Duck population remained precarious until the federal government slapped a closed season on it. Then Wood Duck numbers rebounded, and they are today one of the most common ducks in North America. But they might have been loved to death.

In college, Tom took a course on wilderness philosophy. The phrase "loving it to death" was used by Roderick Nash in his book *Wilderness and the American Mind,* which was the course's textbook. Nash noted that in the past, wild places had been destroyed because not enough people had valued or visited them. But the current irony of wilderness preservation was that wild places are now ruined by too many visitors. The two examples Nash gave for places being loved to death were the Grand Canyon and the Boundary Waters Canoe Area Wilderness.

The phrase lingered in my mind. Was a portage pleasurable if I worried about the damage my boot was doing? Was it solitude if every campsite was occupied?

Our thoughts about the Boundary Waters became as complex as that fish dinner on Gabbro Lake. We had enjoyed vacations there for a quarter of a century, but perhaps it was time to let it go, to deny ourselves the pleasure. There are other waters to paddle, Tom and I told ourselves. We set out to find them.

Burnt Woods River

....

THE BOIS BRULE RIVER IS AN ARTERY THAT RUNS THROUGH northwestern Wisconsin. It is modest in length at forty-four miles but lavish in beauty. The Ojibwe called it Wiisaakode-zibi, "a river through half-burnt woods." French Canadian voyageurs translated this to Bois Brule, "burnt woods." Today, after centuries of plunder and restoration, the forests surrounding the sparkling Brule are verdant and bountiful, white pine and black spruce spires soaring like steeples over green aspen and birch.

The river originates in a boggy headwaters, which also gives rise to the St. Croix River. The two rivers fall on either side of a watershed, the St. Croix flowing south into the Mississippi and the Brule flowing northward into Lake Superior. A short, ancient portage trail at the source connects the two. This nexus has made the Brule a major route for centuries. Of all the rivers we have traversed, the Bois Brule has perhaps the longest history with the canoe. When we dip paddles into its clear water, we connect with people of many different cultures.

The tough Ojibwe traveled up and down the tempestuous waterway, moving from woodland villages to the great lake. There are accounts of Native Americans bringing their dying elders down the river to rest their eyes on Lake Superior one last time. The Ojibwe and the equally tough voyageurs transported great piles of furs trapped in the interior to trading posts located on Superior.

Early European explorers used it to access settlements on the Mississippi from Lake Superior. The litany of names is familiar for the mark they would leave on a future Minnesota: Daniel Greysolon, Sieur du Lhut; Pierre Le Sueur; Jonathan Carver. Henry

Schoolcraft and his party returned home on the Brule in 1832, after their expedition to Lake Itasca and Fort Snelling. Members of the Schoolcraft party vividly described their trip down the Brule. Several of the men kept journals during the expedition, and in them they recount a ragged journey, canoes battered by rocks and beset by rapids.

In more recent memory, the Brule was the center of the U.S. presidency for a brief summer, in 1928. That year, President Calvin Coolidge opted to perform his constitutional duties *and* go fly-fishing in the months leading up to the stock market crash.

But for my family, the Bois Brule is the river we know the best, the one we canoe several times each year. Because our family cabin is only five miles away, we paddle the Brule in May, when trees on the riverbanks have tiny, green leaves; in August, when summer is full and lush; and in October, when the woods turn austere and dry, just before snowfall. Our photo albums hold images of the children as downy chicks, sitting two abreast, sliding across its silky waters in a canoe; of leggy, stilt-like grade-schoolers, gathered under a cedar tree for a trail lunch; and of teens with paddles in hand, gaining skill and dexterity at running rapids.

The river can be run in several sections, depending on how long paddlers want to be out, the water depth, and how much thrill they seek. Schoolcraft and his party griped about the nature of the Brule's rapids. "The river itself is a perfect torrent," the explorer complained. "[It] might appropriately be called Rapid or Mad River, or almost anything else, but by its popular name of *Brule*." The river's upper reaches, however, are mostly tranquil with only a few, manageable rapids. When the Brule crosses a geological formation called the Copper Range, though, it begins to fall quickly, over three hundred feet in eighteen miles. At some rapids in these sections the Leaf family, with its open canoes, takes to the portage path, having learned the hard way that discretion is the better part of valor.

....

A county road crosses the Bois Brule via a small stone bridge some five miles from its boggy source. Paddlers can drop their canoes in at a landing adjacent this bridge. A four-hour paddle will get them to the next landing, Winneboujou, named for a private group of landowners.

Initially, the small stream gathers water from springs, trickling along, too shallow to float a canoe. The Schoolcraft party complained about this, too. It was nearing the end of a three-month trip, and the men were injured, their feet bruised and bleeding from having walked up the rocky St. Croix River. By Stone's Bridge crossing, though, the Brule runs clear and navigable, spring-fed, so that the water level is always sufficient for paddling.

In these upper reaches, the Brule has a serenity and an intimacy that can be found nowhere else on the river. I thrill to its affinity with the northern boreal forest. Black spruce spires point heavenward here. Alder thickets flush against the banks harbor tiny, northern birds. The upper Brule is narrow, and the spicy scent of balsam fir wafts over the clear stream. Nashville Warblers, White-throated Sparrows, and Northern Parulas sing from the recesses of the deep woods. There is a clean scent to the air.

Some of the Midwest's old wealthy families have summer homes on this stretch. Their ample cottages, wrapped in screened porches, perch high over the water. Classic, functional boathouses rest below on the water with wooden docks extending out, places from which to launch canoes. These estates, too, are oriented toward the canoe as the primary means of engaging with the river. Adirondack chairs cluster on grassy lawns at river's edge. If residents are out enjoying the summer day, we wave as we drift past. The river's current is leisurely, but there's never enough opportunity for canoeists to gawk. Each trip as we float past, we appreciate the window boxes and planters filled with red and pink petunias and impatiens, the spacious screened porches with rattan chairs, and the neatly trimmed lawns, but we are not really able to invade the privacy of the wealthy.

As the Brule widens and loses its intimate feel, paddlers approach a series of small bridges spanning the river. The rustic, pleasing spans connect guest cottages of the Cedar Island estate, owned by the Ordway family, heir to Minnesota Mining and

Manufacturing money. The entire retreat is in a private conservation trust, ensuring their holdings will not be further developed.

Cedar Island boasts of a presidential past. In 1928, the 4,160-acre getaway was taken over by the Coolidge White House. The president spent the summer in the lodge with its eight bedrooms, four baths, Italian oak paneling, and French wicker furniture. Mrs. Coolidge took a staff of fourteen with her. No Secret Service accompanied them. Ten White House detectives and soldiers from Fort Snelling provided security.

According to *Time* magazine, President Coolidge signed a slew of bills into law before he left and held a budget meeting the morning of departure. The real draw of the Brule was the fishing. The river, cool and clean, was then, and still is now, a premier trout stream. Brook, lake, steelhead, and rainbow trout—raised in the owner's private hatchery and hand-fed on liver (according to *Time*)—were so numerous and so tame that they could be caught by a dip net.

Cedar Island was not yet in Ordway hands when it became Coolidge's summer White House. But after the Ordways took possession, they, too, entertained a president: Dwight Eisenhower. Locals claim that the president came several times to the retreat to fly-fish.

Three more presidents can be added to the Bois Brule's list of celebrity visitors: Ulysses S. Grant, Grover Cleveland, and Herbert Hoover, who as the Republican candidate dropped in on Coolidge in 1928.

....

But the current has carried us away from Cedar Island, and soon we are preoccupied with lunch, which we often eat under the boughs of a large, twisted white cedar growing on the west riverbank, still on the Ordway estate.

Although mostly tranquil, there is a standout Class I rapids near our picnic site that must be navigated. It occurs in a gentle bend in the river. There is always sufficient water to carry a canoe safely over it, but the force of the water tends to push a canoe into the outer curve, and paddlers need to put some effort into keeping the craft away from the bank. We have never upset on this mild rapids. Nonetheless, I am always just a bit apprehensive when we encounter it, and that says much more about my timidity than about the rapids, which on many maps of the Brule is labeled "The Falls."

One summer noon, as we picnicked at a lookout spot just above the Falls, with a clear view of it, we saw a canoe approach paddled by three carefree women, laughing and talking. I was intrigued because it was obvious they were going to run the rapids without getting out to survey it, although the water chuckled loudly, indicating white water. I also noted that, unlike me, they were not at all anxious, reinforcing my suspicion that I might be a neurotic paddler. It did not occur to me that perhaps these women had run the rapids many times. They weren't giving off the right vibes.

The kids also watched intently as the canoe, two paddlers and a duffer, a red-and-white plastic cooler standing upright, life jackets and extra paddles in the bottom, edged closer to the rapids. The women were gleeful, the whole thing was a lark, right up until the moment when the canoe lurched and tipped, spilling its contents completely into the bubbling waters. In particular, the red-and-white cooler bobbing, lid off, in the white foaming water, seared in the memory of all of us.

We did not go to their rescue. The Brule is shallow in this section. It was a warm day. A dousing wouldn't hurt anyone. There was screaming as the women hit the water, and more laughter. They began scrambling to retrieve their gear.

My first impulse was smugness. Goodness, what did they think this is? A Disney ride? But my second, more reflective thought was that not everyone takes life as seriously as I, and I might be a great deal happier if I were more lighthearted. Nonetheless, the loss of sandwiches and sitting in wet clothes after a dousing doesn't make anyone happy.

We would not forget the incident and ever after have referred to the rapids as "Women-Cooler Falls." We know exactly what rapids we are talking about when we mention it. It has become a shorthand for heedless women, a floating cooler, and a perhaps rash attitude toward canoeing.

The segment of river beginning at the Winneboujou landing and extending to the Brule River landing and campground is a short, wild ride. On this section, the river roils in a nearly continuous run of riffles, a swift forty-five-minute trip.

One October, when the kids were young, we entertained a cabin full of houseguests, a family with several children. We wanted to show them the Brule, but we thought that some of the seven children were too young for a long paddle, duffing in chilly weather. We solved the dilemma by deciding to paddle this short section of the river. We would do it in turns: a men-and-oldest-sons' round, and a moms' round. While the women were paddling, the dads would take the kids, ranging in age from eight to one, to the nearby state fish hatchery to see the little fish.

All segments of the Brule are rocky in low water. This stretch is possibly where the men in the Schoolcraft party began their lament. They were headed for the trading post at La Pointe on Madeline Island in Lake Superior, and the delicate birch-bark canoes were nearly destroyed. Rocks battered what remained of the vessels, and they were short of spruce gum to repair gashes made by rocks, although they frequently needed to pull out and patch holes. The men had met two Ojibwe families going upriver as the expedition prepared to descend and had tried to barter for use of one of their canoes, but the Native Americans took one look at the condition of the Schoolcraft canoes and were not interested. The Ojibwe agreed to carry some of the expedition's gear a ways downriver for pay and also traded some gum to the beleaguered men. It was quickly exhausted, though. The party then resorted to using red clay from cutaway riverbanks. This proved highly unsatisfactory. Later, fed up, some of the men abandoned the river and walked through the thick forest to the lake.

It was because the Brule in low water is studded with rocks that we decided to buy a second canoe of Royalex plastic. Fiberglass is much lighter, but we felt it would not stand up to the Brule's punishing flow. Royalex, on the other hand, slips like silk over barely submerged rocks, a feature causing many "whews!" in an aftermath.

So the moms are going on a forty-five-minute joyride down the Brule. Both of us are experienced paddlers but accustomed to paddling the bow. Our husbands generally steer. Why is this? Logistically, the strongest paddler should be in front. In our family, we do it because sometimes the canoe needs just a bit of a shove—brute strength—to make the final correction for a wandering canoe, and Tom does brute strength much better than I.

On this trip, however, I will be the stern paddler, navigating the rocks. I am a bit regretful. We will be paddling past an old summer estate, Swiftwater Farm, the former retreat of Elizabeth Congdon of Duluth, heir to a fortune made on the Iron Range of northern Minnesota. It is a big but rustic compound, and it affords a little thrill to canoeists zipping past, but we are always dealing with white water at that point in the river. Certainly as sternsman, I would have no time for rubbernecking.

The final excitement of this segment is the Little Joe Rapids, a Class II that has about a foot drop. When you approach these rapids, you can see that the canoe will actually tilt down a full foot, water pushing it forward and shooting it out into calmer water below. There is a big boulder in the middle of the river at the drop. It is common knowledge that paddlers should aim for the right-hand side of this rapids, to the right of the rock. That's where the flow is.

Rapids can be read by paddlers in the language of Vs. A V pointing at you is a rock (perhaps submerged) with water diverging around it. This is not something you want to hit. A V inverted, like this ∧, is a chute. Water flows freely through that chute and will carry the canoe forward without upset. That is, at least, the theory.

The moms start out and quickly enter the riffles that will jostle us all the way down. The Brule bubbles and chuckles along, and we are impressed by how quickly the riverbank passes by. No time to check out Swiftwater! No time to focus on the eagle high up in a white pine!

In the stern, I pick our path through frothy riffles. Time and again, the canoe scrapes momentarily against a submerged rock, then skims off without deviation of course. Soon, much sooner than forty-five minutes it would seem—we have not yet finished discussing the problems of the world—we hear the thrashing water of the Little Joe Rapids.

Stay to the right! Don't be misled by other options! Don't be pulled into the sphere of emergent rocks singing a siren song! Those standing waves are only that—water, not hidden boulders! Here's the drop! Paddle hard! Stay centered!

Whee! We're through it and skimming along on the swirling waters below. Our children stand on the dock of the campground, watching their mothers triumph.

....

U.S. Highway 2 roars over the scenic Brule on a massive bridge. Once paddlers pass under the structure and before they reach Highway 13, the dual nature of the river reveals itself. The idyllic, winding river disappears and is replaced by a raging torrent. Volcanoes from the earth's violent past are ultimately responsible for changing nice Dr. Jekyll into scary Mr. Hyde. A billion years ago, after a period of volcanic activity, the basin of what would become Lake Superior sagged, causing surrounding rock layers to uplift. In the area of the Brule this formed a ridge referred to as the Copper Range, and after crossing this, the Brule tumbles steeply toward Superior.

There are two sets of Class III rapids on this stretch with drops so pronounced that they are labeled "ledges": the Lenroot Ledges and the Mays Ledges. These ledges are like rock stairs, moving progressively downstream, with significant drops each step. For ten years, we avoided this stretch of river. It is a joy to kayakers but not to paddlers in open canoes. Then one August, after a great deal of rain, so that we knew water roared over the ledges, Tom decided that we ought to attempt to run them. The water was sufficient to carry canoes over boulders that ordinarily would give us trouble, and it was warm. If we tipped, we would not be chilled.

There are very few people I trust to paddle with me in white water. Tom is first on my list, and so strong is my faith in his judgment that later, recalling the day in my journal, I did not record questioning his decision. I did, however, describe looking at the first set of ledges, the Lenroot, with fear, not the usual anxiety, and opting not to run them. Which makes what happened even less in character with my true nature.

We dropped two canoes into the Brule at Pine Tree landing, the girls with Tom in the Old Town, the canoe that slides over rocks; and the boys and I in the old, battered Grumman. Let me mention here that in the movie *Deliverance*, it is a *Grumman* canoe that goes over the waterfall and pops right up again, persistently buoyant in the face of trauma. We were all dressed in quick-dry shorts and swimsuits, river sandals on our feet. We understood that on this trip, we could get wet.

We were astonished at the swiftness of the current at Pine Tree, so unlike anything we had seen previously on the Brule. Water rushed and swirled and was a silty red, carrying a lot of eroded clay.

After a series of warm-up rapids, in no time at all, really, we glided under a swinging walk bridge, a noted take-out juncture, either to portage around the Lenroots or to survey them to see how best to run them. It was at this point that I realized that all the instructions in our well-worn brochure of the river were directed toward kayakers, not canoeists.

The high water obscured the architecture of the ledges, but we could see the drops, including a four-foot waterfall on the second ledge, water cascading in a brown curtain. There was a discernible chute on the first ledge. Easy, we thought, surveying it. To approach the second ledge, the common wisdom was to cross in front of a big central boulder and run it on the left side, avoiding the waterfall. After scrutinizing it, Tom agreed with this, even though I pointed out that the protruding boulder could cut off easy access to the left side. We analyzed the right bank, where we might also escape the waterfall, but overhanging willows would entangle us.

After the reconnaissance, the females of the party immediately chose to portage; the males, to shoot the rapids. Tom chose the Old Town, for its slippery hull, and the girls and I would haul the heavy Grumman over the portage path.

From the bank, we watched Tom, John, age twelve, and Andy, age sixteen, take the first ledge through the chute amid the foment.

Then, with the famous brute strength, Tom heaved the canoe to the left. The huge standing waves kicked up sheets of water as the canoe traversed them. The Old Town wobbled precariously, and John, the duffer, white-knuckled the gunwales, but the craft stayed upright. They avoided the boulder, shot past the waterfall, made the dip, crossed to the right for the final two ledges, and cleared them, the Old Town rocking and rolling and all of us cheering. The boys landed on the right bank, triumphant and soaked.

Well, if one canoe can do it, the other one can do it. Tom had the added benefit now of experience. I reversed my decision to portage and agreed to be his bowman. We left all essential gear, including his precious Canon SLR10 on the bank. At the last minute, Christina, age nine, asked to come along. Tom agreed.

I knelt in the bow to lower the center of gravity, and Tom knelt in the section immediately behind Christina for better maneuverability. We rocked as we shot through the chute on the first ledge, but took on a lot of water as the roaring amber river spilled into the canoe. The added water made the heavy Grumman harder to turn. Even Tom's brute strength waivered in the sharp left past the troublesome boulder that guarded the waterfall. The rocking canoe gathered momentum as the current pushed against us broadside. A submerged rock hung us up momentarily, but in that briefest moment the water won. The Grumman began to roll, hung up between the first and second ledge. As I tumbled out, I glimpsed Tom grabbing Christina around her waist before she even hit the water. "Thank God!" I thought. "She's safe!"

The canoe continued to roll. The spectators on the bank later reported it did a 360. ("I was terrified," Andy added.) I scrambled out of the way, certain that the canoe could do more damage to me than the roiling water would. The water on top of the ledge was only about four feet deep, and I could touch bottom, but the force kept me off my feet. There was a bit of a pause in which I had time to position myself in the water so that my feet pointed downstream just as I had been taught. I watched Tom's yellow paddle precede me over the waterfall and resurface without hesitation. "Good," I thought. "No undertow." Then it was my turn.

It was exhilarating shooting over the waterfall, hitting the river below. I suddenly realized that my life vest was working because I now bobbed in water over my head. A second or two later, having cleared the falls and survived, I thought it might be smart not to go any farther downstream, so I dog-paddled to a big basalt rock in the middle of the stream and perched on it while I gathered my wits. I took stock of my injuries. Nothing was broken. I had a few bruises I could already feel welling. The yellow paddle that had preceded me downriver was probably lost.

From my tiny island, I could see Tom and Christina were already on dry land, and Andy was cautiously treading his way through waist-deep water to reach me. Katie and John, at the river's edge, seemed goggle-eyed with fear, which in retrospect makes me wonder if the upset was worse to watch than to experience firsthand. When Andy and I made it to shore, Tom and Christina were more subdued than frightened. Or maybe for Leafs, not given to dramatic excess, silence is the state beyond fear.

There was a landing on County Road FF, which we had glimpsed as we tossed over the ledges. We could pull out there, because for the younger three, the canoe trip was over. They were not interested in any more paddling that day.

We had lost two paddles in the upset, though, and we had tipped in the *middle* of the Lenroot Ledges. We still needed to clear the last two steps, and now we had only one paddle. Luckily, these last two drops were not an impediment. Tom and Andy paddling, I crouched down and let them carry me over. We regrouped below the ledges, arranged ourselves in two canoes. Katie and Tom soon recovered my favorite paddle downstream and, later, the yellow one. At the FF landing, Tom gave the three younger kids a twenty dollar bill and told them to go buy themselves Cokes at a nearby tavern. He showed them on a map where our car was parked and how to get there, a two-mile walk.

....

Then, we prepared for the second set of ledges, the Mays. With Andy in the bow and Tom in the stern, we set off.

The Mays Ledges are more perfect steps than the Lenroots. They drop discernibly: one, two, three, four. The first drop, we discovered when we got out for reconnaissance, was a big one: four feet with no obvious chute. This one we thought we should portage around. Perhaps the Lenroot upset had made us more cautious, but I think that a four-foot drop would have had us portaging regardless.

We took the next one, though, with an undeniable rush of excitement. It was simply thrilling, the roar, the speed, the sense of being surrounded by water with force and vibrancy.

Then, after clearing the third ledge, we upset a second time. The canoe emptied its contents to the right, close to the bank. I reached out to embrace the water, grabbing my favorite paddle as we flew. Andy hit his back, somehow, and gasped. Tom hung on to the canoe to prevent its descent downstream. An old wooden paddle that had been with us for twenty-five years and had been serving as a spare, took off in the current, though, and we would never find it.

Once again drenched and trying to keep a footing in a torrent of water, we crawled back into the canoe, took the fourth ledge, and said good riddance to the last one.

There were many rapids after the Mays Ledges before we came to our car parked at the Highway 13 landing. They were all child's play to us, jaded as we now were with experience of more daunting drops. We could no longer conjure up a rush of adrenaline. We were weary of white water. It was hard to imagine that stout-hearted Ojibwe families and voyageurs pulled canoes and gear *up* this river.

We reached the landing and our car, hauled out the canoe, and prepared to pick up the other canoe that we had ditched at FF. Katie, John, and Christina were waiting for us, their spirits brightened by Cokes and a round of beer hall pool.

That night we dined on lake trout, caught by Port Wing's local fishery, and baked potatoes, downed by Duluth beer. We ate voraciously. Our senses had been heightened by the intensity of our trip down the roiling Bois Brule.

By bedtime, Tom was talking about renting kayaks and giving it another go. We were all interested. The ledges would be possible in kayaks, we thought.

....

After the tumultuous ledges, the Bois Brule settles down a bit. Paddlers on the last section of river between Highway 13 and its mouth at Lake Superior no longer face exciting or challenging rapids. The river in its last miles oscillates between rocky riffles created by small drops and hidden boulders, and expanses of calm in a sinuous series of S curves. High-strung paddlers like me vibrate in response to these, experiencing in turn tension and release, tension and release, as each new set presents itself on succeeding curves.

So this stretch in its own way wears on the nerves. Nonetheless, we embarked on a paddle one sunny, breezy day after a night of heavy rain. The river ran terra-cotta from eroded clay coming off the banks. Tom and I paddled a new canoe that day, a sixteen-foot red Old Town Penobscot, one foot shorter and ten pounds lighter than our trusty green craft.

Tom considered the new canoe a midlife crisis vehicle. A man facing eleven years of college tuition payments couldn't entertain thoughts of red Corvettes, but he could, perhaps, think about a lighter-weight canoe. Something more devil-may-care than forest green.

We weren't sold on this new canoe, though. It felt precarious to us, more likely to tip than our seventeen foot. We had had it out earlier in the summer, and Tom thought it responded more quickly in turns. So it was like a smaller car: less safe but relying on maneuverability to dodge mishaps.

A unique feature of this section of river is a lamprey barrier about three miles from the mouth. Sea lampreys are parasitic invasive fish that first entered the Great Lakes via the Welland Canal. By 1938, the parasites were killing native fish in Lake Superior by attaching via a sucker to the fish and draining fluid. Native fish populations were decimated, and a fish dinner from Superior was a rarity.

Lampreys migrate up streams to spawn, and the Brule was a natural spawning bed. In the 1950s, biologists began experimenting with various barriers to block the lamprey but not the trout and salmon, which also spawn in rivers. After decades of trial and error, a weir was devised on the Brule that traps lampreys but allows the game fish to run a little obstacle course to travel upstream.

Lampreys by the thousands are caught each spring as they undergo their run. Since the erection of this weir and others like it on streams all around Superior's watershed, the game fish populations have rebounded, and fisheries are once again flourishing. This is a change that we've seen in our time on the river, and it is exciting.

Canoeists come upon the weir as a roped-off part of the river and are signed to a short portage path that skirts the edge of it. The grassy path is hardly trod upon, a visual confirmation that this segment of the Brule sees far fewer paddlers than the upper reaches.

After the endless winding and the riffles and the weir, we came at last to the river's very end, Lake Superior and its sandy shore. The Ojibwe once had a village here at the Brule's mouth, a jumping-off point before parties took off up the river. In 1832 when the Schoolcraft party approached the village at journey's end, they could hear the rhythmic thumping of ceremonial drums.

The last hundred yards of the river flow by curtains of emergent plants lining the banks. When the canoe finally bursts out of the sheltered water, the bright expanse of the great lake feels liberating.

After a picnic on the beach, Katie and John departed, needing to get back to the cabin, but Andy and Christina remained, and we decided impromptu to paddle on Superior the five miles home. It was late afternoon, and the front that had moved through with blue skies and a brisk wind had blown itself out.

The white caps frothing on breakers during lunch disappeared. The waves were gentle and rolling, big heaving water that buoyed us mentally and physically. In our canoes we paddled far from shore, way out where we caught sight of the outermost Apostle Islands and the hulking mass of the Bayfield Peninsula. The Brule and its fussy riffles and hidden rocks were forgotten. We gazed through twenty feet of clear, glass-green water at immense boulders on the lake bottom and big snags, nearly intact tree trunks with many branches. We startled a large raft of mergansers, their rusty ducktail head feathers looking cool and hip. Small, agile Common Terns followed us for a bit, curious about the unusual boats on the water.

For many miles the shoreline east of the Brule River was un-developed. The sandy beach went on and on, punctuated by small streams entering the lake. As we approached Fish Creek, only two miles from our cabin, we saw the first man-made structure. The highway was also exposed at this point, and far, far off, we caught a glimpse of John on a training run. He saw us, too, "way out" he said, on the water.

To the northeast, there seemed to be no limit to the water, to the sky. Superior's stretch met the horizon, blue upon blue.

Paddling with the Alligators

JEAN LAFITTE NATIONAL
HISTORICAL PARK AND PRESERVE, 2001

....

OUR PALE WINTER SKIN SEEMED BLEACHED UNDER THE strong Louisiana sunshine. April, All Fools' Day, and we were experiencing real heat for the first time in six months. Tom's forehead, unprotected by a hat, glistened with sweat. Katie's and my bare arms were white against the dark backdrop of the bayou.

We had dropped into the Pelican State for a brief visit, accompanied by our sixteen-year-old. Tom and I had established a tradition of taking each child on a trip when they were sixteen. Katie, our second child, sandwiched between two noisy and extroverted brothers, often struggled to be heard in family conversations. We looked forward to our time alone with her.

She was excited when we planned a trip to Louisiana. None of us had been there before. She expected the charm of New Orleans's French Quarter and the hanging moss of southern plantations, but here we were, in a canoe, chasing alligators at the Jean Lafitte National Historical Park and Preserve, a short drive south of New Orleans. Jazz and Cajun food would have to wait while we pursued a different kind of local color.

The Jean Lafitte National Historical Park and Preserve is comprised of six units, each protecting one of the Mississippi Delta region's unique features. The park is named for an infamous pirate of the early 1800s, Jean Lafitte, who with his brother, Pierre, began life on the shady side with a smuggling operation out of Barataria Bay. The business brought goods through an embargo to the port of New Orleans, where they were sold on the black market. Lafitte had acquired intricate knowledge of the bayou, which aided him in his undertaking and made him difficult to catch. The pirate had Robin Hood aspects to his character, but he also dipped into the slave trade when the opportunity arose, spied for the Spanish in the Mexican War of Independence, and at different times was variously cheered and decried by the inhabitants of New Orleans.

The Barataria Preserve, where Lafitte got his smuggling start, is twenty-three thousand acres of watery wildlife refuge. Boardwalks wind through portions of swamp and marsh; hiking paths cross the higher ground. The bayou is dredged into canals, and visitors can rent canoes and poke about in them.

When Tom first suggested that we explore a Louisiana bayou by canoe, I was less than enthused. He seemed to think that observation of alligators would be a big attraction. Katie and I imagined six-foot reptiles enraged by our presence, rearing out of the water, our canoe on their back, dumping us into black water to deal with swarming water moccasins and copperheads. Somehow, this didn't appeal.

Undeterred, Tom coaxed us into a visit to the Barataria Preserve soon after arriving in Louisiana. We had toured the requisite sugar plantation that morning, and Katie had enjoyed imagining the life of a southern belle—hoopskirts, parasols, and slow drawls. Perhaps she figured it was now her dad's turn for fun.

Later the same day, we drove to Jean Lafitte National Historical Park and walked the boardwalks through the swamp. One took us into a section with a thick palmetto understory. We found the palmettos amazing, almost as if they had been drawn by Dr. Seuss. The leaves were fanlike, big and rounded, the type of plant that served to cool a pharaoh or Mayan king. Although palmettos are palms, they are more shrub-like, growing in clumps, the two-inch-thick trunks often sprawling along the ground.

From the boardwalk, Katie spied a leggy Yellow-crowned Night-Heron perched on a log, a wetland dweller rarely seen in Minnesota. It had a red eye and a yellow ducktail hairdo, and when it edged down its log, it carefully placed one claw-like foot in front of another, like a slow-motion ballet dancer.

We saw White Ibises and blooming irises, hanging moss and

bald cypress, but what had fascinated us most had been the alligators. Small ones, two or three feet long, rested in the watery swamp off the boardwalk. Most had been partially submerged, with only a yellow eye to sleepily observe us. On some we could detect corrugated backs that looked distinctly reptilian, though certainly like no reptiles we had ever seen in Minnesota. We all thought they were really cool and, obviously, not too dangerous, or the park wouldn't let us near them, would it?

The boardwalk gave me the false sense that snakes, which were undoubtedly out there, could not get at me. Indeed, I deliberately did not look for snakes (a practice I cling to back home as well), and so I had not seen any. Louisiana has a stunning diversity of snakes—twenty species alone in the Barataria Preserve—a number of them poisonous, but I believed park literature when I read that if you didn't bother them, snakes would not bother you. I would not bother them.

Katie was not overly concerned by snakes. Spiders are her bugaboo, and we would not be looking for *them*, either.

....

The next day, we rented a seventeen-foot plastic canoe from a private outfitter and entered the preserve via Twin Canals, a dredged-out waterway through the bayou. Our entire time in the bayou would be on canals originally dredged to allow loggers access to valuable bald cypress stands, or for drainage or irrigation. It was not a genuine back-to-nature experience. On the other hand, it was certainly exotic for Minnesotans—we had never seen a landscape like the bayou—and it was authentic: canals are what many of the bayous in Louisiana have become.

From our canoe on the bayou, we could see what a soggy world southern Louisiana really is. Although trees rose high overhead, their bases were thickened by buttresses that anchored them in the aqueous substrate. Tall trees grew from the flooded floor and beneath them, a substantial understory of shrubs about six feet tall. Spanish moss, which is not a true moss but an epiphyte without roots in soil, hung in feathery plumes from open branches. On the first of April, leaves were small and newly emerged. It looked like spring, even in the bayou, where I didn't imagine distinct seasons.

Wild irises bloomed in certain marshy areas. The giant blue iris is Barataria's crown jewel. A native iris, it once flourished in great profusion across the bayou country. Drainage and ditching have greatly reduced its numbers, as has collection of the iris by commercial interests and home gardeners. Barataria is one of the last places to see this native gem. One of the boardwalks featured thousands of the blooming beauties growing in masses along the water's edge.

The water in the canals was dark and reflected the sky, which was fading in the intense heat of noon. In more open areas, we saw water lilies and lotus not yet in bloom.

We paddled past ragged stands of spindly bald cypress draped with Spanish moss. Bald cypress are the signature trees of the bayou, much like white pines are in northern Minnesota. They are conifers with short needles and broad crowns but lack the regular, sweeping boughs of white pine. Cypress wood is prized for its ability to withstand rot. Consequently, like pines in Minnesota, they have been logged out and reduced to a shade of their magnificence. Still, a silhouette of a line of bald cypress seen from across the expanse of a marsh is a feast for the eyes, and we marveled at it.

Soon we turned our attention to alligators. Like the cypress trees, the gators of Barataria tended to be small and less magnificent than those we would later see in the Florida Everglades. Probably this was because alligators are hunted in Louisiana. There are nearly two million alligators in the state, and the hunt and sale of their hides generate tens of millions of dollars each year. We learned to look for objects resembling floating logs near the water's edge. On second glance, we would see the log had an eye, and the eye was on us.

Tom had his camera ready, and Katie and I tried hard to sneak up on the reptile. But the sleepy look was deceptive. No matter how quietly we paddled, how little our ripples in the water, the "log" sank out of sight before we came within camera range. It was perverse, in a way. Now that we had finally decided alligators were wildlife to appreciate and observe, we could hardly do either. Their retiring nature got in the way of our pursuit. Little bubbles rising to the surface marked their disappearance.

People frequently confuse alligators with crocodiles. The two are relatives but dissimilar in personality. American crocodiles live only in Florida. They are tropical and confined to warm climes. They can be identified by a narrow snout and a large tooth that extends from the lower jaw and lends the animal a toothy appearance even when the jaws are closed. Although they are less likely than Old World crocodiles to be aggressive, American crocodiles are known to attack humans.

While American alligators are members of the order Crocodilia, they comprise their own family, Alligatoridae. They are much more widespread in the United States, living as far north as southern Virginia and all along the southeastern United States coast to Texas. They seldom leave fresh water and are notably nonaggressive. Their snouts are broad and rounded—we checked this out at a safe distance—and all the ones we saw avoided us. My binoculars came in handy, helping us get a good look at them.

In spring, the Barataria Preserve receives bands of migrating neotropical songbirds that cross the Gulf of Mexico on their way to their northern breeding grounds. The birds cross the water in one mighty flight, usually made at night, and land, exhausted and famished, in the bayou country, ready to fuel up and complete the journey. One bird that the preserve is known for is the yellow Prothonotary Warbler, a bright, restless jewel of a bird. The warbler is primarily a southern species whose northernmost range extends to east-central Minnesota. I had never seen a Prothonotary Warbler before and needed one for my life list. I talked incessantly about seeing one. I kept my binoculars hopefully slung around my neck. Every little flicker of life in the bayou's canopy was cause for interest. Yellow in the treetops? Maybe!

A life list is something Katie understood intellectually but did not embrace. Indeed, this Prothonotary Warbler business perhaps verified her worst fears of what this junket with her parents could become. What could she possibly tell her friends back home about Prothonotary Warblers? But alligators on the other hand . . .

now, an alligator story would hold some currency. Perhaps that's why she paddled enthusiastically toward one floating "log" after another.

My sister-in-law, a native Floridian, had warned me that some snakes will climb the lower branches of trees and drop into a passing boat. I just didn't want to think about what I considered a remote possibility. Then I bought Tom a copy of *Paddling Georgia* as a birthday gift one year, and the writer advised paddlers to be alert for snakes dropping into canoes. It advised easing the surprise visitors out with a paddle blade. That cured me of ever planning a trip into the Okefenokee Swamp.

The width of the canals on this trip seemed to preclude this unwelcome event, and it made for a much more pleasant trip. Tom took lots of photos. Katie, a budding artist, admired the many varied plant forms and shades of green. I never saw my Prothonotary Warbler. (Years later, I would get my life bird on the boardwalk at Jean Lafitte, when on a return visit we hit the migration right, and dozens of the yellow birds occupied the trees, ravenously gulping down inchworms.)

The canals are a dilemma for the park, though, and for recreationists everywhere. Dredging clears paths and makes most forms of boating possible. If dredging were to stop, the waterway would soon be silted over, on its way to becoming land. At the same time, dredging speeds up water flow to the Gulf because plant structures are lacking. This lack of a silty substrate and vegetation increases the infusion of salt water into fresh areas, upsetting the salt balance of certain aquatic communities.

The ragged, watery coastline of the Mississippi delta is disappearing from other changes to the river, particularly dams, that prevent sediments from reaching the river's mouth and rebuilding the delta, which ocean storms batter. This is a serious problem that the United States has yet to address adequately. The National Park Service does a delicate balancing act in managing the canals, trying to do right by its ecosystems and the humans who appreciate and want to explore them.

When our sun-starved skin had had all the sun it could handle for the day, we paddled back up Twin Canals to our take-out point. That night, we would be in New Orleans, eating Creole cooking and listening to jazz. We had introduced our teen to a different side of the South. When her friends asked her about Mardi Gras, she could tell them where the real wildlife hung out.

Mother's Day

THE CANNON RIVER, 2002

....

THE MERRY MONTH OF MAY IS NOT ALWAYS SO CHEERY IN Minnesota. The first half of the month can see freezing temperatures and snow, cold rain, and chilly days. Yet I have special leverage this time of year. My birthday falls just before Mother's Day. Combined, these events usually compel my children to acquiesce to my desires. If I say I want to spend the day outside, hiking or canoeing, even though the weather is exceedingly dismal, we do it. I am seldom put off by "bad" weather, and in fact, for inexplicable reasons, I like a good tromp in the chill and the damp.

So it happened that we were out on the Cannon River in southeastern Minnesota on a raw Mother's Day with snow in the air. The river is a lovely little waterway originating in Shields Lake near Faribault, flowing northeast through the communities of Northfield and Cannon Falls, and emptying into the Mississippi at Red Wing. Below Cannon Falls, the river cuts through bedrock—sandstone, dolomite, remnants of an ancient lake bed—and this forms high bluffs rising on either side of the river.

We canoed a very small stretch of the Cannon, from the village of Welch to a landing where Highway 61 crosses over the river. It was no more than a two-hour paddle, but when the day is chilly and windy, that is enough.

Although the very name *Cannon* would hint at a military past, this is not the case. French fur traders making trips down the Mississippi to a trading post at Prairie du Chien had a habit of leaving their canoes at the river's mouth to explore on foot the surrounding river valley. They called the stream Le Riviere aux Canots, the

River of Canoes. Through means of an early game of "telephone," the name somehow transformed.

In spring, I always associate the Cannon River valley with colorful, restless migratory birds. It is a recognized flyway, and the connection was laid into my deep memory from my early birding days as a college student at nearby Gustavus Adolphus. Since our 2002 paddle, the stretch of river bottom from Welch to Red Wing has been incorporated into the Vermillion Bottoms Lower Cannon River Important Bird Area and given formal recognition as a bird haven.

So this was part of the mix when Tom and I planned the day's activities on the Cannon. The slow spring had, nonetheless, produced Baltimore Orioles, Yellow-rumped Warblers, and a lone Tennessee Warbler attempting to sip sustenance out of a cut orange using its thin, insect-eating beak. All had visited my backyard feeder in the inclement weather. I wanted to see more on the Cannon.

However, bird-watching would not be a selling point for our teenagers, who, even so, earnestly wanted to celebrate their mother on Mother's Day. When presented with the proposal, Andy, twenty, who had already spent the previous day, fishing opener, in a boat on choppy water, was enthusiastic. Katie, eighteen, was also game and greeted me with a wide smile. Fifteen-year-old John was much less pleased, and his thirteen-year-old sister, Christina, agreed with him, but as the youngest, she was used to being corralled into unappealing activities. With four kids, we aimed for consensus but sometimes resorted to simple majority rule.

Tom and Andy loaded the canoes onto the car and threw in paddles and life jackets, and we headed south.

We picnicked at the small village of Welch before dropping in. All of us hunched over the lunch, hoods partially obscuring our faces. We wore windbreakers, polar fleece, wool hats. Katie had her winter Columbia jacket. Cocoa steamed in mugs, but the rest of the meal was cold. John turned his sweatshirt-hooded back on the party, disdaining what was clearly a bad idea.

It wasn't raining or snowing, though, and we appreciated that. The thrill of the meal came when we learned that, in honor of

Mother's Day, volunteers were handing out brownies to users of the nearby Cannon Valley bike trail—and our paddling party qualified.

....

The Cannon flows through land that is intensely cultivated and seems thoroughly domesticated. It is usually not associated with adventure and discovery. Its tame setting is misleading, however. The southeastern Minnesota waterway has ties to French cartographer Joseph Nicollet, who led a federal expedition from Fort Snelling to western Minnesota in 1838.

Because Minneapolis's major streets are Marquette, Nicollet, and Hennepin Avenues, Minnesotans tend without thinking to lump Nicollet with the earlier, French Catholic explorers. That mischaracterizes Monsieur Nicollet, who arrived in Minnesota over a hundred years later. Nicollet was more in league with Lewis and Clark and Zebulon Pike, whose interests were in producing accurate, usable maps of land that was largely unknown.

The uplands around the Cannon had been inhabited by a Dakota band, the Mdewakanton, in 1838. The Mdewakanton were facing many socio-geopolitical changes. The once-eastern Ojibwe were moving into traditional Dakota lands; other tribes just to the south and west were succumbing to smallpox. A letter written to Nicollet the winter before he set out described the country between the St. Peter's (present-day Minnesota) and Des Moines Rivers—now southwestern Minnesota—as "an utter desert." Nicollet remained enthusiastic about the venture, but he did have trouble recruiting voyageurs to accompany him.

Offsetting these drawbacks—smallpox, possible violence—were Nicollet's additions to the standard government provisions for expeditions. The Frenchman requested "17 lbs. of the finest sausage," "two cans of sardines," and four containers of soup, prepared by Delmonico's of New York City. While the French gourmand had no brownies along, as we had been unexpectedly treated to, he did ensure the chocolate supply was "excellent" and ordered ten pounds of it.

....

The Nicollet party found the Cannon River banks to be forested with a mix of hardwoods: red and white oaks, sugar maples, black walnut, ash, and hackberry. Away from the river, the men discovered "a mixture of prairie and clusters of hardwood trees"—a savannah. The river had a swift current.

Nicollet's fall venture up the Cannon ended with a sudden snowstorm in mid-October, followed by temperatures near zero. The unexpected winter weather threatened the party, and it beat a hasty retreat back to Mendota.

Our little family on the Cannon in mid-May certainly related to winter weather out of season. Our children, who had not experienced as many Minnesota springs as Tom and I, considered snow in the air on Mother's Day outrageous. I, however, recall a number of birthdays that had snow in some form, and anyway, I have a penchant for slow, cold springs. I like to see the summer approach in leisurely fashion. I like to wait for it. So I was OK with the snow.

As it happened, the halting spring had given the hills along the Cannon a lovely textured appearance that year. The descendants of—or perhaps the same—trees that the Nicollet party had observed were in various stages of leafing out, some brushed with yellows and greens, others still naked as a January day. These were excellent conditions to see small birds.

As queen for the day, I got my choice: paddle or duff? I chose to duff; Andy and John took control of a canoe, and Tom and the girls headed out in the other. I kept my binoculars at hand.

Birding on a river is not ideal. It is very hard to focus quickly on something small that is moving about in brush before the river carries you away. I locate birds primarily by ear, now, and that makes it a bit easier. Yet this drawback does not stop me from wearing my binoculars around my neck every single time I get into a canoe. One just never knows what might appear, and you're almost guaranteed to see something interesting if you don't have the binocs.

But we didn't need field glasses to see the birds on the Cannon that Mother's Day. Despite the cold, insects flitted over the water, and migrating birds swarmed after them. Tree Swallows and Barn

Swallows swooped in graceful arcs. Along some stretches, they were joined by Rough-winged Swallows and Cliff Swallows. Also taking advantage of flying insects were the earliest migrating wood warblers, the yellow-rumps. These little birds with lemony patches on head, wings, and tail fluttered above the water by the hundreds. Everywhere we looked, we saw Yellow-rumped Warblers. Restless and agile, they were fun and easy to watch. The boys and I never tired of them throughout the two-hour paddle. Hundreds of Yellow-rumped Warblers served as a fine birthday present while I anticipated the arrival of their more tropical cousins later in the month.

Less bird-watching and more singing went on in the other canoe. We all finished the trip in good spirits.

Our children were growing up. Andy departed the Cannon River and went back to college. Katie and John were in high school, and Christina in middle school. They were quickly moving beyond the realm of our influence. I hoped we had instilled in them a sense that any weather could be fine for an adventure. "Our family does things in the *rain*," Christina once observed, on an occasion when Tom and I had blanched at the price of high-tech rain gear. Her remark was made to justify the investment, and I realized that it also set the Leafs apart from most other families.

I hoped the kids had learned to love the world as it is, whatever face it presents. Sun, rain, snow, wind. Every day is a good day to be present.

The Eye of the Wolf

ISLE ROYALE NATIONAL PARK, 2003

....

LAKE SUPERIOR SPREAD OUT ABOUT US IN SILVERY SHEETS as the doughty *Voyageur II* made its way from Minnesota's shore at Grand Portage to Isle Royale. The distant island rose like a hulk on the eastern horizon, looming larger as the minutes passed. Tom and I floated through blueness that morning—the dark teal island, the ice blue sky, the cerulean waters catching the sunlight, dazzling us with sparkles.

We were on our way to paddle the shoreline of the least-visited national park in the United States. Isle Royale is the biggest island in Lake Superior. If one thinks of Superior's shape as the form of a wolf's head, then Isle Royale is the wolf's eye, an elongate slit observing the world, running roughly parallel to the lake's north shore.

We were not alone onboard the *Voyageur II*. About twenty people gathered on the dock in Grand Portage at seven o'clock that morning, and they, too, had brought watercraft. The *Voyageur II* took on our Old Town and three other canoes, as well as four or five kayaks. Only a handful of the score of people who mounted the gangplank were staying at Rock Harbor Lodge, the park service accommodations on the island. The rest of us lugged camping gear, paddles, backpacks, and other outdoor trappings. Some people would backpack across the spine of the island; others, like us, would explore the park from the water, paddling in and out of coves, stopping to rest and picnic, perhaps to swim on pebbly beaches, pitching our tents at night at one of the many campsites the park maintains.

Although it was the summer solstice, it was stunningly cold on board. Lake Superior is slow to take on summer heat; water temperatures remained in the thirties. I wore polar fleece, a wind-breaker, and my wool winter hat and gloves. We hoped that the landmass of the island would lend us even a smidgeon of summer warmth, but we were prepared to wear long pants and our winter outerwear the entire visit.

The owners of the *Voyageur II* dub it a "passenger vessel," and this is accurate in the precise sense: it shuttles people. It also brings mail, groceries, and other supplies to the few residents who have been permitted through a grandfather clause to spend the summer in private cabins along the island's shore. The *Voyageur II* is not a luxury boat, though. The interior cabin, where most of us gathered to escape the eye-watering chill, boasted gray vinyl benches and indoor/outdoor carpeting. The smell of diesel fuel mingled with the aroma of perking coffee. Nonetheless, after our predawn rising to pack the Duluth packs and meet the boat, we were thrilled with the coffee.

The *Voyageur II* circumnavigates the island, beginning at the western tip, working its way around the northern shore to Rock Harbor on Wednesdays and Saturdays. The boat docks for the night at the harbor, then completes the circle, and returns to Grand Portage the next day. Our plan was to take the boat to the campground at Belle Isle near the northeastern tip of the island. There were other options, but they involved paddling across a large expanse of water. We might be able to do this if the lake remained calm, but there were no guarantees. Surrounded by the immense expanse of the frigid Superior, we found ourselves a bit intimidated. We didn't intend to take chances in our little seventeen-foot watercraft.

There is a dock at the Belle Isle campground, and the crew of the *Voyageur II* deposited us, our gear, and lastly our canoe, and waved good-bye. It was at least twenty-five degrees warmer on land. Off went the winter hat and gloves! Ditto the polar fleece! Perhaps we might find summer at the summer solstice after all.

Despite the remoteness of the island—it had taken us over seven hours to arrive; the *Voyageur II* putts along at the leisure-ly pace of twelve miles per hour—the Belle Isle campground was filled. We headed for a canoe-only campsite down fjord-like Pickerel

Cove, an hour and a half away. Some of the occupants at Belle Isle had arrived there via motorboat from the mainland; it was hard for a slow-moving canoe arriving on the island in midday to compete with them for campsites.

We reached the remote campground in late afternoon and eyed with pleasure an inviting site on a rock ledge high over the water. The views of the big, blue lake would be spectacular. But as we landed on one side of the ledge, kayakers were beaching on the other. Somehow, without discussing the dilemma, the kayak party got the official site, and we were relegated to a pseudo-site—the kind of place on which to pitch a tent when at the end of the day one can't find another place. Our inferior status may have been due to our lack of numbers. There were four of them and only two of us. We felt the lowly ranking more acutely an hour later, when we saw them observing the cocktail hour with gin and tonics poured from their canteens—while we labored over filtering enough lake water for our dinner.

"Why is it that we never think of gin and tonics on a canoe trip?" I asked Tom as he worked the pump and siphon up and down, up and down. "We didn't even consider beer!" I pondered this as I set up the Coleman and started supper. It was probably due to our family legacies: Tom, the child of a Swedish culture that looked askance at alcohol consumption; I, the granddaughter of a conservative Lutheran minister who did likewise. Our parents seldom drank distilled anything. But here Tom and I were, at the half-century mark, celebrating twenty-five years of marriage and drinking lake water for the toast! At a marginal campsite!

Our neighbors, the gin-drinking kayakers, proved good campers, though. Their kayaks were beautiful wooden craft, silky to the touch. People with such fine boats would be alert, sensitive paddlers to protect their craft, and they exhibited the same subtle behavior in camp. Despite our proximity, we had difficulty hearing their low-toned murmurings, and we never heard the clank of cook kettles.

We went swimming later. The water in the cove was cold but not unbearably so. As the daylight faded, the haunting yodel of a loon hung over the water. Hermit Thrushes tuned up their flutelike melodies, and Winter Wrens let forth the silvery, tinkling cascade of trills and chatters that for me says, "boreal forest." We had seen mergansers and cormorants on the water. There seemed an abundance of birdlife. At night, the stars were brilliant.

....

Isle Royale became a national park in 1931 amid a certain amount of rancor, which lingers to this day. The unhappiness has its roots in the oddity that though Isle Royale is geographically close to Minnesota, it actually belongs to Michigan. Upon learning this for the first time, Minnesotans are often indignant—clearly, a mistake was made back in time.

Michigan became a state in 1837, long before Minnesota. In fact, Minnesota was part of Michigan Territory before Minnesota became its own territory. This was why Lewis Cass, as territorial governor of Michigan, led an expedition to map the headwaters of the Mississippi—the upper river formed the western border of his governance. With copper mines, logging, and a promising fishing industry on the island at the time of Minnesota territorial status in 1849, it was not likely that Michigan would relinquish the island to Minnesota by arguments of geographical proximity.

In the twentieth century, copper mining and logging had run their courses. The cost of transporting these raw materials to the mainland ate into profits and made the industries less attractive. Half the island was logged off. Nevertheless, by the Roaring Twenties, several resorts welcomed vacationers to the island, and there were many private summer homes both on the main island and on the numerous smaller ones flanking its shoreline. A fishing industry consisting of independent families who lived on the island in the summer formed the chief extractive economy, and it was marginal.

The campaign to make the entirety of Isle Royale a national park began in 1924 with a journalist at the *Detroit News*. It was entirely appropriate that the enthusiasm for a national park within Michigan boundaries originate with Michigan residents. By the time the island was made a national park in 1931, a complicated agreement had been hammered out, grandfathering in people who owned property within the new park boundaries and limiting their right to pass it down to future generations. The fishing families, too, were both accommodated and restricted, but the thrust of the campaign focused on Michigan residents. The fishing families wintered in Minnesota, the closest mainland, and furthermore, they did not own their homes on Isle Royale—they were essentially squatters. Always just an accident away from financial disaster, independent fishing died out on Isle Royale, but some resentment remains.

Today, descendants of some of the former fishing families of Isle Royale are involved in the life of the island in other ways. The *Voyageur II,* for example, is owned and operated by a family who first arrived in the region in 1892.

It is not uncommon to have tension between local residents, who have the most to lose—but also the most to gain financially— from the establishment of a new national park or a new wilderness area. We were only superficially aware of the lingering emotional effects of our visit. We did not yet know that the island's past was more murky than the clear waters of its lake.

....

Our first night was blissfully free from the noise of civilization. On the mainland, our world is so permeated by the discord of gas combustion engines that there is hardly a place to escape them. Even in the middle of the prairie, the sound of a truck rolling over gravel will carry on the wind. On Isle Royale, the deep silence was punctuated only by the call of loons.

There was also no light pollution. Under a dark new moon, the night was inky black, and the starry sky, brilliant. If I owned a telescope, this is where I would bring it.

We left the pseudo-site the next morning and paddled a short, easy route to Lane Cove on day two. This time, our site was legitimate and lovely. I was struck by the quietude of the island. Occasionally we could hear a distant whine of motorboats. The island is not so remote that a bigger pleasure boat can't cross the water, even from Copper Harbor on the Upper Peninsula of Michigan, and many do. However, most of the time the only sound was the lap of waves, the susurration of wind through conifer boughs, and the glitter of bird music permeating the forest.

After setting up camp at noon, we packed a lunch and headed out on a hike to the top ridge of Isle Royale. The island is forty-five miles long and nine miles wide, with a central spine, the Greenstone Ridge, running its length. There are no roads (and no motorized vehicles) on the island, but there are hiking trails, notably an arduous one following the ridge. We wanted to take in the interior, to see how the forest recovered after logging, maybe to spot a moose or a wolf, the large charismatic mammals that the island is known for.

We took a trail leading up to the Greenstone Ridge. The 2.3-mile climb put us at Mount Franklin, elevation 1,074 feet. The higher peaks, around 1,300 feet, are farther west down the spine. Nonetheless, from Mount Franklin, the view was sublime. On the clear, sunny afternoon, we could see for miles. Amygdaloid Island, a narrow isle off the main island's northern shore, lay below us. Canada was visible far off in the distance, and of course, the sapphire waters of the greatest lake reached seemingly to the ends of the earth.

Some of the trail we had taken threaded through a low area where sedges and other plants that like wet feet grew. Standing dead spruce hinted that the wet meadow was recent, perhaps the result of a beaver dam. Other parts of the trail passed through boreal forest with spruce and balsam fir. Here, as well as along the shore, Nashville Warblers sang incessantly, thin wiry tunes that lit up the air.

The National Park Service champions Isle Royale as "a wilderness archipelago—a roadless land of wild creatures, unspoiled forests, refreshing lakes, and rugged scenic shores." I was surprised to see the term *archipelago* applied to what seemed like one big eye in the wolf head of Superior, but there are, in truth, a hundred much smaller islands surrounding that eye.

When the park service labels Isle Royale a "wilderness," they are using terminology set out in the 1964 Wilderness Act: land "where the earth and community of life are untrammeled by man." One could argue that this is true today, but the island bears the marks of human activity that has occurred over the centuries. In the 1800s, there were roads, a railroad, and many residents who worked in the copper mines that briefly flourished at midcentury. Park visitors can still detect mine shafts, piles of tailings, and even the remains of a rail line in the vicinity of the abandoned mines.

In fact, Native peoples mined copper from the shallow veins on the island for thousands of years prior to European contact. Stone hammers and copper artifacts such as knives, arrowheads, and fishing hooks have been found in or near the mines.

The ruins of a fire lookout tower can be seen from one trail, and logging roads, obscured by new vegetation, emanate from a former logging camp. At one time Isle Royale was heavily deforested. The emerald spread of islands and the continuous green of forest we could see from Mount Franklin were testimony to the regenerative power of trees and their ability to camouflage a multitude of assaults. They were not the mark of a pristine character.

The last part of the trail ascending to the ridge was quite steep. Tom and I carried only day packs for the hike, but we planned the next day to portage with the canoe over this ridge—albeit on a shorter trail farther down the ridge—and down to Rock Harbor on the other side of the island. The hike to the top was not only for the view but to get an idea of how the portage would go the next day.

We didn't think it would go very well. It was true, the trail leading south off the ridge was more gentle than the trail from the north. It was also true that we would be on a significantly shorter trail off Duncan Bay near the eastern tip of the island. Still, shorter does not mean less of a slope.

In particular, I tried to imagine Tom with the canoe on his shoulders trying to scramble up that last steep ascent. It didn't seem to be physically possible. The back of the canoe would dig into the ground as he tried, vainly, to scramble up a sixty-degree angle. Then I tried to envision myself with a big Duluth pack. Not a pretty sight.

....

Back at camp, we spent a sunny hour on a rocky point, observing wildlife. Birds with ethereal songs—Winter Wrens and Hermit

Thrushes—had lined the shoreline everywhere we paddled and had sung from the interior, but the real excitement of the afternoon was our first encounter with a moose.

The young, antlerless animal was knee-deep in the middle of a marsh on a nearby island, close enough so that we could easily observe it without binoculars. Despite its legendary bad moose eyesight, it could see us, too, and it bellowed in alarm at the sight. Maybe our pale, unimpressive bodies frightened it. It continued to low, rather like a cow, and began tugging on some leaves. Clueless, we discussed this at length. I recalled the common analogy of "a lovesick moose," but Tom, more prosaic, thought it was just hungry, and clearly the behavior of the moose weighed in favor of his theory.

We no sooner had recovered from the close encounter of the moose kind when we had another. The gin-drinking kayakers at the last campsite were now our neighbors at this campsite, and they quietly alerted us to a black fox that was making its way in our direction. A black fox is unusual, and I thought it was probably a melanistic phase of the more common red fox. The little animal, terribly thin, trotted toward us on long, scrawny legs. It had a white-tipped tail and wild yellow eyes, which surveyed us warily but with a familiarity that indicated it frequently associated with campers. Its thinness was pronounced. I had to remind myself that it was *not good* to feed the wildlife. The temptation was great to throw it a crust of bread.

....

Over dinner, we discussed our options for the next day. There was a way to avoid that strenuous portage: we could paddle around the very tip of the big island to Rock Harbor—if the water was flat. We were familiar with canoeing on Lake Superior from two decades of owning a cabin on the south shore. We had experienced many days when the water was like glass, a dream to paddle. We had also seen big, crashing, damaging waves that could swamp a canoe in seconds, and we had seen the Jekyll/Hyde nature of the lake, how it could switch in a matter of minutes. We also knew that the water tended to calm down in the evening. Many mornings, we wake up to a lake that is like a mirror, only to have large rolling waves un-furling on the beach by nine o'clock.

It would all depend on the wind. If it were from the southwest when we rounded that far northeastern tip, Blake Point, we would get blasted and could quickly find ourselves broadside to the waves, the best way to capsize. We had met a hiker on the trail up to Mount Franklin who told us that the previous year, a Coast Guard cutter came around the point and had two windows blown out from the wind. Nonetheless, the hiker endorsed the paddling option, if we did it early in the day.

Not having access to a weather report, we crawled into our sleeping bags that night undecided about what to do. Paddling seemed preferable to portaging, but we would have to see what the day would bring.

....

I sleep lightly and rise early. The next morning at four thirty as the night was graying, a time the early explorers called "first light," I awoke to the rumble of thunder off in the distance. Still, the sky seemed to be growing pink in the east, and the storm might never reach us. Very often, we witnessed dark thunderheads and heard ominous thunder over Lake Superior that never came our way.

So I informed Tom of the impending good day. From the recess of his sleeping bag, he told me curtly that it was "inappropriate" to suggest rising at four thirty. By five o'clock, it *was* appropriate, how-ever, and so I dressed and made oatmeal and coffee. Over steaming cups, we decided to save ourselves the toil of a steep portage and take our chances with the big lake.

From our campsite in Lane Cove, we made a short paddle to a portage trail that brought us into Stockly Bay. From there, we paddled and then portaged into Duncan Bay. We were traversing a series of long, skinny fingers of water and land. The big island of Isle Royale would be the next finger of land to cross, but instead, we paddled up Duncan Bay, toward open water. The water of the bay was still without ripple. Loons, sometimes in pairs, accompanied us at intervals. Mergansers, thin-billed, fish-eating ducks with slick-backed rusty heads, floated in familial groups offshore. The air was quiet, and the silvery-voiced birds that had thrilled me on land could be heard as we paddled along. Tom and I had little to say. It seemed too early for talk. We enjoyed the lake's tranquility.

As we worked our way down Duncan Bay, we picked up the toll of the foghorn on Passage Island off the easternmost tip of Isle Royale. A navigational guide, it alerts boaters to shallow water and the nearness of the archipelago. The tone sounded every thirty seconds. Fog ahead.

Soon Passage Island itself came into view, a gray silhouette that seemed never to get any closer and that rung with the rhythmic monotone of the foghorn. We fell naturally into the foghorn's cadence, our strokes matching the tone. We could see a gauzy fog curtain hanging over the open water as we approached Blake's Point, the tip.

Tom had said there would be two moments of truth for us. The first was when we paddled beyond the Duncan Narrows that protected the bay from open water to the north; the second would be when we rounded the point and could assess the east and the south. He remarked on this as we left Duncan Bay. We already knew, then, the first truth: the northern waters were calm.

No longer in the shelter of Duncan Bay, the air became cold, colder than anything we had experienced since crossing from Grand Portage on the *Voyageur II*. It was, undoubtedly, near the temperature of the water, about forty degrees.

Nearing Blake's Point, I saw with unease that the shoreline of the tip consisted of dark rock cliffs rising straight out of the water—nowhere to land if we wanted to abort our plan. We tried and failed to discern Passage Island's lighthouse as the point unfurled in a series of small coves and rock fingers. I imagined what a big boat might see out in open water, shrouded by fog. Nothing.

The foghorn tolled on.

A canoe moves slowly, and with each stroke, our tension built. We were now riding gentle swells coming in from the north. The lake seemed to be breathing, and the canoe rose and fell. We weren't frightened by this, but we knew with certainty that we were tangling with a beast, and luckily for us, the beast was sleeping.

We donned our life jackets. I couldn't help recalling the legendary observation that fishermen on Lake Superior never even carried life jackets—the lake was so cold, a life jacket would not save you. From our low position on the water, we could not tell if we were still in the lee of the point and realized we might not know until we rounded the tip and met what mood of water lay to Isle Royale's south.

The lighthouse light came into view. Its yellow eye winked on and off at intervals. Then, we spied a Coast Guard boat far out on the water. It was steaming full speed—it appeared the lake was passable.

No portage for us! Heading around the tip and along the southeast shore of the island, we encountered gentle swells from the south that carried us buoyantly along and brought us to the first of a series of smaller islands that form a protective barrier between the big island and the open water. The canoe would now be safe from Superior's breakers.

Once in protected waters, we celebrated our good fortune with a handful of gorp. The oatmeal and coffee seemed to have been consumed ages ago. Then we paddled on to Rock Harbor and our campsite for the night. We arrived, unloaded our gear, and checked our watches. It was ten o'clock. The day was just beginning.

The next days on the island saw the return of the winter jackets—in late June! But the chilliness of the air seemed a minor discomfort as we delighted in the nearness of the wildlife. A cow moose and her spindly little calf visited our campsite and chomped down all the dogwood shrubs in short order. A red fox family with cunning little kits enlivened our supper hour. We walked along a rocky path that ran through a patch of dozens of red moccasin flowers, native orchids that are cousin to the showy lady's slipper. We caught a stunning sunset over the lake.

....

Back home, I pondered the conundrum of the lovely, remote island. How wonderful that there is a national park in the middle of Lake Superior that offers us dark, starry nights and the natural silence of a planet before technology! How wise the people were who dreamed of this park—who envisioned a lasting value for a landscape that was not dramatic, that did not have deep canyons, soaring mountains, or oddities like geysers. How fortunate that they realized that water and woods, wind and isolation are enough to restore a soul and should be preserved for future generations.

On nearly every occasion when land is claimed for the public good, there is private loss. This is true for the widening of roads, the establishment of refuges, the siting of a power plant, and the formation of parks, whether local city parks or national parks. A tension is built into our democracy between the public domain and the private sphere, a tension that will never be resolved.

In the years before the park was formed, Isle Royale teetered on the edge of being taken permanently by private interests. Each industry had had its way with the island, and each had significantly marred it. The last, the fishing community, could not gauge that the fish populations were declining through overfishing, and they could not know that the lake would be dealt a near-fatal blow through the invasion of two nonnative species, the sea lamprey and the smelt, which were already on their way into Superior's waters. The fishing community thought it was fishing sustainably, but hindsight and an examination of catch records in the 1940s say otherwise.

Instead of being lost to the enjoyment of a privileged few, as was the fate of Madeline of the Apostle Islands, Isle Royale and its multitude of lesser islands can now be savored by anyone who climbs aboard the *Voyageur II*, braves the possibility of seasickness on the span across the water, and prepares to spend some time amid the blue, silent quiet of the greatest lake.

The Clarity of Nellie Lake

KILLARNEY PROVINCIAL PARK, ONTARIO, 2004

....

THE PINK QUARTZITE HILLS OF THE LA CLOCHE MOUNTAINS seemed very wrong. Our Minnesota eyes were accustomed to seeing gray basalt jutting out of a conifer canopy, not a girly pink. The La Cloche loom over the north shore of Georgian Bay in Lake Huron, part of Ontario's Killarney Provincial Park. We had traveled a long way to see a northern landscape with pink instead of gray. Tucked into those florid hills were several blue gems of lakes. These were also a draw.

Our trip to Killarney was plan B that summer. Plan A had been Nova Scotia. Then two of our kids suffered mishaps, one involving dental work, the other concerning highway guardrails for which the Department of Transportation billed us. The sum total wiped out our savings and quickly put plan A out of reach. This should have been the first indication that Tom and I were on the downward slope of life: our children were old enough to engage in perilous adult activities but young enough to need us to pay for accidents.

But a canoe trip involving large expanses of sapphire water and gorgeous white pines is hardly a poor consolation prize. We looked forward to several memorable days in Killarney, which was only a day's drive from home. We wanted in particular to see Nellie Lake, one of the blue gems. Among lake aficionados, Nellie has a reputation. Situated high in the La Cloche Mountains, Nellie is a true oligotrophic lake, one of the clearest in North America. Oligotrophic lakes are generally northern lakes, deep, cold, and transparent. They are cradled in bedrock that does not provide many nutrients; hence, the plant life they support is sparse, likewise, the fish feeding on the plants. Most of the Boundary Waters lakes are oligotrophs, too. Oligotrophic lakes are a delight to swim in and to contemplate.

Alas, Nellie's reputation was a stained one, through no fault of her own. Nellie and Grace, an adjacent lake, were legendary for having suffered dramatically from the effects of acid rain. They were, in fact, considered dead. Killarney is situated downwind from Sudbury, Ontario, where a massive copper-nickel processing plant had for decades produced a deadly stream of sulfur-containing air pollution. The quartzite surrounding Grace and Nellie had zero capacity to neutralize any of the acid rain (diluted sulfuric acid) that fell in the region. As a result, the acidity levels in the lakes rose to a point where no life could exist. The tiny aquatic plants and animals disappeared. Food chains were uncoupled. What had been a clear lake before was now excessively so, and was an odd blue color.

Susceptibility to acid rain is something the lakes of the Boundary Waters also share with Killarney's lakes. The two regions are united by the same complex of circumstances, beginning with the underlying bedrock, the Canadian, or Precambrian, Shield. The shield is igneous in origin. It is hard and erodes very little, so that lakes, as mentioned before, do not have many nutrients in them.

At the same time, the shield holds deposits of copper and nickel embedded in sulfur-containing rock. When the ore is mined and the valuable metals captured, sulfur-containing waste is produced. It might be released into the atmosphere as a gas, sulfur dioxide, or it can escape into groundwater in the form of sulfuric acid. The difference between Killarney and the Boundary Waters is that Ontario's copper and nickel deposits were easily mined and quickly exploited. The mineral deposits of Minnesota's northern region are deeper and harder to access, ticking time bombs waiting to be set off.

Sudbury's copper-nickel refinery burned off the sulfur waste and sent it into the air. Once in the atmosphere, the sulfur-containing gases, sulfur dioxide in particular, combined with water vapor and returned to earth as acid rain. The original, pre–World War I refinery smokestacks were relatively small and deposited acid rain in the immediate vicinity of the plant, killing everything. Clearly, the short stacks were inadequate to get rid of the waste, so the plant constructed taller ones, megastacks, which dispersed the poisonous plume across a wider area. It was hoped that the sulfur gases would be diluted and rendered harmless.

Sadly, that did not happen. A wider swath of forest in central Ontario around Sudbury died, and the La Cloche Mountain lakes, Nellie and Grace, died with it. When Tom and I first drove east on the Trans-Canada Highway through Sudbury in 1978 on our honeymoon, we passed through the skeletons of conifers in stunned silence. What had been boreal forest had become a moonscape.

....

As well as a little morality tale in the perils of copper-nickel mining, our Killarney trip would give us an opportunity to canoe on a Great Lake, Huron. The park's southwestern boundary fronts Huron's Georgian Bay, a huge body of water. Some Canadians refer to it as the sixth great lake. Studying the map, Tom charted a route that would avoid crossing a massive expanse of water and still give us a taste of Great Lakes paddling, as we had had the summer before at Isle Royale in Lake Superior.

On this trip we would be portaging to get from one lake to another. In the past twenty years, we had not done much portaging. We had given up trekking across portage trails when we had had children—they require tremendous amounts of gear but aren't able to carry any of it for any distance. Still, we had good memories of portages: the chance to get out of the canoe and stretch one's legs, delicate little ground plants on the forest floor, woodland vistas of bubbling creeks and trickling waterfalls. True, there were some lengthy portages on this Killarney trip: three, to be precise, over a mile long each. However, Tom remembered another mile-long portage out of Horse Lake in the BWCAW. He had taken it as a teenager. It had not been all that tough.

Killarney is a long day's drive from our home. We got up at five o'clock and drove east through northern Wisconsin, across Michigan's Upper Peninsula, and through the "Soo"—Sault Ste. Marie, where Lake Superior narrows to a set of rapids. We retraced in part our 1978 route and were heartened to see that the forest around

Sudbury was beginning to come back. Stronger Canadian environmental regulations had required the refinery to install scrubbers on its giant stack to remove the sulfur waste before it reached the atmosphere. After twenty years of clean rain, the conifers were finding a toehold once more.

We had to hustle to reach Killarney by nightfall. Even so, we arrived in the camp that would serve as our put-in point well after dark. It had been a long haul, and we were eager for a good night's sleep. We had two strenuous portages the next day.

The lodge, outside of Espanola, Ontario, was an old fishing resort that was—and I write this with complete certainty—not accustomed to hosting women. When we arrived, we were shown to a small cabin some distance from the office, with a bathhouse and toilet two doors down. This was not a problem, but it was June, and the mosquitoes were enjoying robust numbers. Great clouds came into the cabin each time the door was opened. I had once heard that early explorers to the upper Midwest had been in danger of suffocation at the peak of summer from breathing in mosquitoes. I don't know if this could be true, but the thought came to me as l pulled on my pajamas under the bare bulb of the cabin.

There was a strong scent of mildew about the bed. Pulling back the dingy spread, I saw the sheets were grayish, the pillows lumpy and intensely odorous. The bed itself was narrow and sagging. I considered unrolling my camping pad and sleeping on the concrete floor—I could not share that bed with my six-foot-four husband—but a night on a concrete slab after a day that began at five o'clock was an unpalatable option.

So on the first day of a plan B trip, we turned to another plan B at the insistence of the paddler in the bow (me): we packed up at midnight and, still wearing pajamas, drove back into town to a motel with a room where the pillows smelled clean and were clad in white cases.

....

What is so rare as a day in June! Everything seems better after a good night's sleep. We forgot the misadventures of the previous night and headed back to the mosquito-infested resort to drop our canoe into the waterway leading into Killarney Provincial Park. Paddling east on a series of long, narrow lakes, we approached the western boundary of Killarney and our first long portage into Grace Lake. Out on the water, we did not notice mosquitoes. Lovely birds sang from the shores: black-throated Green Warblers commenting a buzzy "trees, trees, murmuring trees," Winter Wrens issuing a drawn-out, high-pitched melody, and the true singers of the woods, Hermit Thrushes, sounding ethereal and flutelike.

We psyched ourselves up for the two long portages into Nellie Lake. If you know you will carry a sixty-five-pound canoe or a fifty-pound pack on your shoulders for one mile, you think: we will take this slowly, we will rest when we need to, we will get this done, and then we will be there. Tom took a photo of me at the start. My white T-shirt and khaki pants are clean, and I am smiling. Then Tom packed the camera and flipped the canoe. I maneuvered myself into the straps of the equipment pack, and we headed off.

Our companions, the insects, reminded us that we were not alone. It was June! Mosquitoes and blackflies swarmed in ecstasy at the prospect of such a feast as we presented. Tom and I had long sleeves protecting our arms and bandannas on our heads. We had slathered on DEET over sunblock. No matter—the happy dipterans crawled inside pants legs, under collars, and probed the thinness of a cotton shirt. The portage ran alongside a little stream for much of the way. The creek burbled pleasantly, and birds sang continuously, so there were attractions to take our minds off the blood loss from the biting insects. We did not know that a popular guidebook of the area considered that "compared to the rest of the portages on the route, [this one is] the least strenuous."

The first portage brought us into Grace Lake and the provincial park. The pink quartzite of the hills was visible for the first time. We deposited our loads, gave the quartzite an appreciative glance, and then turned back down the portage to fetch the second load. Even in the spartan days of our youth, we double portaged. We are not the kind of aesthetes that can really pare things down. For one thing, we cook meals from scratch, using real food. The second time over the portage is more like a pleasant stroll through the woods. The heavy items are transferred first.

When all gear had arrived at the shores of Grace Lake, we nibbled a little chocolate and drank water. It wasn't lunchtime, and we weren't very hungry. There was a little chop on Grace as we crossed it, but the wind was in our favor. Great puffy clouds raced ahead of us, and with breezy encouragement, we were soon at portage number two. This portage was 2,085 meters, a mile and a quarter, uphill into Nellie Lake. It was the last portage of the day, and we chose to dwell on that fact.

I could never undertake any of our canoe trips without my faithful partner who carries the canoe on every portage. I have carried the canoe—usually it is a matter of getting it balanced properly on the shoulders, but its seventeen-foot length is unwieldy, and sometimes upper-body strength is required. On every portage, Tom matter-of-factly flips the craft, jostles it a little to balance it, and off he goes. In our family, the paramount rule is that the canoe goes first and has absolute right of way. Oftentimes, I will head off down the portage with my pack ahead of Tom, but when I hear the canoe approaching, I stand aside.

The start of the Nellie Lake portage was like every other. We did not know it would serve as an oracle to us. Tom and the Old Town headed off through a cloud of mosquitoes and blackflies, up the hill to Nellie Lake.

Nellie Lake is high in the La Cloche Mountains. The trail ascended relentlessly. There were canoe rests at intervals, so Tom could get the thing off his shoulders and catch his breath. Then it was onward, up and up. A guidebook that we would read after the fact described it as "one nasty portage," but by that point, we did not have to be told that.

In the course of the portage, we encountered a beaver dam that needed to be traversed. There was water on both sides of it—shin-deep water on the dammed side, muck and emergent plants on the other. The beavers had not been completely successful at stopping the creek flow, or more likely, recent rains had caused the water level to rise so that the creek spilled over the top of the dam. The sticks were slick. The dam was about twenty feet across, so this was no easy crossing. From behind, I watched as Tom edged over the tricky obstacle. Then, one misplaced boot hit a slippery spot, and Tom went down, the canoe bearing on top him. I heard mud suck his foot. His knee hit a log. He hung on to the canoe (this, with a small pack on his back), but it took maneuvering to get back on the dam and inch over to the other side.

I was not encouraged by this spectacle. Tom hadn't broken anything, however—the fall could have been much worse. His pants were muddy to the knees, and he was bleeding from a scrape. I edged my way across by tiny increments, and neither one of us had kind words for beavers for quite a while. When Nellie Lake finally came into view, we rejoiced—but of course there was the double portage. Tom set the canoe down, helped me off with my pack, and we started down the hill for round two. Round two was lighter—a clothes pack and the odds and ends—paddles, life jackets, the water jug. The beaver dam crossing was not as perilous.

It took us two hours from the time we left Grace Lake to when we finally set the canoe in at Nellie, two hours to walk the portage trail three times, a total of almost four miles. We were now deep into Killarney Provincial Park. The two long portages had been made at midday, but we had not had much appetite for lunch. We still didn't. We were too exhausted.

Nellie Lake was a vision of loveliness. Ringed by the pink-ish-gray quartzite and fringed by big white pines, the lake was a peculiar teal color that sparkled in the afternoon sun. We saw no other campers on Nellie and took the first campsite we encountered, one that was on a rock outcropping jutting into the water. Whatever breeze came up, we would get. We hoped it would keep the bugs at bay. The Ontario Parks system had thoughtfully provided a gravel area for our tent, which we applauded, because it would have been impossible to find places to drive a tent stake on the quartzite.

The site didn't look tamped down by too many boots or used up by human activity. Indeed, we had seen no one since embarking on that first mile-long portage out of Grace Lake. Of course, two horrendous portages will do that. Red moccasin flowers, with two-inch magenta blossoms, flourished on the edge of the rock outcrop. Bracken ferns grew lush and green. The big pines soughed overhead. Gazing out across the blue-green water, we could see a loon resting on the surface. In short, this campsite was perfect, and we got to work setting up the tent.

Next, we felt we ought to eat something even though we were still not hungry. It was now dinnertime, so I set up the stove and began cutting up vegetables for a stir-fry. We had packed in some fresh beef and broccoli. The robust aroma and sizzle of the frying meat and onions should have stimulated our appetites, but oddly, they did not. I perfunctorily dished myself up a small portion of instant brown rice and the beef and broccoli topping, and ate it dutifully. What I really enjoyed was water to drink.

Later, after the meal and cleanup, we went swimming in crystalline Nellie Lake. The water washed away the mud and blood from the rough day. Filling a cook kettle with water, we went far back away from the lake to clean up with soap. We were covered by blackfly bites. Strings of red welts formed ankle bracelets above my sock lines. Under normal circumstances, we would have been fretting about mosquito bites, but we hardly noticed them because the blackflies had done so much damage. Blackflies draw a drop of ruby red blood, which beads on the surface of the skin. The welt that appears does not itch, but it hurts for days, and it leaves a reminder for several months by way of a purplish circular blotch with a darker bite mark in the center. We anticipated mementos from Killarney's blackflies for the rest of the summer.

We stashed the unbelievably filthy portage clothes in a corner of the tent. Tom's jeans were encrusted with mud from when he went down; our T-shirts were smeared with mud and blood and stained with the tiny bodies of unlucky biting insects—the ones that didn't get away.

In the twilight, we lay without talking in the tent. Then I murmured, "I don't think we can do this again. We're too old." Tom agreed, "It seems to be a young person's game." Somehow, we were sure this would not have happened in our twenties. Not that Tom wouldn't have fallen with the canoe on his shoulders. Nor that a mile-and-a-quarter uphill portage wouldn't have tired us. But that had we been younger, we would have bounced back. We would have gotten a site, set up camp, gone off for a swim, and been miraculously restored. We would have eaten an enormous supper and fallen asleep like healthy young animals.

Today, we hadn't bounced back. Memories of the day seemed somehow harrowing. I kept replaying in my mind's eye Tom's spill on the beaver dam. What might have happened but didn't. The sound of the muskeg swallowing his boot. The bloodied arm.

....

The next morning we felt cheerful and could better ponder the oddity of Nellie Lake. Its transparent, aqua water was the precise result of acid rain. Such clarity indicates an absence of microscopic life that normally inhabits freshwater. Aquatic organisms require a fairly narrow range of pH, more or less around neutrality, in order to live. Since tiny plants and animals form the base of the food chain in a lake, there were no fish, either. Nellie was no more than a basin of water, not a living lake. It had been so for many years.

Pollution controls were installed on Sudbury's smokestack in 1980, and it no longer kicks out acidic gases. Nellie had had some time to recover. A lake might be able to come back after some acidification. Runoff from surrounding soil that is alkaline can neutralize, or buffer, an acid solution, such as Nellie's water had become. However, Nellie's surrounding quartzite hills had little soil—quartzite is very slow to break down—and its water's pH was about that of cider vinegar. It was going to take decades—no one knows how long, if ever, really—for Nellie to be reborn.

There was one portent for recovery, though: the loon. Loons are fish eaters, and heaven knows what the loons we saw were catching in Nellie Lake. The water was so clear, we could watch a pair swim twenty feet down, doing little froggy kicks with their webbed feet. But Nellie must have suited them—loons can fly away if they're not pleased with a situation. So perhaps there is hope for this pretty lake.

I viewed Nellie Lake with a certain amount of equanimity that was, in retrospect, another indication of middle age. As a young woman, I would have raged against Nellie's plight, sunk into a black mood, felt heartsick over the loons living in a sterile lake. I would have filled the pages of my journal with anguish. But on this trip, I did none of that. I looked out over Nellie's waters with some sadness that I didn't linger on. I took in everything: the oddity of a scene reminiscent of the Boundary Waters but with pink rocks, not gray; and teal waters, not blue. I noted the fresh chartreuse fringe of new growth on hemlocks and the baby leaves of red and sugar maples that were just emerging. I was amazed by the abundance of moccasin flowers growing on the forest floor.

Damage to whole ecosystems like Nellie Lake is no longer a new phenomenon. If I dwelt on such a fact, I would become incapacitated. I believe I could not function. Nellie's wounds, unlike ours from the portage, could not be healed, at least by us. Just like one should choose one's battles, one needs to choose the stories one anguishes over.

....

Imagine our delight when we studied the map after breakfast and remembered that the coming day's paddle included yet another portage over a mile in length. Really, could we have planned this trip any better? We had only a night on Nellie—we were moving forward to other vistas. One thing was in our favor: the portage out of Nellie and into (eventually) a bay of Lake Huron was oriented in the preferred direction, downhill.

Once under way, we encountered yet another beaver dam. The obstacle we had to deal with, though, was the Grand Coulee of beaver dams, four feet high, holding back a vast lake that had killed scores of pines many yards up a hillside. The beavers (which we did not see) had been superb engineers. No unkind words for these beavers crossed our lips. They had so successfully stopped the creek's flow that we crossed on stepping stones.

The weather, too, was cooperating. A cold front had blown in during the night, dropping the temperature and bringing a steady breeze. Biting insects were remarkably quelled by these unfavorable conditions. Even the long, long portage proved pleasant. In the muddy low areas of the trail, we saw hoofprints larger than my hand that could only have been moose. On the path at one point, we came upon ungulate droppings that did not look like moose or deer (we had seen both), and we wondered if they were from woodland caribou. It's unlikely—woodland caribou are thought to have been extirpated from Killarney, and we do not claim expertise in reading scat.

However, despite an agreeable experience with the last long portage, Tom and I would not forget the first beaver dam and the long, uphill slog into Nellie Lake. Chastened, we would think hard about portages in the future. We would wonder if we should act our age, and then wonder what exactly that might mean.

We were headed to McGregor Bay, a small pocket ragged with islands in the larger Georgian Bay of Lake Huron. If you study a map of the north shore of Georgian Bay, you will see a meshwork of small islands and an irregular coastline, so that what would seem to be a vast sheet of water, perilous for a small canoe, is actually protected from winds—a paddler's delight. We planned on spending two nights on McGregor Bay, taking a day to explore the intricacies of Georgian Bay's shore. We would be on the boundary of Killarney, not isolated as we were on Nellie Lake. Cabins, motorboats, and floatplanes were all allowed.

Our campsite on McGregor was high on a rock overlooking water. A gnarled old red oak leaned over the tent site. There was a tree stump for my stove, and blocks of granite to sit on. Again, a perfect site. Now, though, Tom and I began thirsting after luxury, in the form of camp chairs. Before setting out, we had shopped for last-minute supplies at a Canadian big-box store, Canadian Tire, and had seen folding camp chairs with the red-and-white Canadian flag, a big maple leaf in the middle, imprinted on the backrests. They were only $7.95, priced to sell in advance of Canada Day, July 1.

We are attracted to anything with a leaf on it. The Canadian flag has been a favorite of Tom's for as long as I've known him. These were not fancy chairs with cup holders and footrests. They were pared down, with a strap for slinging over one's shoulder. We wanted those chairs.

Was this not a middle-age preoccupation? Those chairs would have been an unspeakable nuisance on the three mile-long portages we had just experienced. We would have cursed the day we bought them. Yet, as the memory of the portages faded, we dwelt on the display of red-and-white sleekly folded chairs at Canadian Tire. We have never lugged camp chairs on a canoe trip, but we fantasized now about sitting around a fire (something else we never have), playing cribbage, sipping wine, acting civilized in a middle-aged way, our middle-aged backs supported. The fantasy was in league with our envy of the gin-drinking kayakers the summer before on Isle Royale. We have always been the most spartan of campers, but maybe it was time to consider the high life.

....

The birdlife was abundant on the north channel of McGregor Bay. A nearby Osprey nest brimmed with hatchlings. Paddling close to it, we could hear the babies badgering their parents for fish. Herring and Ring-billed Gulls paid us visits, especially at mealtimes, and they were accompanied by a Caspian Tern, jaunty with an Elvis hairdo and a blood-red bill. There were cormorants and loons, Great Blue Herons and ravens. From our tent, I could hear the hoarse song of a Scarlet Tanager on the opposite shore.

The cold front that squelched the mosquitoes and blackflies and brought a wind proved to be of long duration. On the first windy day, we rejoiced at our good fortune. On the second windy day, now camping on McGregor Bay, we got waylaid by a white-capped channel while out exploring. Our packs weighed the canoe down and made it ride lower in the water, but also gave it some stability, so it didn't get pushed around as much. Alas, we didn't have them with us. They were back in camp. We took refuge behind one of the numerous small rock islands that dotted the shoreline and caught our breath. White pines on the island were sheared on one side, and all pointed in the same direction. It was abundantly clear why this was so. Eventually, we made it back, battling wind all the way.

The helpless feeling of being unequal to the wind gave us pause, and we began rethinking how we would paddle across wide Iroquois Bay to our west the next day, the end of our trip. We had arranged to meet a man at a landing on Iroquois Bay at one o'clock to get a ride back to our car.

Early mornings are the calmest times of the day. If a day promised to be windy, we could lessen our chances of tangling with whitecaps by starting out early. So we decided to get up before sunrise and leave, as we had done at Isle Royale. After a quick breakfast of granola, fruit, and banana bread, we were on the water before six o'clock. At this hour, the big lake was flat and mirrorlike. The silhouettes of white pine that give me so much pleasure were reflected back from the surface, so that we paddled through a forest both real and imaginary. Great boulders of gneiss rose above the water. Off in the far distance, we could see a thin line of rain clouds. Later in the day, when we were in a motel on Manitoulin Island, we would see showers.

But not now. Now, while the day was still young, the silvery music of a Hermit Thrush sounded through the woods. The water was luminous with the yellow sun's rays. White-throated Sparrows sang from the shoreline, "O, Sweet Canada, Canada, Canada!"

Looking for Snakes

....

"Venomous snakebites, although uncommon, are a potentially deadly emergency in the United States . . ." I am reading out loud from an article taken from *JAMA*, the *Journal of the American Medical Association*. Tom and I are cramming. Heading toward Havre, Montana, our seventeen-foot Old Town canoe strapped to the top of our car, we have planned a trip on the Marias River, forty miles south of town. Back at home when planning the trip, Tom had decided that he needed to brush up on his knowledge of poisonous bites. Now he has elected to do so at the last possible moment, with me conveying the information to him. Perhaps he thinks that I, too, should know what to do, in case he's the bitten one, and I, the first-aid administrator.

When I reflect on it, that is the most likely scenario. Tom is not good at multitasking. He cannot, say, focus on a destination and the path to get there at the same time. Hence, while he is thinking about other, more important things, he is likely to not see the dog dirt in front of him. His boot unfailingly finds it. It would find the rattler, too.

I, on the other hand, am a mother of four, an experienced multi-tasker. I am *always* looking for snakes. And I seldom step in dog doo.

In Minnesota, the most fearsome reptiles we ever encounter are bull snakes, large but harmless. A family practitioner, Tom has never treated a case of snakebite, but he wants to be prepared. Prairie rattlesnakes—a reptile termed *very abundant* by our Peterson field guide—inhabit the watershed of the Marias River in central Montana. Like all rattlesnakes, the prairie rattler is a pit viper, marked by a triangular head and two sensory pits, heat detectors, between the nose and eyes. That means they are aware of the presence of warm-blooded prey, like mice and prairie dogs, but a human leg will also attract their interest. They are moderately long, fifteen to sixty inches, and grayish green in color, with darker blotches, nicely concealing. Unlike some species of rattlesnakes, prairie rattlers are doing well. In fact, their status is listed as a species "of Least Concern." That, of course, would be the U.S. Fish and Wildlife Service's opinion. They are not a species of least concern to *me*.

To be sure, the bite of a rattlesnake is usually not fatal. A lot depends on the snake: How big? How irritated? How hungry? Bigger, angrier, hungrier snakes deliver more venom. Usually, a prairie rattler is not anxious for a confrontation. Between seven thousand and eight thousand people suffer snakebites—from all kinds of poisonous snakes—each year. Only five people on average will die from them. Coral snakes are much more venomous.

The Marias River cuts through high plains furred with short-grass prairie, arid and unoccupied. The watershed is generally grazed but not cultivated. The snakes will be there. We seek solitude on our sixty-mile trip down the isolated river, and the Marias promises this, but once we drop in, there will be no take-out points for four days. Solitude is appealing, but there are drawbacks.

"Oh, here's what we need to know," I tell Tom, scanning the *JAMA* article. "First-aid measures for snakebite include avoiding excessive activity, immobilizing the bitten extremity, and quickly transporting the victim to the nearest hospital." Hmmmm, I think. How would I transport Tom with any speed to the hospital if he got bitten? Time would be of the essence here. A vision of me astern, paddling dead Tom with a swollen extremity down the Marias rises before my eyes.

"Well, at any rate, the article says that making a cut and sucking out the poison doesn't work," I conclude, as we approach Havre.

We need maps available at the Bureau of Land Management office in town before starting out. At headquarters, the ranger is enthusiastic. "You folks have made a good choice!" he tells us. "The Marias is beautiful and secluded. You won't see a soul." But then he adds, "Have you got a snakebite kit?"

"No, indeed," we think silently, smiling politely. *JAMA* has spoken: snakebite kits don't work.

"The rattlers will be out!" he continues. "We've had a long spell of wet weather, and they've been holed up. Now it's turned hot and sunny. Watch for them on the rocks! Watch for them in the grass! Get a snakebite kit!"

We chat with him about water depth, possible campsites, public versus private land issues. Five times he brings up the subject of snakebite kits. Five times we nod, Minnesota-nice fashion, and think, "We do not need a snakebite kit."

One hour later, in the local Safeway, picking up other supplies, we encounter a $9.95 snakebite kit packaged in yellow and green. Called "The Extractor," the kit consists of what looks like a suction cup attached to a plunger. It claims it can create a suction so effective that "no cutting is necessary." It includes a razor "for removal of body hair when the maximum level of suction is desired." There are alcohol pads and benzocaine, for pain relief. It can treat bites from snakes (a coiled rattler with fangs is shown on the front of the package), bees, wasps, yellow jackets, fire ants, scorpions, and mosquitoes. Independent toxicologists have proven scientifically that it removes significant quantities of venom (this in bold letters).

We hesitate. We waver. Would we ever use it? Who could say? We think about the advice from the experienced BLM ranger. Had he ever used the Extractor? Suddenly, a deeply felt ancient need for a talisman, something to ward off snakebites, possesses us. The *JAMA* article is just words on flimsy paper. We need more than that. The Extractor will be our talisman. We toss it into the cart.

At Loma, where the Marias joins with the Missouri, we meet up with the outfitter we have hired to shuttle us to the drop-in point, about sixty miles upstream, just below the Tiber dam. We transfer our packs and canoe to the outfitter's pickup and head out on a rutted road. A native Montanan, the outfitter has good stories to tell about the river, and we settle back to listen. It takes a couple hours to reach our destination.

As we bounce along, I assess the country we are about to paddle through. A silhouette of lavender mountains smudges the horizon, but otherwise, the landscape is a vast, unbroken plain of dusty sage and nascent grass. The only trees are ragged cottonwoods, clinging to the floodplains of the rivers. There are outcroppings of limestone and a big sweep of sky brushed by wispy clouds. There is a grandeur to what we see, as if great deeds could happen here, as if we could be bold and courageous with the beauty of the world laid bare in this wide expanse.

As we near our destination, the topic turns mundane—to rattlesnakes.

"You've got a kit, right? There's lots of snakes out there; you've got to keep an eye out for them."

Dang! I had forgotten that there are snakes in this Garden of Eden. I have the distinct feeling the outfitter feels duty bound to warn uninitiated canoeists from tame, docile Minnesota: Beware, you greenhorns! These are Montanan reptiles!

Now somewhat rattled about snakes, we are nonetheless able to appreciate our first glimpse of the Marias: a dreamy blue waterway coursing off into the distance between rounded gray cliffs. Cascades of Cliff Swallows with rusty throats and buffy foreheads circle above us, chittering and swooping as we carry the canoe to the river. The swallows are nesting under the bridge, our last avenue out of here until we reach Loma and the Missouri River. We wave goodbye to the outfitter and ease the Old Town into the water. We're off!

Sunlight glints off the water, and birdsong drifts from the dark groves of cottonwoods as we float by. I hear robins and wrens, Cedar Waxwings and warbling vireos. In June, with water levels regulated by the Tiber dam, the river is navigable in most stretches. We pass gravelly islands on which rest a plethora of wading birds: here a Great Blue Heron, there a Willet, leggy and dowdy, but flashing a black-and-white wing pattern in taking flight. On one island, we pass a remarkable gathering of thirteen Marbled Godwits, their cinnamon-colored plumage rosy in the afternoon sun.

The banks are lined with new emerald growth on the narrow floodplain. There are no designated campsites on the Marias. We can camp anywhere below the high-water mark and on all public land. The BLM maps clearly designate public and private ownership.

We feel a primordial sense of freedom at being able to simply pull out our canoe and set up camp. We're not tied to fire grates or required tent sites.

The gravelly islands where the birds are gathered actually seem appealing as campsites. There's a verdant brush of new grass atop them, and certainly no snakes would be out in the middle of the river. We Minnesotans, of course, know this factoid of rattlesnake preference. But although it is past lunchtime, it is too early to stop just yet and destroy the Marias's magic with the domestic acts of rattling cook kettles and staking a tent.

We're not the first to be captivated by the Marias. Meriwether Lewis took a shine to the pretty river on his famous expedition to the Pacific in 1805. In fact, the Corps of Discovery wondered if it was actually the Missouri River. The Hidatsa who overwintered with the Mandan in North Dakota were familiar with the area, since they headed west every summer to hunt. The Hidatsa had mapped in detail the route for the expedition, and the maps had been very accurate up to this point. But they hadn't mentioned a major tributary coming into the Missouri from the right-hand bank, west of the Milk River. The corps had passed the Milk River, as mapped, and then encountered this mystery river.

Lewis and Clark camped nearly two weeks at the confluence of the two rivers, pondering what to do. The expedition could not afford to make a wrong decision in this matter. A wasted two weeks up the wrong river might mean they could not make it over the Rockies before winter storms set in.

At issue was water clarity. The one river, what we now know is the true Missouri, runs clear; the Marias, the "mystery" river, carries a great load of sediment and is milky gray, exactly like the lower Missouri, through which they had trudged upstream for months. The entire corps, including Sacagawea, thought that the Marias, whose waters look like the Missouri, was the true river. But the expedition's leaders, Lewis and Clark, were of a different mind. The Hidatsa had told them that the Missouri's source in the Rocky Mountains is just above the Great Falls. The leaders thought that the mystery river's milky color meant it had flowed through a considerable stretch of high plain in order to have picked up so much sediment. A clear stream meant that the river had only recently emerged from its source.

They decided to scout out the options. Lewis chose to head up the mystery river atop the cliffs on foot while Clark, the better boatman of the two, went up the Missouri. Lewis and the six men accompanying him did not travel overland long, though. Thick prickly pear cacti impeded their progress, and the cactus thorns pierced their moccasins. Further, the cliff's rim was penetrated by dry ravines, which soon made walking tedious, and the hikers descended to the river to slog through the bottomland. Lewis, acting on President Jefferson's charge to record the wildlife he encountered, described three new species of birds: the Long-billed Curlew, McCown's Longspur, and Sage Grouse. The trip, undertaken in early June, was made miserable by cold rain. Yet, at the end of the venture, he would write, "It is a noble river . . . which passes through a rich fertile and one of the most beautifully picturesque countries that I ever beheld." He was so sure it was not the true Missouri that he named the river the "Marias" in honor of his cousin Maria Wood.

The captains chose rightly and led their expedition up the clear-running option. Later, Lewis would come back to the Marias as the expedition retraced its journey, headed home. Lewis's return trip to the river was notable for his party's encounter with Blackfeet Indians, the most powerful tribe on the upper Missouri. They skirmished when two of the Blackfeet attempted to steal rifles and horses from them. The ensuing fight, taking place at night in the dark, resulted in two Blackfeet deaths. Lewis and the three others beat a hasty retreat to the Missouri, traveling under moonlight and the lightning flash of far-off storms. They met with others from the corps and headed downstream by canoe to safety.

Now, as those same river cliffs loom over us in our canoe, I imagine Lewis's silhouette pacing along, his dog at his heels. An hour passes, then two. As the late afternoon sun slants across the milky water, laden with silt, we begin to think about campsites and, unlike the Corps of Discovery, about rattlers lounging in grass.

When Tom points out an inviting expanse in the shadow of

gnarled cottonwoods, I'm the first one out of the canoe, paddle in hand, ready to ferret out snakes. This is the work of the bowman, and I make sure I do a good job. Whoosh, whoosh! I sweep the grass back and forth, making as much noise as I can, on the premise that rattlesnakes are, at heart, nonaggressive and less interested in confrontation than I. When I am satisfied that the site is snake-free, we pitch the tent, but I keep my paddle at hand. I will need it on visits "to the latrine," camp shovel in one hand, paddle in another (whap, whap, whap through the grass), to the equipment pack (whap, whap, whap), and when I wind my way down to the river to swim.

Because it is our only option for bathing, we swim in the Marias. The water is turbid, the color of coffee with cream, but the temperature tops out at ninety-five degrees each day, and we slather on sunblock, even while protecting our skin with long sleeves and hats. The mosquitoes are often kept at bay by a stiff prairie breeze, but on still mornings, we use DEET to fend them off. The clay in the water seems more benign than the chemicals we use to protect ourselves. We don't drink it, though, or wash dishes in it. We carry five gallons of clear water for cooking, drinking, and washing up.

Camping is so pleasant in the arid west. Accustomed to humid Minnesota, we marvel how everything dries—the towels, the dishrag, the dishes themselves. After supper, which always tastes wonderful, we spread a clean towel on the overturned canoe and lay out the washed plates, cups, and silverware. Our little nesting cook kit lines up like a matryoshka doll. Then we settle into our camp chairs, red and white with a Canadian flag on the back, to watch a waning moon rise over the sere khaki cliffs opposite our campsite.

The Marias River, viewed from above, resembles a length of ribbon candy on some stretches. To paddlers, this is frustrating, since it is not conducive to making progress, when progress is defined as nearing the mouth of the river. One morning, we awake to a northwest wind, and since the Marias flows nearly north–south, we think the wind might benefit us. This is actually true about half the time. But for the other half, we battle a headwind and two-foot waves as we round one hairpin turn after another, so in the balance we do not rejoice.

On one stretch of hairpins, we witness a little drama. A female Mallard appears ahead of us, scrambling to and fro. She looks injured. I wonder if she has a broken wing. Feigning a broken wing is the oldest trick in a bird's book of defense. It draws a potential predator's attention away from vulnerable young and toward the seemingly injured bird. As we watch, a fuzzy little duckling head pops up alongside her. We have been had! She has been protecting babies, who begin reappearing.

The duck then precedes us, leading us away from her flock, and we paddle at a leisurely pace, feeling a bit like bullies, bearing down on the little mother. Then, we hear a squawk behind us and turn around to see two Golden Eagles feverishly circling the water. The eagles themselves are mobbed by a kingbird, but they ignore it, intent on nabbing the now-unprotected ducklings. We are helpless to intervene. All we can do is watch. What we see is that the kingbird is successful in harassing the eagles, and they fly away, their talons empty. The ducklings are safe—for now.

Along one stretch of the river, the cliffs rise high above us, taupe-colored clay topped by a layer of ochre sandstone. The sandstone has eroded away, leaving behind irregular columns that geologists call hoodoos, a comical name for elegant structures. There are hoodoos all over the world—famously, in Bryce Canyon National Park in Utah, in Cappadocia, Turkey, and in the Badlands of the Dakotas. The hoodoos of the Marias River are formed in textbook fashion, where the soft clay erodes faster than the sandstone cap. A small column of clay is protected by a cap of harder sandstone. However inelegantly named, the columns are graceful, looking like the remains of an ancient civilization. We feel as if decrepit and abandoned temples and civic buildings tower over us as we paddle past.

Sometimes these cliffs seem to murmur to us, the soft utterances carried on the prairie air. Pigeons, ordinary pigeons, are hidden in the recesses of the cliffs, with nests composed of sticks, and we marvel that a bird so associated with cities and barnyards would be found in such a wild place.

....

At our daily lunch stops, we continue to look for snakes. I wonder at times if I would recognize the warning rattle of an agitated snake's tail. The common wisdom is that it sounds like a baby rattle. But once in a natural history museum, as I bent my head over a display to scrutinize a live horned toad, I inspired the excitement of the inhabitant in the cage above the horned toad's: an albino rattlesnake. Its tail was vibrating at warp speed, and the sound was nothing like any infant's toy—more like a cicada buzzing high in the treetops. It is unnerving to think that we would not pick up on the one protection we have against these reptiles—their own warning.

Tom and I would perhaps be more confident if we were clad in jeans and heavy boots. That would be sensible dress, but each day the temperature soars into the nineties. We wear quick-dry shorts and river sandals, for the occasional stop to walk the canoe over a gravel bar. On lunch breaks, we seek the shade of cottonwoods, which grow on the floodplain. We set up camp chairs—for comfort and to raise us above the grass (at least, this gives *me* peace of mind)—and spend the hottest hour out of the sun.

We also continue to marvel at the abundant birdlife attracted to the river: scores of Spotted Sandpipers, flocks of Marbled Godwits, a Long-billed Curlew—one of the birds first identified by Meriwether Lewis—streams of Cliff Swallows in undulating ribbons.

Mammals are less conspicuous. At one camp, a beaver is in residence and has tried to gnaw through a giant cottonwood. At another, a small muskrat swims through the milky water. Mule deer, singly or in herds, frequent the floodplain.

....

For four quiet days, this is our world. We watch birds, we look for snakes, and we admire the broad sweep of the arid high plains. The only sounds we hear are the river, the wind, the wildlife, and those we ourselves generate. We see no other human beings.

On the fifth day, we approach the confluence with the mighty Missouri. The Marias has widened and carries even more silt. The day before, we had paddled past a hefty herd of cattle, some individuals standing hock-high in the river. We cross swimming off our list of activities for the evening.

Cornfields appeared atop the bluffs. They must somehow be irrigated. We know our trip is ending, without a single rattlesnake sighting. Somehow, I'm a little regretful. We were so prepared. The snakebite kit isn't even opened. The Extractor remains sheathed. It would have been exciting to have just seen one snake . . . sleeping . . . at a distance. Later, we would learn that the gravelly islands that enticed us as campsites are unusually favored by the snakes, where they can rest and sun, undisturbed.

At the take-out point, I find myself anticipating a hot shower and cold milk, as I do at the end of all canoe trips. The landing isn't as romantic a place as our put-in. There's a parking lot, a paved ramp leading out of the river, grassy verges of a meager park. As we pull gear from the canoe, the intact snakebite kit falls out of the equipment pack onto the grass.

I stuff it back into the pack, and we begin hauling our gear to the car. Tom, ahead of me on the trail, the canoe on his shoulders, gives a little jump. He's been startled by a snake! I catch just a glimpse of black and yellow stripes silently slipping into the weeds.

Abundance

THE UPPER IOWA RIVER, 2006

. . . .

THE SUMMER HAD BEGUN WITH GENEROUS RAIN. TREES
and grass and vines responded vigorously with verdant growth.
June had the feel of abundance, the press of humidity a constant
presence on our skin.

Our last child at home was attending a weeklong music camp
in northern Iowa, and we decided to spend that week paddling a
nearby river that had long been on our list: the Upper Iowa. We
wanted to immerse ourselves in the summer's bounty. Our photos that we took on the river show a dense overhang of box elder
and honeysuckle brushing a dark, silvery waterway. Birdlife was
vibrant. In the initial two hours on the river, we saw or heard fifty
species. As the journey continued, we would pass an astonishing
number of Yellow-billed Cuckoos, a generally shy bird I had never
seen before.

The Upper Iowa has its source in southeastern Minnesota in
Mower County, right on the border with Iowa. The river winds
south and eventually cuts through a limestone rock layer that
forms towering vertical cliffs along some stretches. The stream is
well-known among savvy canoeists, who regard the Upper Iowa as
scenic and remote.

We dropped in at Lime Springs, near the Minnesota border,
on an afternoon that was not cheerful with sunshine. The overcast
sky only deepened the verdure of the riverbanks. The humid air
lent a tropical cast to the midwestern waterway. This stretch of the
Upper Iowa can become unnavigable later in the summer because
of low water levels. We attempted the Lime Springs to Kendallville
segment only because it was June and the weather had been rainy.

We found the river shallow but deep enough to paddle. Grateful not to have to walk the canoe over ankle-deep gravel beds, we settled back to enjoy the float and admire the birds. Belted Kingfishers, with their oddly big heads and wild hairdos, flew back and forth across the river, rattling off a raucous call. Indigo Buntings, little sapphire jewels, sang sweetly from exposed perches, and scores of catbirds riffed with wild abandon from thickets.

Our destination the first night was a county park outside of Kendallville. The park was accessible to cars by a gravel road, but on a Tuesday evening, we had it to ourselves. We set up our tent on a grassy lawn, under the protection of two large bur oaks. The sturdiness of the trees was testimony that they had been there a long time. They reminded us that before Iowa grew corn and hogs, it was an oak savannah with rolling hills and waving prairie grass.

Near the park was an old gravel pit that exposed the Galena limestone rock layer, close to the surface along this stretch but appearing as striking cliffs farther downstream. Limestone is sedimentary rock, laid down as a substrate of a vast inland sea that once covered much of North America. Galena limestone is very old, Paleozoic in origin, and it is famous for its abundant fossils. Tom was a fossil hunter as a boy and had collected trilobites, ancient invertebrates that today have no living descendants. There are trilobites to be found in this rock layer, and so after supper we trotted down the road to explore.

The limestone was a rosy buff color, and it formed the walls of the gravel pit. Big chunks of it lay scattered on the ground, ours for the taking. Tom picked through the rubble for a while and came away with several good-sized specimens of what looked liked crinoid stalks. Unlike trilobites, crinoids do have living descendants. They are related to starfish and sea urchins; modern crinoids are called sea lilies or star feathers and are found in shallow seas around the world. One of Tom's finds showed the animal's length and cross section, which intrigued us. Later, we learned that throughout northeastern Iowa, wherever a road cuts through this limestone layer, fossil hunters can sift through a feast of ancient sea creatures.

The open, grassy campsite overlooked the dark moving river. The lack of brush alleviated some of the humidity in the air, at least until sunset. It was the summer solstice, and the light lingered long after the sun sank behind the trees. After the gravel pit visit, we returned to our camp and got out the cribbage board for several rounds. The park washrooms had running water, a luxury for campers. After showers, we crawled into our bags and slept uncommonly well. There were no paved roads, no cars, no campground lights. At four thirty, the first bird, a mournful Eastern Wood-Pewee, roused us from our slumbers.

....

In the tender morning light, the Upper Iowa River shimmered faintly, indicating a hidden current that had proven swift and strong. We calculated it at about three and a half miles per hour, clipping along by our flatlander standards. Translated, a current this fast means that even without paddling, without any work at all, we would travel three and a half miles an hour downstream, about the speed of a person walking.

A canoe trip is an opportunity to step out of one's normal life for a short time and think about something else. Holidays in general should afford the vacationer this, but canoe trips are especially good at doing so, in large part because paddlers live in the immediacy needed to detect snags and rocks below the surface. If you focus on the river and its features, you have no time to worry about other things.

Then, too, people almost always camp on canoe trips, so you front life in the most elemental way. You carry all necessary clothes with you in a small pack. The menu options depend on what you packed in the food box. The weather becomes more significant. It can control the menu (do we really want to put up a tarp and cook oatmeal in the rain?), it can control movement (it's too windy to paddle across the lake—best to stay here), and it can control recreational plans (let's paddle on while it's sunny). A heavy dew means a later start if you want the tent to dry. A light breeze means less bugs.

The weeks leading up to this trip down the Upper Iowa had had their quota of stress. Tom and I grappled with the opening stages of a chronic illness in one of our kids, a distressing situation that I struggled to come to terms with. A parent, once vigorous, had become an invalid. We had two children in college, one studying abroad. I was in the last stages of writing a book, and Tom kept up the always-frantic pace of a family practitioner. So we were happy for a little breather, one in which the most pressing issues were what we would cook for supper, and whether we needed the rain jackets accessible near the top of the Duluth pack.

....

On the second day of the trip, we paddled past green banks of mixed forest and flat banks of waist-high reed canary grass. The trees on the banks were every shade of green, some bright with yellow undertones indicating new growth, and some bluish in the shade, leaves that had emerged in the opening weeks of the spring.

I was thrilled when I first spied a Yellow-billed Cuckoo perched on a dead branch of a slender elm that had succumbed to Dutch elm disease. I had never seen the bird before, but it is unmistakable: the long tail with the striking white circles marking its length, the white throat, and, most vivid, the yellow ring circling its eye. I didn't have binoculars at hand, but I didn't need them with the bird so clearly visible. The tangled bank of vegetation behind it was perfect habitat. Yellow-billed Cuckoos range as far north as central Minnesota, where we live and do most of our bird-watching, but they are not common. Perhaps this is why: Minnesota is not as lush as northern Iowa.

Almost on the heels of seeing that first cuckoo, we rounded a bend and beheld another Yellow-billed Cuckoo. We felt uncommonly lucky! Two of the birds in a single morning. As we paddled on, we soon discovered, however, that the cuckoos were numerous. The ones we encountered were all sitting on exposed branches near the river, taking in the sunshine in a slow cuckoo way, all easy to see and tally. They didn't startle and fly off. They regarded us with yellow-ringed eyes, as if wondering in a jaded way what manner of creature had taken to their stream.

As we approached the town of Bluffton, we entered a region that is referred to broadly as the Driftless Area. Tom and I were familiar with the unglaciated regions of southwestern Wisconsin and southeastern Minnesota. They are marked by a hilly landscape that was not smoothed over by large ice sheets. We did not know the Driftless Area extended into northeastern Iowa as well. This unglaciated landscape through which the Upper Iowa River runs is marked by the Galena limestone cliffs one hundred to three hundred feet high above the river. They create an intimate, canyon-like feel. The limestone bedrock is very close to the surface here, and the river has cut through it over the millennia to form the cliffs.

That night from our campsite, we had a wonderful view of a limestone tower, Chimney Rock. Sitting in our camp chairs, the river gurgling at our feet, we studied the cliff. Its top was crowned by white pine, red cedar, and basswood trees, which were in bloom in late June. The sweet scent of flowering basswood wafted in the damp evening air. The conifers—the pine and cedar—were new to the river's landscape, and we would see more of them farther downriver.

Our campsite was in a private campground, and the owners had agreed to help us shuttle our car so it would be waiting for us at trip's end. We had left the car at the drop-in site upriver and needed to retrieve it. Tending to the car meant interrupting our river experience, during which we had seen no one, and reentering the everyday world for a few hours.

Off the river and traveling over the countryside with the campground owner reminded us that the Upper Iowa runs literally through people's backyards, through farms, and through bordering county parks. We had seen no other souls in the two days we had been on the river, and it had seemed remote and pristine to us. Our river experience was much different from the human experiences on just the other side of the banks, where people fretted over soybeans, fed hogs, drove on paved roads, and hung laundry on clotheslines. We had seemed to paddle through a wilderness, but had we, with roads so close by?

Mulling this over begged the question of what really defines wilderness. Is it an actual place, or is it a state of mind? I once read a short essay, "The Wilderness Experience" by naturalist Robert Finch of Massachusetts, in his fine little book *Common Ground*. He had entered a scrubby patch of familiar woods by his house one evening, woods he had walked through hundreds of times. He was without a flashlight that night, though, and became unaccountably confused. He stumbled about for some time, feeling sheepish and yet truly lost, until he came upon a boulder that he recognized, sat down, and thought to look up. There, the Big Dipper shone in the night sky, pointing the way to the North Star, and telling him how to get home. "Wilderness," he concluded, "is where you find it, or perhaps where you lose yourself."

I have lost myself in Finch's manner more often than I would like to admit. On the Upper Iowa, though, we were losing ourselves—our anxious, schedule-driven selves—simply by letting an underappreciated river carry us downstream, with only cuckoos and catbirds as spectators.

Our bird list, which we were compiling both by sightings and by hearing songs as we floated past, was up to sixty-four species. We added another bird to the life list at Chimney Rock: Bank Swallows, little brown-backed swallows with brown "belts" across their breasts, were nesting in holes they had excavated from the cutaway riverbanks.

....

The stretch of river from Bluffton to Decorah on the third day of our trip took us past the Bluffton Fir Stand State Preserve. This ninety-four-acre preserve protects Iowa's largest stand of balsam fir—a tree not generally found in Iowa at all. Balsam fir is a boreal species, a major member of Canada's expansive northern forest. These trees are relicts, members of a plant community that had grown up near the icy glacial sheet ten thousand years ago and had been left behind as that sheet retreated. Associated with the left-behind firs are other boreal species, Canada yew and Canada mayflower. The little relict community grows mostly on the lower slopes of the preserve, in crevices where it is cooler and shadier, reminiscent of the glacial climate. On the upper slopes of the preserve, the maple-basswood forest of present-day northeastern Iowa has taken over. The western portion of the preserve has bur oaks, the vanguards of the oak savannah directly west, so the state preserve is at an intersection of three major plant communities, and as might be expected, the plant diversity is very high—340 species of vascular plants on the ninety-four acres.

The limestone cliffs are particularly impressive along this stretch also, so much so that they have been singled out and designated the Bluffton Palisades. All along the river, little springs drip down the limestone cliffs or spurt out in mini-waterfalls. We had been noting them since entering the Driftless Area. Sometimes we could catch a waft of cooler air as we paddled past, hinting at an origin deep in the limestone layer. Other times, we noted a mist marking a stream's entry into the warmer river water. Between Bluffton and Decorah, the most significant of these springs emerges from the bedrock and feeds the widening river.

At the pretty college town of Decorah, our trip ended. The city has an attractive municipal campground, Pulpit Rock, with grassy tent sites next to the river. We had enjoyed the evenings out in the open area and the breakfasts of coffee perked on the Coleman stove and oatmeal bubbling from the cook kettle so much that we stayed another night. The getaway had been both modest and great. We had been given a respite from everyday cares and treated to the abundance of nature.

We seldom ask ourselves if we are happy. Perhaps that lack of questioning is as indicative as anything of a happy life. In the morning, feeling renewed, we undid the tent stakes, rolled up the fly, and stuffed our home away from home in its sack.

Sea Caves

....

THE AUGUST AFTERNOON GREW LONG IN THE TOOTH. LAKE Superior was remarkably calm on the south shore, and we drowsed in a golden light that was all too rarely seen. Not a ripple marred the mirrorlike surface of the water, and a summer haze obscured the Minnesota shore twenty-two miles opposite. When our torpor got tiresome, we felt the need to rouse ourselves. Perfect weather, then, for the sea caves.

The sea caves, part of the Apostle Islands National Lakeshore, pocket the western edge of the Bayfield Peninsula, which protrudes into Lake Superior in northern Wisconsin. Excavated by wave action from erodible sandstone, the caves can only be approached from the water. Squaw Bay, which encloses the caves, usually freezes over in winter, and then visitors can hike, ski, or run snowmobiles over the ice to reach them. In summer, however, one needs a boat. Most visitors to the caves paddle kayaks; indeed, the National Park Service, which oversees the caves, frowns on canoes on Lake Superior. When the conditions are right, though, a canoe is a fine way to explore the nooks and crannies of the caves.

The most direct route to the caves is to launch from Meyer's Beach within the national lakeshore, about four miles northeast of the town of Cornucopia. From the white sand beach it is about a mile paddle on crystalline water—you can see twenty feet down— to reach the caves. When the lake is flat, it is a dreamlike trip, gliding between sky and sea. When the water is choppy—well, you shouldn't be out on Lake Superior in a canoe on choppy water.

Lake Superior enjoys a certain lassitude on many August days. But because winds can pick up seemingly out of nowhere, we plan our visits to the sea caves for the late afternoon or early evening hours. By that time of day the weather is set. Winds tend to die down with sunset, and we can be as certain as we would ever be that the weather won't change suddenly when we are on the water.

The hour of our visits also means that the caves, carved from red sandstone cliffs, nearly always glow in the most vivid hues, bathed in the yellow rays of a low-hanging sun. The greens of the northern forest that grows atop the cliffs assume a brilliant emerald, especially in the deep shadows, where the irregular shoreline casts some parts in shade. And the lake picks up the reflection of this brilliance and transforms it to a watery teal. Every trip is a feast for the eyes.

But a sea caves visit also offers an auditory treat. Water rolling into the caverns roils about and echoes. Paddlers can hear the round, hollow booms on the approach to the caves and the liquid sloshing as water is momentarily contained.

....

Anticipating being on the water, we arrive at the parking lot for Meyer's Beach around six o'clock. The National Park Service paved over a once-gravel patch and built outhouses, formalizing visits to the caves that had once been casual. Visitors must pay for their parking place, and there's a little kiosk adjacent to the lot. The place looks empty—most of the kayakers have gone home to dinner. We will have the caves to ourselves.

We unfasten the straps anchoring the canoes to the cars and hoist them off the roofs. Two by two, we lug them down the stairs to the white sand beach. The sun is a yellow orb in the western sky. The water is calm on Squaw Bay.

....

The sea caves had a beginning in ancient outwash from streams flowing out of present-day southern Minnesota into a basin where Lake Superior is now. These streams carried sandy sediment, which was laid down in a thin bed. Over the eons and with pressure, this sandy layer became a sandstone, later to be called the Devils Island formation, for nearby Devils Island, the outermost of the Apostles, which itself has dramatic sea caves carved out of sandstone. Although the sea caves are specific to the Devils Island formation, other sandstone layers above and below it, the Chequamegon above and the Orienta below, form a fairly thick sandstone layer, the Bayfield Group.

The Bayfield Group is a pervasive rock layer throughout Lake Superior's south shore, and it was extensively quarried to build the cities of Duluth, Minnesota, and Superior, Wisconsin, as well as Bayfield, Ashland, Marquette, and Ironwood in northern Wisconsin and the Upper Peninsula of Michigan. The stone is rosy, ranging in hue from terra-cotta to a deep plum. The redness indicates iron content, and indeed, analysis of sand grains from the stone show the grains are coated by iron oxide—rust.

Other Apostle Islands have exposed layers of the Bayfield Group of sandstones. Basswood Island had a very early quarry, begun in 1868, and it produced a lot of stone, but business declined with the panic of 1893. The stone did not regain its popularity after the panic. In the later 1890s, paler limestone came into vogue, due in large part to the dramatic White City of the 1893 Columbian Exposition in Chicago. The massive reddish stone used to build Pillsbury Hall at the University of Minnesota and Duluth Central High School in downtown Duluth was passé.

....

On the water, we dig our paddles in, appreciating the sea-green clarity of Superior. The northeastern shore of Minnesota is visible on the horizon. We can see the southernmost Apostle Islands, too. Tiny Eagle Island and the larger Sand Island are far-off specks that grow bigger as we cross the distance between the beach and the caves.

There is a restful quality to the large expansiveness of Lake Superior. Nothing hems the viewer in. One's eyes can sweep the sky and water without confronting barriers. It invites a sense of limitlessness. I think this is why I prefer the spareness of horizons to the grandeur of a mountain range. A horizon—the edge of the water fading into sky—holds a promise of unfettered possibility.

There is freedom here, and especially so when unencumbered by a bulky boat. The paddler sits just inches from the water, the sleek canoe slicing through it.

....

When we spy the first cave, we are nearly upon it. Its dark recesses look cool. It is hard to see through to its depths because of the brightness of the early evening. This is not a cave large enough to enter, but soon we will encounter chasms that can accommodate a canoe. There is an arch. We maneuver the canoe through it, peering up into the darkness to see the sandstone underside. There is a deep cleft. We approach it bow first and feel a slight thrill as the reddish walls rise high over our heads.

The Devils Island sandstone has ripples in it. We can see the individual horizontal layers within the rocks. I wonder if long ago the sandy deposits were delivered to this basin in spurts. A sudden immensity of flowing water, followed by a quiescent period? We marvel at the pattern of sand layers and shadows cast by them as they follow the curve of a hollow. Color variation is apparent. Some layers are pink, some are darker, the color of clay pots.

Cliff Swallows dart out from a deep niche. I can detect their globular nests constructed from mud that the birds collect in their beaks and transport to the nest site. I try to imagine a mother bird incubating eggs inside one of the mud nests, listening to the crash of Superior's waves during a storm. Then I think of the fragile nestlings, huddled together, the liquid music of the lake the unceasing marker of "home."

Water seeps out of the sand layers at some points in the cliffs, and there bright-hued ferns grow, staking their claim. In contrast to the rust-colored sandstone, they are incredibly green.

....

Today the lake is unusually placid, but if there are waves at all, paddlers have to beware of the bounce-back of water from the cliffs. These interference waves are at odds with those rolling in off the lake. The interference waves themselves are not regular. Water hits against the cliff, or it enters a cave and returns at a different interval, and there are many caves. All of this happens at once, and the confused water rocks canoes irregularly. The Park Service warns paddlers to be aware of this. Inattentiveness and a particularly big wave can send a canoeist overboard.

After an hour or so, we have not exhausted the caves, but we have run out of time. The sun has sunk low on the horizon, and it is time to return to the beach. Tonight we will dine on whitefish from a local, family-owned fishery. After satisfying our need for color and beauty, the lake will provide a meal as well. Superior feeds us in many ways.

Transition

KEJIMKUJIK NATIONAL PARK, NOVA SCOTIA, 2008

....

WE FACED A TIME OF TRANSITION. OUR YOUNGEST CHILD was heading to college, and we would be empty nesters at last. Tom and I had been sending offspring away to school for years, but because there were four, the dwindling of our brood took a long time. Our empty-nest friends had warned us about the house that seemed to echo when the baby of the family left home. The vacant bedroom suddenly became a shrine to a past of sporting events and prom dates. Milk soured in the refrigerator. There was leftover food at dinner. Some couples had taken several years to adjust to life without children. Some had felt it necessary to work through a whole new definition of marriage. At least one had not successfully made the transition, and split.

The in-betweenness of being a couple on a daily basis, but with a large and perhaps extended family at holidays, is a marker in the progression of middle age. I had long pondered the metaphor of life being a river. I came across the idea in a news magazine as a child. I had thought, at that tender age, that it was a novel idea. At the beginning of the waterway, the stream is small and slow moving. You splash and play in the sun-dappled waters, unaware that you have begun drifting downstream. Later, you realize that the current has quickened. The banks of the river pass swiftly. There is less time to study them and certainly no time to splash. But still you man the boat competently, steering here and there, avoiding rocks and whirlpools. Then, imperceptibly, you detect a distant rumble, soft at first, but gradually louder. There is, you realize, a waterfall somewhere downriver, a waterfall that would be best to portage around, but of course, you can't. The current carries you with increasing haste, your paddles no match for what has become a formidable river. You will go over that waterfall.

The empty nest is not the Waterfall. I likened the transition Tom and I were approaching to a rapids. Rapids are classed on a scale from I to VI, Class I rapids being mere riffles, Class VI being more or less unnavigable waterfalls. (I want to add here that some incautious people do run waterfalls in kayaks, but I am not one.) We were unsure what class rapids confronted us.

I am not particularly fond of any rapids, even riffles, unless I know them well. When I anticipate encountering rapids, I strain my ears for their first murmur and fret and stew in the bow until we actually have plotted a way through them. Then I dig in and paddle hard, no longer worried. "Enough already!" I wrote in my journal, contemplating for the nth time the empty nest. "I just want to be in the rapids!"

After waving good-bye to the youngest in front of her dorm, driving down the hill of the college, Old Main at our backs, and passing the orientation volunteers, who were handing out Kleenex packets to weeping parents, we headed home to our quiet house. When all four kids had been at home, Tom and I had peered down the length of the dinner table at each other while the noisy ones chattered on about school, athletic workouts, homework, and friends. Now we were excessively polite to each other. "Would you like a glass of wine with dinner?" Tom would ask. "How was work?" I might query, and then listen for the first time in years to the experience of a harried physician who saw sore throats, uncontrolled diabetes, and possible cancer in the course of one day. We took walks into town. We watched movies, cuddled on the couch. We made an effort to converse. We paid attention to nuance. The first weeks in September were riffles, when we had expected Class IIs.

No longer tied to the public school schedule, we were free to vacation in the fall, and we planned a driving trip to Nova Scotia. The jaunt would include a three-day canoe paddle in Kejimkujik National Park southwest of the provincial capital of Halifax. We had visited Nova Scotia eight years before and paddled a canoe on Mahone Bay, a protected cove of the Atlantic Ocean off the eastern coast of the peninsula. Returning home, our small plane had flown low, and from it we glimpsed beyond Halifax a vast, undeveloped area of bogs and forest. Scarcely a road penetrated this quaggy lowland. The wilderness stretched on and on. Nova Scotia is sparsely populated. Most people live along the coasts. Our view from the air underscored the point.

The large, wild expanse we had flown over was the Tobeatic Wilderness Area and Kejimkujik National Park. The park is both a natural preserve and a national historic site, protecting the cultural heritage of the First Nation of the Mi'kmaq Indians, who have lived in the area for thousands of years. About two thousand Mi'kmaq still live in this boreal place, some on reservations. Others of the Mi'kmaq First Nation live on Cape Breton in northern Nova Scotia, in Maine, and in Newfoundland. The Tobeatic (Mi'kmaq for "the place of the alder") Wilderness Area is nearly three times bigger than the national park, but the park was developed for canoeists.

There is wonderful continuity in twenty-first-century canoeists plying the waters of Kejimkujik. The native Mi'kmaq were early developers of the canoe, and images of the graceful craft suffuse their ancient stories. In one, the first human being, Glooscap, paddled the world in a stone canoe. Some tales take Glooscap across North America to the West Coast; others have him arriving in what is now Nova Scotia from afar to teach the Mi'kmaq how to make a canoe out of native materials—birch bark, spruce, and cedar. In one story, he appoints a bird, a partridge, to be the designer of a boat so light that it can take to the air.

The Mi'kmaq are not the only people to have built and perfected canoe-like boats, of course. First peoples across the world use dugouts, hollowed-out logs that are one forerunner of the canoe. In northern North America, where lakes and rivers form a mesh of water, many different nations still use canoes and have a wealth of legends concerning them. Petroglyphs drawn by the ancients on rocks often show canoes engaged in various work.

A common, recurrent thread to these stories casts canoes in a spiritual light. One Canadian chronicler of tales termed them "liminal vehicles"—boats on a threshold. Frequently they are used to carry paddlers from one world to the next. They are barks of transition. They are trustworthy. In their airiness, they are capable of transporting something as delicate as a soul.

....

Tom's and my instincts were correct in turning to our canoe on this vacation. What better way to traverse a threshold? For many years, we had taken canoe trips alone, as a couple, with the kids enjoying Grandma's hospitality. We had an informal goal of paddling in all fifty states, an achievement we were not likely to complete, but it gave form to our travels.

It wasn't practical, though, to haul our sixty-five-pound Old Town halfway across the continent. Someone else's canoe would have to carry our souls. We planned a trip through the park service and arranged to rent a canoe at an outfitter associated with the park. We would bring our own packs and gear. It was not until we reached upstate New York that we discovered we had not carried this plan through to completion.

"Hand me the stove and I'll get the stew on," I had said, after we pulled into a rest stop for a supper break. We had been on the road since six o'clock that morning and were nearly groggy with the miles we had put under us.

"It must be stowed under something," Tom had replied, rummaging bearlike through the trunk. "I thought I put it on the side of the cooler. . . . Well, that's just dumb. I can't find it." I watched as his lanky form disappeared into the far reaches of the trunk, thinking that I would have put that stove on top.

Alas, the Coleman stove was missing. We now remembered it was standing ready to be packed back home in the garage. We made an emergency plan to swing by Freeport, Maine, to L. L. Bean, for a replacement and ate cold sandwiches that evening.

We took a fast ferry, a hydroplane, from Bar Harbor to Yarmouth, Nova Scotia, on a bright blue morning with sunlight glinting off the Atlantic. From the ferry we saw skeins of small shorebirds in great numbers flying in undulating waves, migrating south. As a midwesterner, I had only heard of these iconic flocks, and it was fascinating to see them skimming the water, dipping and rising, all birds of one mind. They were themselves on a transition from their Arctic breeding grounds to their winter haunts.

Kejimkujik Park is heavily used. By visiting in September, we avoided crowds. When we arrived midmonth, red maples were brilliant against the dark green of the conifers. The spruce bogs, those wet, low areas we had seen from the plane, were still dressed in summer verdure. Misshapen black spruce, draped with lichens, edged the blue eyes of open water fringed with arrowweed and sphagnum moss. Kejimkujik—Keji, to the locals—looks boreal, northern, with its spires of conifers and the boggy sphagnum mats. It is, in fact, lower in latitude than Minneapolis. When we commenced the trip, the air was cool, but the sun was warm. The lakes were still bearable to swim in, at least for us, who are accustomed to frigid dips in Lake Superior.

Because the park has so many visitors, every campsite has features to lessen human impact. After an initial portage and a short paddle, we arrived at our first site (#3) on Big Dam Lake in the northern corner of the park. There we discovered a picnic table, a fire grate, a tent pad, and an outhouse with four walls (in provincial parks, and also in the BWCAW, biffies are simple boxes). We were also intrigued by a complex cable system resembling a jungle gym. This was the means by which we were to string up the food pack. We are always scrupulous in hoisting our food out of the reach of bears each night. The jungle gym arrangement with carabiners and a pulley would make the night's duties an easy task and was probably more sustainable for the surrounding trees.

To canoeists used to the Boundary Waters, this seemed an intrusive bit of civilization on the wilderness experience. However, Kejimkujik is a national park, not a wilderness area. A comparable situation might be Voyageurs National Park in northern Minnesota, west of the Boundary Waters Canoe Area Wilderness. At Voyageurs, there are also tent pads, picnic tables, and fire grates at every site. The Yanks provide a bear-proof food locker, rather than the string-'em-up approach, and the toilet scene is not quite so private.

I was immediately taken with Keji as we paddled to our first campsite on Big Dam Lake. When we silently approached the shore, a young river otter crawled out of the water on to a large rock directly ahead of us. It began grooming itself in the late afternoon sun and was so preoccupied with fur matters, and so little accustomed to people in canoes, that we edged very close before it startled and slipped into the lake. Almost always the wild animals I see are aware of my presence. There's a kind of biologic observer effect in that—the animals are either wary or posed for flight, on edge in some way. You can't see them as they really are. The opportunity to watch up close a young animal acting naturally was very moving, a peek into its world.

Site #3 on Big Dam Lake was ours by reservation long before we picked up a paddle. The highly structured approach of the Canadian national parks was foreign to us. It was a bit like procuring an outdoor motel room, and we felt it cut both ways: it was nice to be guaranteed a spot. We didn't feel anxious about the late start to our trip. On the other hand, what if we had wanted to paddle farther that day? We didn't have a reservation for another site. We could imagine a dreadful scenario where we simply moved into an unoccupied site, later to be accosted by very late arrivals, waving legitimacy with their reservation slip. "Dumb Yanks!" they would yell, disturbing the peaceful park. "You can't be here! Get out!"

Happily, site #3 was lovely. We set up camp and started dinner on the new L. L. Bean single-burner backpacking stove.

At this site, we soon discovered that Kejimkujik is also a backpacker's paradise. One of the hiking trails ran the length of Big Dam Lake, directly behind our campsite. It is possible for backpackers to take this trail and circumnavigate the entire park. The Big Dam segment is close to the park entrance and easily accessible for day hikers, so it sees a lot of boots.

The next day, we took an early morning hike on the trail. We found a large portion of it to be boardwalk through a primeval stand of giant hemlocks. It inevitably brought to mind the opening lines to Henry Wadsworth Longfellow's epic poem *Evangeline*, which is set in this very area. "This is the forest primeval," the poem begins. "The murmuring pines and the hemlocks, / Bearded with moss, and in garments green, indistinct in the twilight, / Stand like Druids of eld, with voices sad and prophetic."

I had never walked through an old-growth hemlock forest before. Underneath the drooping boughs of the ancient trees scarcely a whisper breathed. So little light came through the canopy to the forest floor that there was no understory. One might easily have traversed it unhindered—except for the mounded hummocks of tree roots, covered with sphagnum moss draping the ground, creating a knobby terrain. Tiny boreal plants—wintergreen, pyrola, and bunchberry, and the trailing double leaves of twinflower—grew amid the shaggy moss. The air under the hemlocks was cool and green, and there was abundant moisture. Mushroom diversity was unexpectedly delightful. Tom went off with his camera and returned enthusiastic over coolie-capped cliffs of fungi, apricot-colored mushrooms, red-capped ones with white stalks, rosy ones with peaked caps.

I craned my neck to the treetops to check out the birdlife. There was little activity in the hemlocks, but in an adjacent area that had been logged and was second growth, I found small birds atwitter: Black-and-white Warblers, which may well have been summer residents; Golden-crowned Kinglets in migrating flocks; and a striking male Black-throated Blue Warbler, a bird I seldom see. The ubiquitous bird, though, the one peeping all day long, was the jaunty little Red-breasted Nuthatch. A bird of the boreal forest, these tiny graybacked birds with peach-colored waistcoats yank-yank-yanked continuously. I watched them travel in small bands. I wondered if the unit consisted of Mom, Dad, and the kids. One couldn't know for sure. Male and female nuthatches look much alike. Sometimes it seemed like some of the nuthatches begged food—fledglings late in the season. There were so many of the elfin avians that whenever I think about Nova Scotia's woods now, I think of Red-breasted Nuthatches.

....

The route for our trip took us through a winding river connecting Big Dam Lake with Frozen Ocean Lake. We had reservations at site

#8 on Frozen Ocean. It was not an attractive name, and in fact, we were finding the mid-September nights chilly. In addition to pajamas, I wore a wool sweater, socks, and a hooded sweatshirt when I crawled into my new mummy sleeping bag, a bag we had bought specifically for fall camping. It was supposed to be comfortable to nighttime temperatures of twenty degrees.

I was coming down with a cold, so the chill might not have been attributable to the bag. I was, in fact, enamored of the new bag. It was called the Cat's Meow and was a pretty powder blue, lightweight but with nice loft. I liked that it had an internal hand-warming "muff" for my hands and a built-in pocket for my watch. The alternative at the store had been something called a Big Agnes. I am sure it was a perfectly fine bag, but who would choose Big Agnes over the Cat's Meow? Not me, a feline aficionado, even though at five feet eight, I am probably a bigger Agnes than most female shoppers at REI.

Chastened by the long, steep portages at Killarney Provincial Park a few years before, we had planned a route at Keji with short, level portages, nothing that would challenge us. We then felt encouraged to bring a cooler—yes, a cooler—along on the trip, an unusual luxury. This sheer extravagance can actually be put down to our frugality. We started the trip with milk to use up and cold beer. As we packed the Duluth packs at Keji, we looked at the milk carton.

"It seems a shame to toss perfectly good milk," I commented, "but I don't want to drink it now."

"We could take the cooler, you know," Tom replied. "It wouldn't be that big of a deal on these dinky portages."

"Hmm," I said slowly, thinking through a new idea. "Yogurt would be a great, easy breakfast—with oranges and granola. We could even take lettuce and salad stuff, why not?"

Constraints aside, we tossed in carrots and peppers. On the first portage, we merely carried the cooler. By itself, though, the big hulk unbalanced the canoe. Subsequently, we shoved the cooler into the bottom of our number four Duluth pack, a vast canvas sack about four feet across. We piled the food and equipment boxes on top—number fours are really big—and then shouldered it. This would never have worked had we known we would encounter white water or long portages. As it was, the trip was easy, and we assumed the attitude "Hey, we're empty nesters! Approaching decrepitude! We're entitled to cold beer in camp!"

....

Luxury upon luxury in this national park: the site on Frozen Ocean had an Adirondack shelter to sleep in. Adirondacks are classic, three-sided shelters, sometimes with a wooden platform floor. They offer protection for outdoor enthusiasts all over North America, no longer just in the Adirondack Mountains. The roof can protect from rain or snow; the open fourth side is often oriented toward a fire pit, so it is also a warming hut. We had never seen one on a canoe trip anywhere, but having the shelter meant we didn't need to set up a tent.

The shelter proved cozy. We positioned the stove on one edge of the platform and sat on the deck itself to eat and to read. We had not packed any camp chairs when portages were planned. Our Coleman lantern cast a rosy glow and gave off a comforting hiss, and we needed its light. The September nights were getting longer. No bugs disturbed our tranquility. The insect season was over. Far off, a Barred Owl asked us, Who who who cooks for yoooou? Quietly, companionably, we turned the pages of our books. I was deep into a novel set in Nova Scotia, written by a native son, Alistair MacLeod. Tom was reading an account of lobster fishing in Maine.

We would rise early the next morning and hoped to head out before rain set in. The evening's sunset had told us it was on its way. We would paddle immense Kejimkujik Lake, counting on a gentle, all-day rain to keep it calm. The hemlocks and pines would murmur from the shore. The transitioning canoe would carry us to our new life.

Nerve-Wracked

THE WHITE RIVER OF WISCONSIN, 2010

....

THE WHITE RIVER OF NORTHERN WISCONSIN IS A LOVELY little waterway arising in the Bibon Swamp, a glacial lake remnant southwest of the town of Ashland. It flows northeast into the Bad River, which continues northward to Lake Superior. As the crow flies, the river is very near the Great Lake—no more than fifteen miles distant at its most southern point—but because of its many S curves, the river mileage is considerable.

The river has two distinct natures, much like the better-known Bois Brule River of northwestern Wisconsin. Both rivers arise in inland wetlands and flow toward the Great Lake; both reach a point where bedrock breaks away toward the lake, and the rivers tumble rapidly as elevation declines. The waterways trace the volcanic basin that took its initial shape a billion years ago, an echo of its ancient geologic past.

On an earlier paddle through its upper reaches, we found the White to meander placidly to and fro. We spent a pleasant, if slightly dull, day, wandering with the stream, collecting watercress for a dinner salad, and hoping, after hours spent on S curves, that the landing was just up ahead.

One August, however, we took a swift jaunt down the much different lower White, below the geological break. We discovered a challenging river, where the attraction of watercress paled in comparison to the rapids and riffles that demanded our attention from the minute we dropped in.

Despite years of paddling, I have never overcome my anxiety about white water. The sound of rushing water starts my heart racing. When I happily agreed to canoe the White that day, I had no idea that the stretch from Maple Ridge Road, outside of the tiny burg of Mason, to the Highway 112 dam would be continuous white water. I read the disturbing truth in the car as we hastened toward the dam, our ending point of the trip, to drop off our bicycles.

At the dam, we unloaded our bicycles from the car rack and stashed them in the weeds. The plan was to drive to the point of embarkation, paddle to just before the dam, take out, don bike helmets, and cycle back on gravel roads to the car.

As we locked up our bikes, we met a pair of kayakers just ending their trip. One was a woman. I am always happy to meet a woman; believe it or not, they are not all that common on most rivers, and I pay more attention to their assessment of a river, thinking, perhaps wrongly, they will be less inclined to machismo. The kayakers assured us that the river would be kind to our canoe, but that we might get wet from standing waves. "It's not as bad as the Ledges on the Brule," the man remarked. This was not comforting, since running the Ledges years ago in open canoes was perhaps one of the worst ideas we had ever conceived.

....

At the put-in point, we left in the car what should not get wet: Tom's camera and my binoculars. We put the cell phones in a tiny dry bag—a high-tech, waterproof pouch with an interlocking clasp that does not come undone under stress—the lunch in a larger one, and extra sweatshirts in a still larger one. These we tied to the central thwart of the canoe, insuring they would stay with us should the canoe tip. Muttering a favorite mantra from Thoreau ("I did not want to live what was not life, living is so dear"), I put on a windbreaker, for a strong wind blew from the northwest, and my life jacket.

It took Tom three tries before he was set. He put the car key into a dry bag, and then realized he had forgotten to lock the car. He had to fish out the little dry bag from the big dry bag. When the car was locked and the bags repacked, he realized he had not put on sunblock. Fish out the little dry bag again. Then when it seemed we were ready to push off, he realized he had not yet changed into river sandals . . . which were in the locked car. So he undid the nesting dry bags a third time. When he went to the car for the sandals, he discovered he had left them at home.

Meanwhile, I kept muttering that mantra, assuring myself that "living was dear" and "real life" involved white water. My confidence in my forgetful fellow paddler wasn't shaken, really it wasn't, because navigating rapids has nothing to do with sequential planning. It just doesn't.

We pushed away from the bank.

....

Almost immediately, we encountered bubbling water, and for the next several miles, it did not let up. We riveted our attention on the stream, dodging rocks, looking for chutes, and shouting instructions over the din of rushing water.

"Rock on right!"

"Paddle on the left!"

"Paddle hard! Paddle hard!"

"Is this nerve-wracking or exhilarating?" I yelled to Tom. I may have been laughing.

"A little of both!" he yelled back, grinning broadly.

That August had been a rainy month, and the White was running high. Usually, this softens the rapids. Menacing rocks are submerged and become less a worry. But with increased volume, the rate of flow increases. Things happen more quickly; paddlers need better reaction times.

After an hour, we reached a point in the river that was calmer. It was time for a breather. We beached the canoe on a sandbar and pulled out sandwiches and peaches from the dry bag. The birdlife all around us was rich and diverse. Red-breasted Nuthatches, a hallmark of the northern forest, yent-yented high in white pines, sounding as if they blew tiny tin horns. A flock of Cedar Waxwings trilled overhead. Young mergansers floated by, miniature versions of their parents.

This entire stretch of the White flowed through a narrow, undeveloped valley. A thick growth of red and white pines, basswoods, birch, and often spruce and alder created a leafy tunnel, shaded and intimate. The river seemed pristine. *Paddling Northern Wisconsin* calls this "a beautiful stretch of river," and it's true.

....

After the lunch break, we encountered another lengthy stretch of rapids. The terrain declined more precipitously as we approached the confluence with the Bad River and edged closer to the big lake.

The biggest drop—the one labeled The Ledge by some maps—caught us by surprise. We rounded a bend, having successfully navigated a slew of challenging runs, and spied a slender doe and her young fawn in the water. We were close to them, since the chuckle of white water had masked our approach. The pair was a vision of loveliness, picture-perfect. Focused on the deer, we were both astonished to see a one-and-a-half-foot drop in the river, a rock shelf, immediately under us. Tom had just time to shout, "Hang on!" when we shot over the ledge. The canoe nosed down, the stern poked up, we listed to starboard, and then the White's dark water filled the interior. With the weight of the water, we began to roll.

I gripped my paddle as I plunged into the river. We hadn't brought a spare, and I didn't want to lose it. With the other hand, I hung on to the canoe, as did Tom, who was somewhere behind me. Clutching our craft tightly and dripping with water, we edged our way to the riverbank. Breathless with the exertion and the surprise of the upset, we took a minute to settle down. Then we placed the precious paddles on land, untied the dry bag, and with much effort, raised the canoe up and drained the water out. Canoes don't sink completely even when filled with water, and once most of the water is out, they bob back in fine form.

Then we secured the dry bag once more, reclaimed our paddles, and took a minute to assess the lower part of the rapids. We were not yet through them, and Tom studied the flow for the best path through. After the ledge, the remaining rapids seemed like child's play. During the next twenty minutes, we discussed what went wrong. Nothing, we decided. We had done everything right. There had been no better chute to take. In fact, there had been no chute at all. Next time, we decided we would portage—if we could remember when the big drop was coming. That would be key. There had been no signs indicating a portage might be a good idea.

When we ended the trip just before the dam, our bicycles were waiting. Tom started the hour-long ride ahead of me because he could pedal harder and faster. The dousing had soaked us through. Our T-shirts were still wet, and we were getting chilled.

As I pedaled my bicycle alone on the back roads, I waxed philosophical about the experience. Another favorite mantra of mine is "The only way through this, is through." Nowhere is this more true than in the middle of a rapids. You can waste a large amount of brainpower trying to think through a rapids, but once you have embarked on the descent, you are committed. You cannot abort. The only way through this is through.

Teamwork is critical to a successful outcome. Trust is primary. And there is no room for negative thinking. It distracts and can endanger you. Lastly, you can do all those things and still tip the canoe. That's the existential risk of canoeing, and of life.

Wild and Scenic

THE UPPER ST. CROIX RIVER, 2011

....

THE ST. CROIX RIVER REFLECTS TWO DIFFERENT NATURES, depending on human proximity. Close to the communities of Stillwater, Minnesota; Hudson, Wisconsin; and the Twin Cities, it is a waterway of gaudy paddleboats, jazz, and merrymaking, of boaters, lift bridges, and fireworks on the Fourth of July. Farther north, however, the narrower St. Croix is a green, undisturbed river, lacking pizazz but offering refuge from modernity to canoeists and wildlife.

The upper St. Croix begins in the northern reaches of Wisconsin as a barely discernible trickle, gathers strength in a lake created by a dam, and runs southwest, forming the upper delineation between Wisconsin and Minnesota twenty-seven miles after the dam. This young river, together with its major tributary, the Namekagon, was one of the original eight waterways in the United States to be designated a Wild and Scenic River in federal legislation of the same name passed in 1968.

The designation "wild and scenic" is at once true and ironic: ironic because the river and its watershed carry the scars of abuse and disregard from a brutal past that rendered it profanely unwild; true, because the passage of time has a healing effect. It is possible for beauty to rise from ashes.

....

The St. Croix River shares a beginning with another northern stream, the Bois Brule of northern Wisconsin. The twins arise in a watery tamarack bog near the town of Solon Springs, Wisconsin. The two actually share a glacial beginning. A single river once flowed south out of Lake Superior, draining a melting glacier. The icy waters carved out a deep valley. As the glacier continued to recede, a subtle divide arose in the land south of the great lake. The river draining Superior reversed its flow, and two rivers formed, one continuing southward and one flowing north into the lake, both sourced in the new, barely perceptible high point. The north-flowing Bois Brule empties into Lake Superior and eventually the Gulf of St. Lawrence. The south-flowing St. Croix feeds the Mississippi River and then the Gulf of Mexico.

After twenty-five years of paddling northern Wisconsin, Tom and I hiked the historic portage trail that links the two rivers. The connecting path is ancient and has been trod by human feet for centuries. In a world before roads, the rivers and their portage were the means by which people traveled between Lake Superior and the Mississippi River.

Our family is intimate with both rivers, plying the Brule while at our cabin on Lake Superior and living near the St. Croix at home in Center City. We frequently canoe the St. Croix, hike and cross-country ski on its banks, keep an eye on its eagles and Trumpeter Swans, and picnic on its sandy islands. We often feel that we straddle two worlds in our cabin/house existence. They seem not to have anything to do with each other. At home, we don't think about the cabin. At the cabin, we don't think about home. The portage path linking the two rivers is a tangible tie to both places.

....

We came to the portage in late fall on a dark day that portended winter's approach. Parking in a lot on the northern end of the St. Croix Flowage, we took our Sheltie and a picnic lunch, crossed Douglas County Road A, and ascended the steep path, leaving the St. Croix and heading to where the Brule River arises.

Initially, the path cut across a grassy opening studded with scraggly red and pin oaks that still clung to dry reddish leaves. Following Tom's broad back (blue jacket, army-green backpack, don't lose sight of it), I scuttled to keep his pace, but the path invited dallying. The portage bore the marks of countless feet, and I tried to imagine them all—ones clad in moccasins or leather leggings, others in sturdy boots with Vibram soles. The surface duff was soft and powdery. The rut had been tamped down about ten inches beneath the surface.

When the trail leveled off, the character of the woods changed. Here the trees that dominated were conifers: red pine and jack pine, dark-needled spruce, and wispy balsam fir. On the floor, we noted the Lilliputian flora of the northern forest. Wintergreen still had a few red berries clinging to its shiny dark leaves. Tom knelt to examine *Linnaea borealis,* twinflowers, a favorite because his sister bears the name Linnea. In June, its two flowers would be tiny pink bells, but in October, only green leaves twined across tuffs of sphagnum moss. The divide, we saw, was not only topographical. This was a point at which the boreal forest mingled with a more southerly mixed woods of needled and broad-leaved trees.

The path angled left, and we skirted a large bog below us. Here the two rivers are born. The source was brown with marsh grass. Spears of flaming tamaracks thrust upward through the tangle. Alders and red osier were thick. We listened to the sparse calls of birds that remained after summer—now a chickadee, then a nuthatch, a noisy Blue Jay, a crow.

At the end of the portage, as we neared the Brule, the trail descended to a substrate of dark, peaty muck. We saw footprints of people who had recently tromped here. A thin layer of ice sealed the prints. The muck was stiff with frost and held firm as we followed the path to the edge of open water, where it might be possible, we thought, to plunk a canoe down and paddle away. The Sheltie lapped at the stream.

The portage was 1.9 miles long, a trudge with beginning and ending hills if one was carrying a canoe, but a short, pleasant hike if one was not. We had traversed it in less than an hour.

It was lunchtime, so we found a log and sat down, pulled out the lunch, and ate our cheese sandwiches, apples, and gingerbread. Big wet snowflakes began to fall, and we rejoiced in the first snow of the season. Never too old, I hope, to be thrilled with the first snow. The dog nosed about and looked hopefully at us for handouts.

After lunch, we retraced the portage back to the car, this time paying attention to the fair number of large rocks lining the path at intervals. Each bore a plaque with the name of a notable explorer on it. The earliest date was 1680, when Daniel Greysolon, Sieur du Lhut, an early French explorer and diplomat, roamed the area. He was the first to mention the portage in an official report. The city of Duluth is named for him. Pierre Le Sueur took the portage in 1693; Jonathan Carver, in 1768; and Henry Schoolcraft, in 1820 and again in 1832, when he returned after his expedition to the source of the Mississippi. On that trip, Schoolcraft portaged from the St. Croix to the Brule, reaching the latter about six o'clock in the evening. The party loaded its canoes, thinking it would soon reach a clear, unimpeded stream—but it did not. Instead, they found themselves in a kind of watery limbo as darkness fell and were forced to spend the night—during which it rained—in their canoes.

Somehow, it is always cheering to learn that others more experienced than we are can also make bad calls.

It was still snowing when we reached the end of the portage and arrived at the car. The waters of the St. Croix Flowage were still and silvery. A fine mist rose from its surface.

....

When we canoe the St. Croix River on a day trip, we never paddle its uppermost reaches. Our favorite put-in point is at river mile 104, Norway Point Landing, about an hour's drive from our house and about fifty miles downriver from its source.

As a federal Wild and Scenic River, the upper St. Croix is maintained under the auspices of the National Park Service. It keeps the landings in good shape, services the restrooms, provides taps for drinking water, and mows campsites, which are dispersed at intervals along the river. The sites are almost always lovely and not heavily used. The Park Service also has great maps of the river, its landings, and amenities.

A frequent trip for us is to drive to this section of the St. Croix, through Grantsburg, with canoes and bicycles, stop first at Fox Landing, river mile 99, unload the bicycles and hide them in the woods, and then drive to Norway Point Landing and begin our trip. When we get out at Fox Landing, we hop on the bikes and pedal back to the car over a flat, paved, empty road.

The river on this stretch north of Grantsburg is narrow and undeveloped. Public lands flank its banks. Mature trees of a mixed forest—white and red pine—mingle with big red and bur oaks. Box elder and soft maples, species that can get their feet wet, cling to banks that might see spring flooding. The water is clear, and the substrate is sandy, almost reddish. It is a legacy of the last glacier. The ancient river draining the glacier carried off stones and sand that the moving ice had picked up and ground fine, depositing it as outwash as it retreated. The reddish color hints at an affinity with the Gogebic Iron Range of northern Michigan.

The river has sandy spots for swimming. Often, we pull out at an empty campsite for a picnic and a dip. It is not uncommon to find empty freshwater mussel shells along the shallow sections of the river. The olive-green shells splay open to reveal a pearly white interior, but the animal that made the shell is long gone, perhaps as a meal for an otter or raccoon.

The upper St. Croix River is known for its diverse community of freshwater mussels. Forty-one species can be found in the river, but many populations are in trouble, and five species are listed by the federal government as endangered. All of the listed species were once widespread through the midsection of North America, and all have diminished as dams impede the free flow of rivers, intensive agriculture silts the water, toxins poison their surrounding environment and their food, and invasive species, like zebra mussels, take up residence.

The woes of the St. Croix's mussels are caused by their method of obtaining food and their sedentary life: adult mussels don't do much traveling. The animals are filter feeders, gleaning small orts through large amounts of water. Dams restrict the flow of water—less orts come the way of the mussels. Runoff caused by farming, logging, and poor maintenance of the watershed carries small particles that clog their filtering organs. Pesticides and other chemicals dissolved in water are disastrous to creatures that filter large amounts of water. And invasive species like the zebra mussel horn in on their beds.

Their troubles are compounded by the way they reproduce. Sex in a watery medium is not the issue, even taking into account sturdy, armor-like shells. After fertilization, females release tiny larvae into the river. But these minute larval mussels need to cling to the gills of fish until they are mature, and this is the problem: many mussel species are particular about their host. For some, only one specific fish species will do, and these themselves are declining in population. Others are less fussy and may utilize several different species of fish. The less-fussy ones have a rosier future.

The St. Croix's mussels bear evocative names. The five on the endangered species list illustrate: the Higgins eye, the sheepnose, the snuffbox, the spectaclecase (long and dark), and the winged mapleleaf. All are proving difficult to recover in other parts of their range, like the Mississippi River, and restoration biologists are aiding the little animals in reproductive efforts and transplanting individuals and larval forms in (mussel) unpopulated areas in hopes of recolonizing.

The U.S. Fish and Wildlife Service, in charge of protecting endangered species from extinction, sees the St. Croix River as a last holdout for these imperiled animals. Its website states, "In a sense, the St. Croix watershed is an island of near-pre-settlement conditions surrounded by the more developed and altered North America of the 20th century." How true is this observation? Is the watershed unaltered?

....

When we reach Fox Landing, we paddle to the bank and haul the canoe away from the water. We drag our hidden bicycles out of the weeds, hop on, and head back to our put-in at Norway Point. The rough asphalt road, flat as a pancake, skirts the boundary of the Crex Meadows Wildlife Area, a whopping thirty-thousand-acre expanse of marshland and pine savannah owned by the State of Wisconsin.

Crex Meadows, wholly undeveloped, hides past abuse. After the last glacier retreated, a large body of water, Glacial Lake Grantsburg, pooled where Crex now lies. The lake's legacy of a flat, sandy terrain, interspersed with low, extensive marshes, was good for cranberries, blueberries, and scattered pines. Pines do grow well on sandy soil but grow back after logging only if certain conditions are met.

Wildlife flourished in what was considered a barrens: Sharp-tailed Grouse and other brush-prairie birds, mammals large and small. The native Dakota and Ojibwe hunted in the barrens, drawn to the wealth of game.

The St. Croix watershed had abundant pine forests, some of the best in the state. The Ojibwe signed away their rights to the land in 1839, even before Minnesota was a territory. Logging was unregulated, ruthless, and complete. Gleeful newspaper articles from the time recounted the immense logjams on the St. Croix resulting from the phenomenal winter logging efforts. Men got rich, and many settlers found employment in the region's logging camps in the winter, when they couldn't farm. Section after section of pine forest was logged off, leaving only stumps and towering piles of slash—the frothy pine boughs, undesirable brush, and roots—to burn in furious wildfires when conditions were right.

The sudden denuding of the riverbanks caused tremendous erosion, resulting in siltation of the once-lovely St. Croix River. Sawdust from the mills also clogged the St. Croix. Loggers often relied on small dams to raise the level of small streams to float downed logs to the main river, so the flow of water was impeded. We can only wonder at the effect of this activity on the St. Croix's freshwater mussels and their host fish. No one was observing the effects of their habitat destruction.

In the Crex region, the pines were also logged and did not return. In 1872, the Crex marshland north of the town of Grantsburg was eyed for its prospects for cranberry production. Cranberries grew there naturally, but of course not in the abundance that exploiters desired. The marshland was ditched and dammed to control water levels on artificial cranberry beds. But the wildfires, like the 1894 Hinckley fire, which periodically swept through the cut-over land, also burned the cranberry bogs. Pest worms infested the berries. The whole operation foundered in drought years.

Although cranberry production was spectacular for a while, the abundance, like the abundance of the pines, ran out. Within decades the cranberry fields were abandoned. People then attempted to drain thousands of acres of marshland for agriculture. This, too, failed on the sandy soil, and in 1911 the land was bought by the Crex Carpet Company to make grass mats out of native wire grass. This failed within two decades. The ravaged land, mostly tax-delinquent, was bought by the state after World War II.

During the Great Depression, the New Deal's Civilian Conservation Corp had a significant presence in the St. Croix watershed. It built fire roads and fire towers, improvements that aided control of fires that were devastating the land. The men replanted enormous expanses of forests, cleared streams of brush, and repaired riverbanks to halt erosion. A fish hatchery produced juvenile game fish, and with the cease of sedimentation in the waterways, fish were successfully reintroduced. When the State of Wisconsin acquired Crex Meadows, habitat restoration was the chief goal.

As I pedal past Crex Meadows after a trip down the St. Croix, I have lots of time to reflect on how the land has suffered at the hands of shortsighted individuals who were so consumed by the pursuit of money. It is disheartening to ponder how things have not changed much in a century.

And yet, much of Crex Meadows has been restored to abundance. Trumpeter Swans, which were nearly extinct in North America, have been successfully reintroduced at Crex, and their offspring now populate the St. Croix valley, to the extent that we commonly see them on the river in the winter as we ski along its banks. There's a wolf pack that frequents the refuge. Other upland brush birds are coming back, and Sandhill Cranes, once very rare in Wisconsin and Minnesota, now use the vast expanse as a fall staging ground before migration. In late October and early November, visitors to Crex can witness the spectacle of ten thousand cranes wheeling in formation overhead and landing in gangly elegance, all the while croaking and bugling in a cacophony of crane music. When I see the cranes, I believe that the abusive past century did not have the final word in the St. Croix valley.

Although we usually paddle the St. Croix on summer days with friends or family, one Sunday in July, Tom and I felt the need to see the pretty river and headed up to Grantsburg alone, just the two of us.

It was a lovely paddle, I am sure. I don't remember much about it. The woods were lush and green. We left the river, made the bike trip, returned to pick up the canoe at Fox Landing, and were making our way down the sandy back road that leads to the main county road, when I looked up from the map I had been scrutinizing to see five capuchin monkeys cavorting in the middle of the road. They were small and gray, and they seemed to be standing on hind legs, dancing and frolicking. Then, just as quickly as I saw them, they were gone. Nature does that. You catch glimpses that you don't get a second chance at.

I was stunned. Several seconds passed, with silence in the car. Then I asked Tom, "What did you just see?"

"I saw monkeys," he replied. "Dancing in the middle of the road."

More silence.

"So did I," I told him. "Monkeys in the middle of the road."

We drove on. Silence reigned.

When we reached the paved road, I said, "Mine looked like organ grinder monkeys, but they didn't have the little caps."

"Right," Tom agreed. "No caps."

We have not wanted to tell anyone of our sighting, for obvious reasons. Now, could we have seen gray fox kits? It is possible our eyes were mistaken. Recall: we were leaving Fox Landing.

But now while other paddlers may take out or put in at Fox Landing, the Leafs frequent The Place Where We Saw the Monkeys. That's our story, and we're sticking to it.

....

On a hot July Sunday, we are on the St. Croix with friends. Neither has been on this stretch of river before, and we all are anxious to escape the summer heat in town.

It has been a hot, dry month. We haven't had the succession of thunderstorms we are accustomed to, and rainfall for the summer is below average. Alas, this is not something we consider before driving north to the river. But now that we are under way, we note that the stream is lower than it usually is in July. Numerous tributaries that are spring fed and not directly dependent on rainfall feed the St. Croix, but the watershed is large, and when it doesn't rain, the river level goes down. Soon our canoes scrape a gravelly shoal.

The water is clear and sparkles in the sun. We are all wearing river sandals, so we get out to walk our craft over the gravel, a pleasant chance to cool off. The water is ankle deep. At first, this is enjoyable, a part of the river. The forest all around looks thriving. Giant white pines growing here and there wave their furry branches in the light breeze. Flycatchers hawk insects over the water. A pair of Bald Eagles attend a huge, brushy nest. But after five or six river walks, we weary of the interruption.

"Oh, we should have warned you!" our friends laugh. "Things go wrong when the Petersons are out adventuring!"

We stop for a picnic lunch. We swim, we sun. The afternoon matures, and still we are nowhere close to the landing. Walking in the river, pulling and shoving canoes over the shallows, takes a lot more time than paddling does. Finally, as the sun's yellow rays skirt the tops of the trees on the opposite bank, we see the landing. What should have been a two-hour trip has taken us four.

When I recall this afternoon years later, though, I realize that not once did I mourn the loss of the magnificent pines or dwell on the ruined river that now has been resurrected. We can never regain the pristine forests. We cannot reenter Eden.

We can, however, recreate. Having fun restores us. Water, sun, forest, breeze renews us. The land, once devastated, rises to new life. It is once more wild and scenic. Like a sundial that records only sunny hours, life on the St. Croix knows only that it is living. That is enough.

Pursuing the Group of Seven

ALGONQUIN PROVINCIAL PARK, 2012

....

WE FIRST ENCOUNTERED PAINTINGS BY THE CANADIAN ART movement the Group of Seven on Manitoulin Island, a large Canadian island in Georgian Bay of Lake Huron. We were heading home after a canoe trip in nearby Killarney Provincial Park and had stopped at Manitoulin to dry out a tent and bags and all the rest of our gear that had experienced a June storm. The island was hardly a cultural center, boasting of three motels, a handful of housekeeping cabins, and two trinket shops with curios made mostly in China. Nonetheless, one of these shops sold boxes of note cards with landscapes of Ontario painted in the 1920s. It seems that some Canadian artists, including A. Y. Jackson, had enjoyed a special affinity to Nellie Lake, in Killarney, a lake we had just visited. Two of the note card scenes were autumnal, with golden poplars and tomato-red brush flanking a roiling Montreal River of western Ontario; one was summery, with cool greens and darker jack pines; and one scene, by Lawren Harris, was, well, difficult to describe. Titled *Lake Superior,* it was composed of a big expanse of blue, with stark, naked trees and somewhat geometric clouds. It was not a conventionally pretty picture of the Great Lake, and yet when I got home, I found myself wanting to share that particular note card with friends.

The Group of Seven, the note card box told us, "shared a passion for Canada's landscape." They painted a northern landscape of rocks and lakes, rugged forests, and tumbling rivers. Rebelling against a Canadian art scene after World War I that still embraced a European vision of what Canada was, they hoped to create a national sense of identity that arose from the land itself, its vivid autumns and snowy winters, the long shadows of a low-slung sun in November, and the sop of melting ice in March.

Tom and I were becoming increasingly conscious of our affinity to what I can only term *northernness*. We liked bedrock exposed or draped in the thinnest of soils. We appreciated twisted little white cedars that find toeholds in granite, low-lying bogs with tamaracks and muskeg. We thrilled to the look of a land that is still rising, released so recently from the pressure of a glacier. The idea that there were artists in Canada who once thought that these things could define a nation intrigued us.

On a second trip through Canada, also returning from a canoe trip, we stopped in Ottawa at the National Gallery, hoping to see some of the Group's pictures in the flesh. We expected to find these Canadian artists displayed front and center and were surprised to see them tucked away in a corner with little to announce their presence. However, we bought from the bookstore a thick book with illustrations of some of their work, and we paged through this tome off and on for several years.

That was how we learned that the Group of Seven was a tidy term for an assemblage of artists, not necessarily seven, based in Toronto, who worked together and encouraged each other for about twenty years. Prior to the Great War, they had been derogatorily referred to as the "Algonquin Group" because one of the artists, Tom Thomson, a skilled outdoorsman, drew his inspiration from Algonquin Park, a wilderness area north of Toronto. From September through November, Thomson roamed the semiwilderness with canoe and backpack. As the Group coalesced, Thomson drew other artists along on the outings. He was a largely untaught artist, but his rough, vital depiction of Algonquin's raw beauty expressed the soul of what the artists were trying to express.

Most of the artists earned their living working in Toronto as commercial artists and painted on the weekends. Thomson met others like him at this trade and transferred his enthusiasm to them. While Algonquin was a favorite haunt of Thomson, Georgian Bay was also close enough and wild enough to attract the painters.

The crafter of the odd Lake Superior scene that I found compelling against my better judgment, Lawren Harris, was also Toronto based. He inherited wealth, however, and didn't need to work commercially. Well-educated and talented, Harris best articulated what was needed for Canada: a national identity based on its northern wildlands. It was Harris and an enthusiastic benefactor, Dr. Mac-Callum, who together sought out young artists who seemed to share that vision. In 1913, Harris began construction of a studio in Toronto that would provide inexpensive workspace for the artists and an opportunity to share ideas.

The restless artists, eager to make their mark on the world, were in their twenties when the Group coalesced. In reading about them, I recognized my own male friends in their twenties. They, too, gravitated to wild places and were seduced by the pounding of waves against bedrock. They, too, lived for the jostle of a canoe on a heaving lake and pored over maps, plotting an escape from their work life whenever possible.

Harris's studio was completed in 1914, and Thomson and another artist, A. Y. Jackson, were already at work in it when events across the Atlantic intervened. Europe was at war, and Canada entered it that summer. The artists who had hoped to shape a national psyche with paintings of trees and rocks and water were wrested from their intentions and thrown into the conflict. Several enlisted; others served as war artists for the Canadian War Memorials Program and produced profound, moving sketches of the worst atrocities in Belgium. Plans for an art movement were put on hold.

But perhaps the most influential event affecting the Group of Seven—not officially named as such—that occurred during the Great War happened at home. In July 1917, Tom Thomson drowned in a canoeing accident on Canoe Lake, a part of Algonquin Park he knew well. Thomson's death came as a great shock to the others. It was they who experienced the dangers of war-ravaged Europe or worked on a heavily militarized east coast of Canada. Thomson lived in apparent safety. His studio mate, Jackson, later wrote that Thomson was an expert paddler with all the skill and techniques native to the craft. He supplemented his income by guiding fishing parties during the summer. It hardly seemed possible that he could accidently drown on a placid lake.

After the Group was officially named, in 1920, a mythology sprang up about Thomson and the manner of his death—had it been accidental? Might he have been murdered? But these were whispers, nothing more. A cairn dedicated to his memory was erected on Canoe Lake.

In all, at least ten artists (counting Thomson) belonged at one time or another to the movement. The book we had bought in Ottawa had lush reproductions of their work in gorgeous oranges and teals, forest greens and ochers. Harris's weird paintings of Lake Superior continued to haunt me. Thomson's series of the northern lights in winter thrilled me.

Tom and I know nothing about art. We were science majors, spending most of our college hours in required labs. The fulfillment of our liberal arts degrees was achieved mainly with music credits. Still, we wanted to view the work of the Group of Seven with our own eyes. We wanted to see what Tom Thomson saw. That is how we found ourselves hurtling down the Trans-Canada highway on a chilly September evening in 2012, our seventeen-foot Old Town canoe strapped to our roof. We were on our way to Algonquin Provincial Park, in pursuit of the Group of Seven.

....

To this day, there is no quick highway into eastern Ontario from Minnesota. But on this trip, getting there was part of the experience. The trees of Ontario's boreal forest were beginning to turn in mid-September. Slender red maples showed bright bursts of crimson here and there off on the hillsides. Massive hunks of rocks jutted up along the roadside, suggesting perfect lunch spots. They were exposed sections of Canadian Shield, the bedrock that underlies much of Canada. This was not farming country—much too rough for that.

I had bought a copy of A. Y. Jackson's autobiography, *A Painter's Country*, and we passed the miles reading out loud from it. In one passage, Jackson summed up his friend Thomson's art with an aphorism: "Gazing man is keenest fed on sparing beauty."[1] The maxim arrested me, and I repeated it. "Sparing beauty"—yes, exactly. This was most certainly what Tom and I were chasing. It summed up what we called northernness.

On the trip to Algonquin, we drove east through Michigan's Upper Peninsula and entered Canada at Sault Ste. Marie, where Lake Superior narrows into rapids. The highway skirts the northern shore of Georgian Bay of Lake Huron and leads directly to the northern part of Algonquin Provincial Park. We could have then followed the park's western border down and entered the park at its southern end. That is where Canoe Lake is, and the cairn to Thomson's memory. There is even a major, paved road through the park in the south, which would ensure us easy access.

But we were more inclined to enter from the north. We did not want to run into many people; Toronto and its millions lay directly south of Algonquin. People intent on a short weekend paddle would undoubtedly enter from the southern routes. Also, Algonquin is far from pristine. Logging roads and railroad tracks crisscross the land closest to Toronto. We had read from paddlers' guides that bombers from a nearby air base can blast the calm without warning. To enter from the north, we would have to drive twenty miles on a gravel road to reach the drop-in point, the park office at Kiosk. That was a good thing. Twenty gravel miles is a deterrent to many.

Tom had bought a small book, *A Paddler's Guide to Algonquin Park,* which suggested possible routes for canoe trips in the park. Pondering the options, we debated the features of each. A big lake, especially one with an east–west axis, could be heavenly with the wind at your back but hellish and even treacherous headed the other way. Paddlers could get wind bound on such a lake and their time schedule disrupted. Did we want to take that chance?

We didn't relish mile-long portages anymore. And some routes that interested us were footnoted with a warning that they might

---

1. A. Y. Jackson, *A Painter's Country: The Autobiography of A. Y. Jackson* (Toronto: Clarke, Irwin & Company, 1958), 33.

not be navigable in low water. Low water levels are not a problem in the spring, but they are something to take note of in the fall. Minnesota had been in continuing drought. Was that also true of eastern Ontario?

Finally, we settled on a route that started on the big lake of Kioshkokwi and headed east for a portage into Mink Lake, long and narrow with many campsites on it. We had the option of making the trip a circle route or of merely paddling in and out. We would see what the weather would be like, and what we felt like once out on the trail.

A night spent in Ontario before dropping in convinced me that my flimsy flip-flops would not be needed in camp. It was cool enough in September to want socks on when the sun went down. But it was warm and August-like when we started out with a clear, blue sky and a landscape that was still mostly summer green. Algonquin at first glance resembled the Boundary Waters with the long, narrow lakes and outcroppings of bedrock. We hadn't been to that wilderness area in a very long time, and I was unsettled by how nostalgic I became at Algonquin, a Canadian cousin.

At the first portage, we saw that summer's verdure was beginning to concede to the waning day length in advance of the equinox. Speckled alder leaves were yellowing, sassafras on the forest floor was mottling. Not much—just enough to cast a wistful air over the woods, to cause a canoeist lugging a heavy pack over the portage to mull over the transitory nature of life.

But we were cheered when we noted that Canadians mark their portage trails clearly with a big saffron sign and the silhouette of a man with a canoe on his shoulders. No waffling with sixty-five pounds on one's shoulders, trying to decipher a fork in the trail. The first sign we encountered adamantly stated, "Mink Lake," with an arrow to the left fork.

Algonquin's forest, like the Boundary Waters', is boreal, with pines, spruce, and fir. There are plenty of deciduous species as well: birch and aspen, appearing after a clear-cut, sugar and red maples. But unlike in Minnesota, hemlock also grows here. Hemlock is an eastern species, and we passed some that were enormous, three feet or more in diameter. Hemlock needles are short and darker than balsam fir. They give the big trees an incongruous, lacy appearance. Because our Minnesota eyes seldom rest on hemlocks, the trees also make the woods seem ever so slightly foreign, reminding us, if we needed it, that we were not at home.

The forest floor community is a Lilliputian one similar to the BWCAW: tiny twinflowers, bunchberries (red berries produced in August, eaten by September), shining club moss, and wintergreen with its shiny, dark leaves that release a minty fragrance when crushed.

The sunny afternoon, summerlike warmth, and lack of a wind made us feel leisurely, as if we had an abundance of time in which to select a campsite and set up camp. We paddled down a strip of sparkling water, alone on the lake, just the two of us. As we dipped our paddles into the water, though, we felt an odd sensation that the warmest air was closest to the surface. This hinted that the water temperature was actually warmer than the air—it was only the strength of the sun that made us feel warm. It would cool off quickly when the sun went down. All around us, clues of impending fall were there to decipher. We opted to ignore them and basked in the moment.

Our camp on Mink, when we finally chose one, was splendid. High above the lake, it was protected by a number of towering red and white pines. It looked like something Thomson might have painted. His *Pine Trees at Sunset,* the elongate pine silhouettes framed by an apricot western sky, came to mind. We were pleased to find a grassy place for the tent and a suitable place for the Coleman stove. Someone had thoughtfully provided a flat piece of plywood resting on rock. In the States, it would have been deemed inimical to a wilderness experience, but we liked it. Among other advantages, the plywood made it harder for chipmunks to get at our dinner.

For we were not alone at the campsite. As soon as we hauled up our packs, eastern chipmunks appeared, bright-eyed and quick. They assessed us with obvious savvy, calculating our value. Did we carry peanuts? Sunflower seeds? Gorp? Were we susceptible to charm? Given to inattention? Wielders of weapons?

Well, one of us thought they were cute, and one of us considered them pests. The sun was low on the western horizon. The one with the pest attitude set up the tent, and I started dinner without delay. The chipmunks were companionable and demanded vigilance. They were bold. They were numerous. One crawled on top our plates to peer into the big cook kettle. The aroma of the trail mix in the food pack must have been irresistible. I felt I could not turn my back for a second, and brandished a spatula in my hand.

By dusk, as we ate our supper overlooking the quiet lake and observed the growing darkness, the little rodents were gone. It was bedtime.

....

The weather forecast had been for mild, sunny days on our paddle in and the day following, but on the third day, rain was expected to move in, followed by a blustery wind and a temperature drop into the thirties. This prediction of impending doom did much to make us savor the sunshine we experienced. After the sunny drop-in day, we awoke to a lake swathed in fog, another indication that the longer September nights were cooling the land. Water retains heat longer than air. The temperature differential produced the fog. In the morning, the rising sun tinted the fog a rosy pink as I went down to the water to wash up.

The previous night, we had donned our headlamps to navigate our way around the campsite. Headlamps were new to us. The young generation of outdoor enthusiasts—our children—introduced us to their benefits: how you can wash dishes and tidy up a campsite in the dark with your hands free to put away food and equipment, string a food pack high in a tree with ease (this we did, for we knew the chipmunks would wake up before we did), and arrange things just so in a small tent. For the after-dinner cribbage game, we used the Coleman lantern, but the headlamps were employed everywhere else. We felt very modern and up-to-date, even though Tom looked like an odd sort of Cyclops.

Though the campsite on Mink Lake had been lovely and we seemed to be the only souls around, we were eager to see new country. In the morning, while a band of migrating Golden-crowned Kinglets twittered overhead, we packed the Duluth packs and left.

The Canadian park authorities request that campers make reservations ahead of time for the lakes they plan to camp on. We had reservations for a campsite on Mink and then asked for space on the next lake, Cauchon, for our second night. We wondered what would happen if we did not camp on Cauchon but continued on. How flagrantly do Canadians flout the rules? That morning we passed a party of young men on Mink Lake with a small motor attached to one of their canoes. Tom had read that Mink was a non-motorized lake, and this seemed to be illegal. Maybe the authorities wouldn't care if we camped somewhere without reservations? We are Good Campers Who Follow the Rules, but really, it didn't seem reasonable to be held to a certain lake when apparently the entire provincial park was nearly devoid of people. We had seen only a handful of campers, and everyone was headed back to civilization.

On Cauchon, we renewed the debate: camp so close to our last site? Or push on? At noon, we spied what we thought looked like a nice site. Although the day was weakly sunny, the first rain clouds, small and harmless, puffed up on the western horizon. We wanted to swim, and it was lunchtime, so we stopped, went into the water, which was comfortably warm, and ate a trail lunch of bagels and chèvre. When we investigated the campsite, we discovered that the latrine was situated up an impossibly steep hill, a hill that we had to use hands and feet to scramble up, an incline that would be disastrous in the rain. So we paddled on down Cauchon.

The lunch break had been fortuitous, though. We had been given enough time to believe that the forecast was correct, that it would indeed rain. As we paddled the shoreline, we assessed sites for a decent, nonslippery place to land a canoe and the ability to support a tarp and provide a dry place to cook meals under it. Cauchon had no such sites, so giving up on a circle trip, we paddled back to Mink. Tom now called it "Our Lake"—we saw no other campers on it and found a "perfect" place.

A unique feature of Mink Lake is an abandoned railroad bed skirting its entire eastern shore. There is enough of a woodsy expanse between it and the shoreline that campers might not be aware of the intrusion of the line. But the latrine on the second site we occupied overlooked the abandoned bed, and after the dishes, we took our binoculars and strolled its length. We found many little kinglets in the woods and a roving band of Palm Warblers moving through the understory. In the fall migration, the larger birds, the ducks and geese, claim our attention, and we found it very satisfying to be present to witness the southward movement of the songbirds, too.

That night, we watched a winter constellation, Orion, rise in the east. In the dark, from time to time, we heard the cluck-cluck of a migrating robin, settling in for the night, a pleasant and familiar sound. We knew we perched on the cusp of change.

....

The next morning dawned dark, but rain had not fallen, so I set about getting breakfast before it did. Tom, hardy Viking, went in for a swim, the last swim of summer, while I stayed on shore, tending his scrambled eggs. By ten o'clock, it was sprinkling, and we moved all the gear under the low-slung tarp: packs and stove, cook kettle and lantern, life jackets. The rain was gentle and intermittent, waxing and waning. It was warm, fifty degrees, and we read, played cards, drank tea, and gazed at the soft gray curtain that had fallen over Mink Lake. It was pleasant, really. We could envision spending a day doing this, fixing a supper of sausage jambalaya in the rain, then turning in early. Near our overturned canoe, a small red maple was just beginning to flame, its scarlet lower branches draped protectively over a small balsam fir.

Red maples turn earlier than their kin, the sugar maples. They streak a Canadian countryside that in September is still largely green. The Group of Seven and especially Tom Thomson had an eye for red maple. The brilliant, singular trees appear here and there in their work. The artists were also drawn to seasonal change, summer into fall, fall into winter, winter into spring. The Group was interested in change in general. They painted clouds high in the sky or lowering over water. Where people generally think of clouds as obscuring the sun, the artists saw them as heralds of change, or movement, ushering a new season.

By noon, the soft, gray, tentative rain had morphed into an emphatic pounding, and with the change, our benignly philosophic mood vanished. The tarp collected water competently but needed draining every few minutes. Tom experimented with various designs, each drawn from his experiences with Japanese gardens and bamboo fountains that fill up and self-empty. Soon, our tarp was doing that too, but in the process, Tom's rain gear had become soaked.

The three questions that campers need to ask themselves, particularly in adverse weather, the ones we had taught the kids, are: Are you warm? Are you dry? Are you fed? If the answer is "yes" to all of them, a camper is in a good place. If the answer is "no" to all of them, one should worry about hypothermia. If the answers are mixed, then there are things one can do to make life comfortable.

Under the tarp at lunchtime, the answers were still "yes." But then, around two o'clock, a west wind began to blow, and to our consternation, the temperature began to drop noticeably. Suddenly, hands that were wet became chilled. Damp hair clinging to the forehead felt stringy. I mentally sifted through my packs, assessing how many layers I had brought.

Tom is not given to impulsive decisions, so as we chewed our bagels and sipped hot tea at lunch, I could tell he was balancing the pros and cons of packing up soggy wet gear and leaving. Our sons, we knew, would scoff at us. Thirty-five years ago, we would have scoffed at ourselves. But we imagined a cold, wet night with no enlightening benefit and the odds tipped in favor of leaving.

Once the decision was made, we acted. We began dismantling the tent and discovered that it was leaking through an overhead seam. We had bought it used, thirty years ago, so this was not surprising, and I silently rejoiced that at last we could get one of those cute little domed tents at REI. Wordlessly, we pulled up the fly stakes, the tent stakes; we folded a sodden fly, a wet tent. We dropped muddy stakes into their little bag, rolled up the miserable whole, and pushed it into the stuff sack. There was a point in this process when the stuff sack that held the tent poles got misplaced and we spent time looking for it. Immediately after, I left to tend the "kitchen" in order to diffuse incipient cross words. Really, in pouring rain, one must keep track of the sacks.

Then we started on the packs under the tarp. A cook kettle that we had kept out in the rain had an inch and a half of water in it—that much rain had fallen in four hours. Piece by piece, things got loaded into the sturdy Duluth packs. Then we hauled everything down to the canoe, tucked the already dampened packs under a tarp, and pushed off for the boat landing, three lakes away.

Honestly, it is almost never as bad paddling in the rain as it is contemplating paddling in the rain. We were well protected by rain jackets and pants, and I wore a wool tam that could get wet and still keep me warm. We discovered that the wind was shifting direction and now blew straight down Mink from the northwest. We leaned into the headwind. It was going to be a long paddle.

The colors looked more vivid in the rain. The leaves, shiny with water, were scarlet on the maples, bronze on the birch, emerald on the delicate mosses draping the forest floor as we took the first portage. We paused to take photos. On the second lake, the waves were high, flirting with white caps. We began to sing. "I've got a mule her name is Sal," I belted out, hoping my sternsman would join in (his is by far the better voice). "Sixteen miles on the Erie Canal!" We went through our repertoire of work songs, of folk songs, of spirituals. We may even have sung "The Star Spangled Banner," and what did it matter? There was no one, no one at all in the northern part of Algonquin Provincial Park. Loons sidled nervously away from us. Otters popped their heads up and peered at us.

Arriving at the landing, we checked our watches. It had taken us three hours to paddle out, and we were so, so glad we had done it. The temperature had continued to drop throughout the afternoon, promising a wet, miserable night to campers in the park. They were few in number. In the parking lot, three cars remained where on Sunday there had been fifteen. With stiff fingers and feet cold in wet boots, we threw our gear into the Jetta, strapped the canoe on top, and left.

That night, safe and dry in a motel room, we strung a clothesline from the base of a television to the door's security lock and hung up the wet clothes, sleeping bags, towels, and packs. The next morning, in bright sunlight, we laid out our faithful tarp, the plastic sheeting that goes under the tent, and the still-damp Duluth packs.

Then we repacked it all and headed to Toronto. We knew of Algonquin's loveliness. Now we wanted to know what the Group of Seven thought of it.

....

Two of the three galleries in Canada that have large collections of the Group of Seven are in or near Toronto: the Art Gallery of Ontario (AGO), near the University of Toronto campus, and the McMichael Canadian Art Collection at Kleinberg, Ontario, now an exurb of Toronto.

The McMichael began as a ten-acre country retreat of a wealthy Canadian couple. They were art collectors, focusing on the Group's artists. Their first acquisition was by Lawren Harris, *Montreal River,* a fall scene with four black spruce and a powder-blue river beyond. Then they acquired a Tom Thomson, *Pine Island,* a picture with lichen-crusted rock in the foreground and an iconic succession of white pines tossed in the wind. The collectors were hooked, and over the years, they accumulated 194 paintings of the Group. They donated their estate to the province of Ontario, and it has grown into a renowned collection of Canadian art, including other artists who were associated with the Group or who painted in opposition to the Group.

The graves of six of the Group's artists can be visited on the grounds of the McMichael: Arthur Lismer, F. H. Varley, Lawren Harris, Frank Johnston, Alfred Casson, and A. Y. Jackson are all buried there, in a small cemetery with big, irregularly shaped stones marking the graves.

There were few visitors to the McMichael on an overcast day in September. We strolled the galleries and gazed at the paintings.

There were many, many of the quick sketches, the little works that Jackson in his autobiography said took twenty to forty-five minutes to produce. Often these hung next to a large, refined painting that had evolved out of the sketch. We could see how the artist retained some features, like a craggy stump in the foreground or a distant feathering of pines, and jettisoned others. Almost always, the big painting was the one that we would have wanted in our home.

It has taken me many years to appreciate that visits to art galleries are simple exercises in pleasure—soaking in the vibrancy of color, experiencing that little thrill in a well-executed form (like a sweeping white pine), being amazed at technique that can accurately reproduce the feel of a maple sapling or lichens on rock. But walking through the McMichael's collection, we saw hundreds of paintings in a few hours' time, and it became a crash course on the Group. We saw how Thomson liked to lay on the paint, creating a deeply textured canvas. Jackson, too, was a bold technician. His snowfields were thick swirls of white. Harris, the highly educated heir to a fortune, produced works of refinement, very modernistic, his mountains and trees increasingly cubistic. Johnston seemed to use a technique of little dots, like the Impressionistic Pointillists. We saw heaving lakes, like the turbulent Mink Lake we had paddled only the day before. We saw landscapes on the cusp of autumn, red here and there, big rocks, hills. We saw houses from a Toronto of the 1920s, portraits of women in fur hats (Varley liked portraits), and everywhere we saw Algonquin Park as we had lived it, hours ago.

The second gallery, the Art Gallery of Ontario, is located in the heart of the city. When the Group was active, this institution was a champion of their efforts, and today it has an impressive collection, particularly works by Thomson. We gave ourselves a day off from art and then went early in the morning a day later, when our eyes were still fresh.

I was intrigued to find that the geometric pictures of Harris were growing on me. Harris spent some time later in life painting on the north shore of Lake Superior, not the North Shore in Minnesota, a place I know intimately, but the wilder north shore of western Ontario. Some of his big pictures, and Harris liked a large canvas, seem almost primitive. Stripped down, the trees take on stark forms, the hills are rounded curves, the clouds become lumpish. Cerulean blue floods the space. Yet, Tom and I were both startled to see that somehow the soul of the Great Lake was perfectly depicted in the stylized, not-so-simple works. We spend a lot of hours staring out at Lake Superior in all seasons. Harris captured its essence.

The AGO also had on display two short films running in continuous loops. One was a movie from the 1920s, showing the urban scene of Toronto when the artists were most active there. People stream all about the city streets. Model As and Ts teeter down the roads, weaving in and out of the pedestrian flow. Toronto looks bustling, a major city. It was hard for us to imagine that their little studio, which still stands in the midst of a city that has completely engulfed it, was then on the outskirts of town. When he resided at it, Thomson would strap on his snowshoes and take nocturnal tromps up Rosedale Creek far beyond the city.

The other film, from 1941, was a newsreel, and it showed the artist who served as narrator to Tom's and my current quest, A. Y. Jackson, at work. We watched him paddling a canoe with a guide, whom he called McIver—McIver was mentioned in the book. In the movie, we could see Jackson did a perfect J stroke—no greenhorn, he. Then we watched as he shouldered a heavy Duluth pack over a portage. He was dressed in knee-high, laced-up boots, jodhpurs, and a heavy plaid shirt. It was fall, and he hiked through the Cloche Mountains of southern Ontario. We saw him settle in to paint lake, sky, and trees on a blank board and turn it into something that looked like a Jackson painting. In 1941, Mr. Jackson would have been fifty-nine—still camping, still hiking and paddling, still finding beauty and meaning in the northern landscape. I watched the film twice.

....

To us, the appeal of this long-ago group of Canadian artists lay not only with their interest in the spare, northern landscape, the changing weather and seasons, the massive blocks of Canadian Shield sticking up looking primitive and geologic. We liked that the men were active and physical. They endured rain and snow, freezing temperatures, and snowstorms. They painted outdoors while their hands became stiff with cold. They slept under rough conditions and ate simple camp fare cooked over an iron stove. When frustrated, they were known to throw their sketch kits into the woods in despair—then spend the next morning picking through the sphagnum and seedlings, looking for paint tubes. Eventually, some of them traveled into the high Rockies of Alberta. Some went on government steamers to Arctic outposts to paint the ice and glaciers beyond the Arctic Circle. Jackson lived out his years in Manotick, near Ottawa, where he found rocky hills rising out of farmlands to paint.

I read recently that the current crop of Canadian art critics decry the stranglehold that the Group has on defining that country's art. Although we in the States are largely unaware of the Group of Seven, Canadian schoolchildren have had the artists' work drummed into their heads for decades. Those following the art scene in Canada claim that today's artists have moved on. After all, the Group officially disbanded in 1933.

Perhaps it seems quaint that a group of artists once thought that a country's soul could be defined by its latitude, that falling in the upper reaches of North America, where the Canadian Shield provides a solid bedrock to the underpinnings of civilization, would make for a certain outlook on life. Canadians, like all of us in the West, spend increasing amounts of time indoors. We don't think of ourselves as connected to the land, and perhaps it is wise not to. Can a damaged environment offer any sustenance? When global warming really bites into us, Canada will be dramatically transformed.

Canadians, too, have an especially divided mind when it comes to seeing their national identity as a northern country. Even as climate change threatens every defining feature of their northernness, Canadians anticipate great riches from their wealth of natural gas and oil shale, and the promise of a northern coast as the ice in the Arctic Ocean disappears.

The Group of Seven, then, will seem an anachronism, a voice receding into a past that no one will remember. To recall their vitality, we have a wonderful photograph taken of the original members in the 1920s at the Arts and Letters Club in Toronto. The men sit around a glossy table. There are coffee cups, salt and pepper shakers, matches to light cigarettes and pipes. They all wear three-piece suits, with ties or bowties and pocket handkerchiefs. They are relaxed. They are comfortable with each other. You can imagine one making a quip, a witty observation on a critic's review of their work, others throwing back their heads and roaring. I think of them consuming a lot of coffee, ready to paint the night away.

"We lived," Harris observed, "in a continuous blaze of enthusiasm. We were at times very serious and concerned and at other times, hilarious and carefree. Above all, we loved [Canada] and loved exploring and painting it."[2]

2. David Silcox, *The Group of Seven and Tom Thomson* (Richmond Hill, Canada: Firefly Books, 2006), 46.

Chronos and Kairos

THE LITTLE MISSOURI RIVER, 2013

....

AFTER A COOL, RAINY SPRING, THE NORTH DAKOTA BAD-lands are very green. New plant growth paints the bluffs with clean strokes of lime, of chartreuse, of willow. Tom and I are paddling the Little Missouri River, the waterway that cuts through the core of the desertlike badlands on the western border of the state. The morning sparkles with liquid sunlight spilling over the craggy cliffs and brightening the air. The sky is blue with scarcely a wisp of cloud.

The water we dip our paddles into is milky, the color of a latte. If I were to take my caffeine in liquid of that color, I would be chided for having a little coffee with my cream. So laden is the water with silt that I imagine it difficult to paddle through. It is silly, I know, but each stroke seems more laborious than it would in clear water.

Above us, the riverbanks rise high, rock layers exposed in bands of pink and khaki. They anchor this river decisively in the West, more kin to the Missouri than the Mississippi. The Little Missouri's source is in eastern Wyoming, near Devils Tower. From there it flows northeast into Montana and then on to South Dakota and its badlands, before heading into North Dakota. I feel a shiver of pleasure at being once again on a western river winding through grassland, not forest. It has been a long time.

Both Tom and I are a little surprised to be here now, in early June. Forty-eight hours ago we were still undecided where to go on our thirty-fifth wedding anniversary canoe trip. We had vac-illated for weeks between the Little Missouri and the Au Sable River in Lower Michigan. Both appealed in different ways. The Au Sable flows through white pine forest. There was the prospect of encountering a rare bird, the Kirtland's Warbler, on the river and seeing the "mitten" of Michigan, a region unfamiliar to us.

The Little Missouri, on the other hand, links two units of Theodore Roosevelt National Park. The former president had written movingly about it, and the river had beckoned Tom for decades. He had considered canoeing it for so many years that he couldn't remember what first triggered his desire.

The Little Missouri River is distinguished by highly seasonal water levels. Fed by runoff, not subterranean springs, the amount of water running through its channel fluctuates greatly, and it dwindles to an intermittent flow in the summer. The river can roar, though, in spring, when April and May's rainy days bolster the meltwater. It is navigable then and in early summer. The government posts water gauge readings online to give hopeful paddlers information on the flow.

Spring 2013 had been exceptionally wet. Western North Dakota had received a whopping eight inches of rain in May alone. It stewed in more rain the weekend immediately before we left home. Reading weather reports at his desk Sunday night, Tom made the snap decision to head west toward the North Dakota badlands. Michigan could wait. It was the time to paddle the Little Missouri. We left early Tuesday.

The ancient Greeks had a word to describe opportune moments such as this: *kairos.* They had pondered time and knew it to be big and unwieldy, beyond human comprehension, really, and so they made distinction between time that is measured and orderly, *chronos,* and time that is flexible in duration, where events coalesce into a rightness. Our vacation time had been arranged as chronos—Tom had requested five days off. But canoeing the Little Missouri? We were living in kairos.

We would both turn sixty this year. Our thirty-fifth wedding anniversary was upon us. It was difficult to believe so much time had passed. We hardly felt any different, hardly looked any different (how we kid ourselves). Now when we looked forward, though, we saw our time on earth as limited, perhaps two more good decades. We could benefit from thinking about time in a different way, and we knew we should not put off our dreams. The Little Missouri was waiting for us.

．．．．．．．．．．．．．．．．．．．．．．．．

In North Dakota, the Little Missouri River winds its way through national grassland (the prairie equivalent of national forest) and Theodore Roosevelt National Park, as well as private ranch land. There are few roads in this part of the state, but a gravel road south of the freeway ran very near the river. We would start our trip at this point, paddling through the national grassland. We planned to be off the river before we reached the national park. The town of Medora, population 131, on Interstate 90, is perched on the river and would be our end point. The national park abuts the town, so tiny Medora is also the gateway to the park.

Theodore Roosevelt National Park operates a visitor center in Medora. We stopped there when we arrived in town, to ask locally about river conditions and get tips on paddling. It was the start of the summer season, and novice staffers had just arrived. We quickly discovered that the information booth was manned by a young crew of twenty-somethings who knew almost nothing about western North Dakota. No one had canoed the river; one ranger had rafted from Sully Creek State Park to Cottonwood Campground inside the national park the weekend before, and it had been a quick trip. No one had, as yet, hiked the park. No one knew anything about prairie birds, wildflowers in bloom, or dangers we should consider. They had only a textbook knowledge of rattlesnakes. Recalling our experience paddling other western rivers, I was worried about barbed wire strung across the river to control cattle. No one knew about that.

We were on our own in this kairos moment.

Before we left home, we had called the owner of a Medora campground and arranged to have them drive us upriver—which was south of Medora; the Little Missouri flows north—and then drive our car to the Medora landing and leave it there for us when we ended our trip. Although we had hoped to get out on the river immediately upon arrival, the weather dissuaded us. After a day of passing squalls, which we had met head-on as we drove west from

Minnesota on I-94, the late afternoon in Medora was damp with rising winds. We holed up at a motel in town, setting our camp stove on a small stand outside the room and eating spaghetti indoors at an end table.

On a walk about town later on, we wore wool and heavy polar fleece, windbreakers, and winter hats. That night, the food that we had frozen to keep the cooler chilled—rhubarb sauce, apple cider, meat—remained in icy blocks.

However, the next morning dawned blue and clear, not a cloud in the sky. The wet weather had drifted off to the east. We ate yogurt and granola in the room and packed up. As an experiment, Tom packed the tent, sleeping bags, and his personal gear in two rubber dry bags. We took only two canvas Duluth packs—the small number two, which was mine, and a larger number three for the food, lantern, tarp, and other equipment. We wore our warmth. The packs felt roomy without the bulk of sweaters and jackets.

We planned only two nights on the river. Kairos moments may expand without regard to a clock, but chronos ticks on. Neither of us could afford to be away for more than five days.

We had to haul the canoe through a damp floodplain of knee-high grass to reach the river from the gravel road. It was our only portage. We waved good-bye to our car and its handler and pushed off into the milky water.

The North Dakota badlands are undeniably arid. Even the fresh growth of a rainy spring was sparse to our Minnesota eyes. The canoe drifted past high river bluffs the same khaki color as the water. The bluffs were banded showing different rock layers. There was a broad upper band of sandstone that was relatively hard, eroding less than the bluish layer below it, which we had learned was a clay, bentonite clay. We would come to ponder bentonite clay later in the trip but not on this first day of a bountiful river basin.

Occasionally we saw a black band between the clay and sandstone representing a vein of coal. The coal sometimes catches fire and can smolder for years. A burning coal vein might be so hot as to color the surrounding rock, creating reddish scoriae, injecting color into the landscape. The palette in general, though, was subtle and pleasing in taupes and tans. It seemed durable and unchanging, beyond the reach of the contemporary cultural scene of shifting political turmoil, evolving social norms, and the ravages of time. I felt that Tom and I were making a genuine retreat in choosing to paddle the Little Missouri. We were taking a time-out from life.

One of the unexpected pleasures of the first day was the ubiquitous song of the Western Meadowlark, which rose up on every side as we floated along. Its lovely carol is sweet and melodic, rising from the grass and hanging on the wind. I had grown up in a first-ring suburb, where a Western Meadowlark sang from a vacant lot outside my bedroom window every summer. Today, the bird is dying out even in rural areas of Minnesota. Western Meadowlarks are ground nesters. Suburban sprawl wiped out birds that tolerated close human presence, and intensified haying has eliminated them from hay fields throughout the state. Attempting to reap maximum yield from their hay fields, farmers make the first cut of hay in late May or early June, which destroys the first nest; the birds then renest, only to have the second attempt stymied by the second cut in July.

Western North Dakota is rangeland, where the land use is much kinder to ground-nesting birds. The national grassland through which the Little Missouri flows is all grazed by privately owned cattle, and not mowed for hay. Cattle might step on a nest, but the odds are not great. Meadowlarks are evolutionarily adapted to another grazer—bison—which could also destroy a nest with a misplaced hoof. That is one reason they will quickly renest if their efforts are quashed early in the breeding season.

The music of meadowlarks accompanied us our entire time on the river. Sometimes there would be several males singing at once, all determined to hold territories in an open, grassy world. The many meadowlarks seemed to be an avian embodiment of an abundance that reflected the wider abundance of sky and sun.

When the afternoon grew old and shadows elongated, we pulled out on a flat prairie patch above the river and set up camp. The public is welcome to pitch a tent anywhere on national grassland without a formally designated campground. We had a map that delineated public and private lands and were able to maintain a rough idea of our progress down the river. We chose a spot that was flat and grazed—indeed, Black Angus cattle nosed about in the distance. We stepped around dried cow pies as we set up a cook station and the tent. Soon a broccoli-beef stir-fry was sizzling on the Coleman.

Our home for the night was opposite a high sandstone cliff. We arranged our red-and-white camp chairs to look out over the river and settled down to dinner. From our perch, we watched White Pelicans drift past. A pair of kestrels flew back and forth over the water. We both had our binoculars trained on them at the very moment that the two birds, male and female together, disappeared for the night into a dark hole in the cliff and did not reappear. We had not known before where kestrels nest.

After the dishes were washed and stowed in the pack, we took binoculars in hand and wandered in back of the campsite, toward the oblivious cattle. Much of a prairie's beauty is tucked away, hidden amid blades of grass. We sought the early prairie flowers that were in bloom: buttery yellow puccoon, and white bastard toad-flax, a buffoonish name for a delicate flower. There were lupines just beginning to leaf out, their palmate leaves spreading like tiny hands, and one species of electric blue penstemon, a "beardtongue" with trumpetlike flowers flaring out from a central spike. We came across prickly pear cacti and brushy clumps of sage. Tom turned his camera, and his medical eye, on a variety of dried, white bones: pelvic bones with a tailbone and vertebrae, a mandible, a skull, the remains of cattle. We chased an elusive Grasshopper Sparrow song and never found the singer. We watched a pair of Lark Sparrows from afar. They are high prairie birds, ones we don't often encounter, and with two, they undoubtedly tended a nest. Time seemed to expand as the evening grew darker. The western horizon paled to pink. Meadowlarks sang late into dusk.

Tom and I love poking about for this secret beauty and realize that our affinity for prairies is an acquired taste. We were fortunate to have had a college professor, Ward Tanner, who introduced us to prairies when we took courses under him. Ward himself was a city boy, so we were unclear how he had developed a penchant for prairies, but he had passed it on to us—forty years before. We had had forty years of pleasure from knowledge we had gained in our teens. We wondered if Ward ever knew what impact he had had on our lives. He was a shy, secretive man, a bachelor, a loner. Improbably, we both appreciated him, and he liked us. Tom and I reminisced about this unlikely friendship as we meandered from flower to flower, listening, admiring, breathing in the sweet scent of evening. Later, back in camp, we heard turkeys gobbling and later still, coyotes. In the morning, there were canine paw prints near the tent.

....

The rising sun filtered through fog the next day as we crawled out of the tent to greet the dawn. The diffuse light turned the Little Missouri silvery and hung the prairie architecture with dewdrops. Tom grabbed his camera and headed out in search of spider webs made visible and other transformed structures. I revved up the stove for breakfast and discovered, while rummaging about in the cooler, that the rhubarb sauce I thought I had grabbed from the freezer at home was, in truth, chicken broth. What a useless item to haul along on a trip. I readied the oatmeal and coffee.

But the big surprise of the morning was the state of the river. At the water's edge, we saw that the Little Missouri had dropped a foot overnight. This is what happens with a river that relies on runoff, not springs, for its flow. People in Medora had told us to expect this, but we hadn't appreciated it. A lot of water still ran past us, but when we loaded the canoe, preparing to leave, the newly exposed sand kept crumbling beneath our feet, making it difficult to edge close enough to the canoe to swing the packs in. The kairos moment, the time of paddling, was passing.

Crumbling sand was an annoyance. Far worse was the bentonite clay that now appeared flanking the river as the water level dropped. Clay particles are tiny and can absorb a lot of water. When the clay layer in the cliff becomes heavy with the added water, it sloughs off and collapses. This has happened many times in the past, and that morning we saw that what had been a riverbank the day before was now an emerging mudflat.

Bentonite clay has a volcanic origin. The clay along the Little Missouri is a testament to the eruption of volcanoes sixty-five million years ago, about the time of the uplift of the Rocky Mountains and the die-off of the dinosaurs. Volcanoes in what is now Montana, Idaho, and South Dakota spewed large amounts of ash. The ash was carried into the Little Missouri basin via wind and water to settle and become clay as the rock layers formed. Today's clay has a reputation for becoming a nuisance when wet.

We quickly discovered this on our first break from paddling, when we disembarked to stretch our legs. We had to cross an expanse of the muddy clay and found it perilously slick, a slimy goo that clung to our river sandals. It would be easy to take a misstep and do a pratfall into the slime.

Furthermore, it was nearly impossible to remove. After a gummy walkabout, I tried to pry the mud from my sandals with my pocketknife. Now the knife was covered and so were my hands. Dipping my hands in the latte-colored river scarcely helped. It was already carrying a fair share of clay. We already knew that if river water splashed on anything—the packs, the sides of the canoe, the paddles—it left a fine rime of powdery clay when it dried. Our Duluth packs, which we always take pains with, were becoming filthy.

That morning, with the emerging clay layer, we became filthy, too. We washed off most of the clay on our sandals, but it got under toenails and fingernails. It lined the creases of hands and feet. Arms and legs began sporting smears. Remember the Cat in the Hat, who left a pink bathtub ring, which subsequently dirtied Mother's dress, the wall, and Dad's ten-dollar shoes? ("It may never come off," Sally said. "It may not!") We, too, needed Little Cat Z and some Voom!

The deplorable qualities of bentonite clay are not immediately obvious to visitors to the Little Missouri. We had to be up close and personal to the stuff to truly appreciate it. Yet, we had been warned. Pamphlets tell visitors that clay can be treacherous. Dried clay is hard, like rock, and hikers readily traverse it. The surface is solid, sporting cracks like the striations on an alligator back. But in a July cloudburst or after days of steady rain, the hard substrate becomes the slimy clay. It can mire a horse or strand hikers for days.

Under different circumstances, bentonite clay is an admirable substance. Herbalists value it highly, considering it the most effective cleaner found in nature (oh, the irony!). They claim its absorptive property pulls toxins from the body. They tout it as a toothpaste. It is used cosmetically as a facial mask. Some say it is effective in treating the stomach flu. I later discovered I could buy it at the food co-op. It was sold in the same section as the herbs, teas, and spices.

After that first tussle, however, we thought it would be wise to avoid bentonite clay.

....

The river continued to drop. When lunchtime arrived, we landed on a gravel beach that had also been exposed by the receding river. We set up our camp chairs facing the opposite bank so we had front row seats observing the Northern Rough-winged Swallows that flitted to and fro, hawking insects and apparently feeding nestlings tucked into cavities in the sandstone. The gravel was littered with bits of reddish scoriae, petrified wood, and moss agates, the petrologic offerings of the badlands. Tom picked through the rubble for choice specimens.

Immediately upon pushing off after lunch, our canoe drifted past the Maltese Cross Ranch and a little cabin nestled beneath towering cottonwoods. When Theodore Roosevelt made his first trip to western Dakota to hunt bison in 1883 at age twenty-five, before he had entered politics or considered a life of public service, he became enamored of the western ranch. With a flair that only one with a personal fortune can manage, T. R. bought the Maltese Cross Ranch and commissioned a cabin to be built on this site. Sadly, the cabin quickly became a refuge from unanticipated tragedy. The following winter, Roosevelt's young wife and his mother died of different causes on the same day in the Roosevelt family's Manhattan townhouse. T. R. fled to the cabin for a stay of several months while he recovered his equilibrium. Later, he bought a second ranch and raised cattle, spending long stretches of time on the Little Missouri. His experience in North Dakota changed him. It cemented his love of wilderness and his appreciation for its healing power. He saw firsthand the ravages that Americans were inflicting on their virgin country and understood the impulse both to destroy it for monetary gain and to preserve it as a legacy for future generations.

The cabin under the cottonwoods that we passed was not T. R.'s original place, but it looked like it could have been. Its roofline was uneven. Windows were missing, and it was weather-beaten from many winter storms. The original cabin, still in existence, went traveling. T. R.'s domicile was dismantled and moved to St. Louis for the World's Fair in 1904. From there, it went on to Portland, Oregon, to be on display at the Lewis and Clark Centennial Exposition in 1905, and from there, to Fargo, North Dakota, for the state fair in 1908–9. Then it was dismantled a fourth time to move to the state capitol grounds at Bismarck, where it remained for fifty years. It made one more trip, back to the badlands, and today, visitors to Theodore Roosevelt National Park can walk through the building at the park's visitor center in Medora.

The Maltese Cross Ranch itself is still operating. The rancher uses the four-armed symbol as his brand.

After passing the cabin, we began looking for campsites for the night. There was no urgency. There seemed to be plenty of available public land and no competition for tent sites. Indeed, we had seen no one on the river for over twenty-four hours since dropping in, save for a rancher and his enthusiastic collie, which pursued our canoe from the riverbank for quite a ways. We had planned for a short day and time to relax at our camp, to read or write, take photos, watch birds.

The newly exposed gravel beds similar to where we had stopped for lunch seemed like good candidates for a campsite. Three times we pulled the canoe over, and I clambered out to scout the area. It took three times for us to decide they were all alike and all lacking. The substrate was rocky, few plants grew, and no shade beckoned to shield us from an afternoon sun that had turned scorching. In addition, we wondered if we would be at risk if a thunderstorm to the west or south suddenly sent runoff our way. There was also a lingering worry about rattlesnakes preferring these sites. When we paddled the Marias River in Montana, we were told the reptiles gravitate to them. Why wouldn't North Dakota rattlers do likewise?

We next considered camping farther away from the river, but every suitable site involved crossing a mudflat. It took no effort to imagine slipping with a pack and ending up like pigs in a sty.

We held out hope for the state park, Sully Creek, which we were fast approaching. The park is only one and a half river miles from Medora. We hadn't planned to be this close to town. It had just worked out that way. We might hear freeway noise from I-94—but Sully Creek had showers. That knowledge made my heart beat faster.

However, as we approached the park, we could see no formal landing—only endless bentonite clay to plod through to reach solid land. The very fact that the park had no designated landing underscored how little recreational use the river saw. We passed by and headed for Medora.

....

We knew the national park had what is termed a primitive campground, Cottonwood, on the Little Missouri, about three miles from town. It was late afternoon, and we would have sunlight until nine o'clock. Cottonwood Campground seemed our best hope, although we could pull out anywhere in the park and camp as long as we carried water, which we did. We called the park to see if Cottonwood was filled. It was not. The ranger paused a moment when we told her we would be coming in by canoe, then laughed and said that there was a lovely open site overlooking a bend in the river.

We paddled on as the western sun drew nearer the distant hills and lost some of its heat. Cottonwood Campground would have no RV hookups and no showers, but there would be taps with cold water. Even this, a prospect of unlimited clean water, cheered us.

The campground was on a bluff, and yes, we hauled gear and the canoe through the slimy clay to reach it, but it was worth it.

"Primitive" in national park lingo means, among other things, "unmowed." We set up the tent on long, green grass that provided soft, luxurious padding. I arranged a cook station on a picnic table.

Then, we set about removing the grime that had collected on our hands and feet, the canoe, the gear.

At the national park campground, we discovered a mother bison and her calf were neighbors of ours. The park doesn't fence out its wildlife, so they wandered about the campground unrestricted. Tom took her photo—with his zoom lens. We gave them wide berth.

....

We were off the Little Missouri. The next morning the river carried less water still and continued to recede. We went to the visitor center to plan a day hike. There we learned that hikers are frequently routed over a riverbed that carries at best a trickle of water most days of the summer. Bison, deer, elk, and feral horses cross the shallow river without hindrance. We ourselves drove to the western edge of the park and hiked to the petrified forest, gazing at stone-like tree stumps and trying to imagine a much different landscape that existed eons ago.

We felt a mark of distinction, having witnessed the beauty of North Dakota's badlands as few have been able to. The green Old Town strapped to our car was an oddity here. I slapped its clay-smeared flank with satisfaction just to hear the hollow thud. Then we got in the car and headed east.

We had seized the opportunity to canoe an iconic river that had carved out natural beauty deserving of a national park and that had shaped a president and, through him, a nation. We had taken only two days on the Little Missouri, but the experience seemed much longer. When one becomes immersed in the landscape of an unfamiliar world, the tick of a clock is forgotten. The position of the sun in the sky, the status of stomachs that are either satisfied or empty, the level of a river that depends on rainfall are all more reliable indicators of exactly how much time is passing and how much remains. That a moment can expand to assume significance is wisdom I will remember as we sense our time running out.

Ancient Valley

THE KICKAPOO RIVER, 2013

....

THE COUNTRYSIDE WAS BRUSHED WITH OCHRE, AS IF IT were aging, the threads of a tapestry yellowing, darkening, which indeed it was, as summer drew to a close. Goldenrod blanketed the fallow fields of the Kickapoo River valley in western Wisconsin. Acres that had been planted to row crops wore the golden stubble of oats and the tired green of corn that was past its prime.

Through the placid vale, the Kickapoo River wound a serpentine path, cutting into the sandstone cliffs of the Driftless Area, that region of southwestern Wisconsin that remained untouched by glaciation. Bedrock of the area is exposed and is very, very old, dating from before the Age of Fishes, almost five hundred million years ago. For that reason, it has been claimed that the Kickapoo is one of the oldest river systems in the world. The sandstone cliffs that border lengths of the river are the sedimentary remains of the floor to a great inland sea that once covered midcontinental North America.

We planned a leisurely eleven-mile trip down the scenic little river. It was a birthday activity. Our oldest child was turning thirty-one, a fact that confounded Tom and me. Andy is a hydrogeologist by training, a groundwater enthusiast by inclination. Tall and dark, he speaks with conviction from an already deep well of knowledge. His forceful personality assured that we all would be appreciative of the value of groundwater by the time we had paddled an afternoon on the Kickapoo River.

The river had been on all our lists of rivers to canoe for a long time, and for Andy, the interest lay not only in its unique geology but in the fact that by September its flow came entirely from groundwater. Fall is the low point in the hydrologic cycle, he explained to us. The past winter's snow buildup had cycled through and was gone.

This year, the reliance for flow on underground springs was especially apparent. The entire upper Midwest had experienced a grueling six-week drought. We had had no rain in a month. Vegetation on the riverbank looked parched. Leaves hung limp and dusty, some plants were prematurely yellow, and the forest floor was powdery with a fine dust.

Because of the drought, we expected water levels to be low and were prepared to drag the canoes over gravelly shallows, as we often do in late summer on the St. Croix River. How pleased we were to find that there was enough groundwater seeping into the river to maintain adequate levels for paddling. The water temperature was cold, too, another indication that it came from deep in the earth and not the surface.

The Kickapoo River is distant from any major city, and communities in this sparsely populated area are small. On these canoe outings Tom and I try to elude the masses; plying a river far from a population center tips the odds toward solitude. We put in at a landing outside the unincorporated town of Rockton, Wisconsin, and paddled to La Farge (population 754), which though small, is famous in the natural foods world as the headquarters of Organic Valley—the largest organic dairy co-operative in the world.

Our party consisted of Andy and his girlfriend, the red-haired Katherine, Tom, and me. Andy and Katherine took one canoe, launched, and began the patter of canoe partners—jive that would last the afternoon—good-natured squabbling, Andy's emphatic directives, Katherine tossing her curls, not taking any guff. Tom and I followed in the green Old Town, paddling without comment, feeling aged and sedate.

We had gotten a late start and headed out about noon, so the first task was locating a lunch spot. It wasn't long before we found a sandy take-out on the bank. We hauled up the canoes and pulled out a lunch of pretzel rolls, turkey, and chèvre; pears, the late-summer fruit; and more chocolate than could reasonably supply four people. One could guess, rightly, that women packed the lunch.

The sunlight had that watery quality about it common to mid-September. It warmed but not as in July. We turned our faces upward, soaking in the rays, appreciative now for what was a waning phenomenon. Katherine took out her camera and began snapping photos of the fading colors and the sunlight on the water, trying to capture what had suddenly become a bittersweet day as we all realized it was one of summer's last.

After sating our hunger, we continued the trip downriver. As the first of the sandstone cliffs appeared, casting greenish shadows on the river, we realized that they were the defining feature of this river. They ranged in color from a creamy white to an earthy terracotta. Near the top of the cliffs, small saplings clung to life. But what was especially interesting was the plant life growing on the lowest level of the cliff face near the water.

From the river surface extending upward at least six feet grew a carpet of water-loving terrestrial plants. There were ferns, lacy and delicate, and soft, emerald mosses. What really intrigued me, though, were the liverworts, a primitive plant lacking the specialized structures to transport water to tissue. Liverworts can take many forms, but generally they are not pretty, as one might gather from their name. These were gray-green, quarter-sized, and flat, with edges that rolled upward. They hugged the substrate that anchored them and draped it like a carpet, in the same manner as moss and lichens. I seldom encounter liverworts in nature. I guess I don't go looking for them, but they interest me because they made the pages of my General Botany textbook decades ago, and it is always fun to scrutinize in the flesh something you spent some time thinking about abstractly.

The liverworts formed a tapestry upholstering the cliff face. I did not know it at the time, but there was a story to be told of the drama occurring between this ancient plant and its almost equally ancient moss neighbors. Moss expert Robin Wall Kimmerer of SUNY College of Environmental Science and Forestry also was taken with the luxuriant plant growth of the Kickapoo's cliffs. As a graduate student, she had a trained eye that picked up something mine had not: that the mosses grew in bands of individual species parallel to the water. A small, wiry moss occupied the lowest level. About a foot higher, this moss was replaced by several other species, silky and glistening in a collage of different greens. Above these mosses grew the liverworts. They completely covered the cliff at this point. There seemed to be a definite demarcation between moss and liverwort.

Kimmerer was interested in what caused the growth patterns of these several nonvascular plants. She collected individuals of the various species and took them home to the lab. She found that she could easily grow each species in the lab by itself. But when the lowest moss, the small, wiry one, was grown adjacent to the liverwort, it was repeatedly overrun by the scaly, flat liverwort.

Kimmerer is a professional scientist, determined to remain unbiased, but she is also a bryologist, a moss specialist, and as she related the story of what she termed a "power struggle," words like "reptilian" and "snaky" began to describe the liverwort hostile takeover. She had a dog in this fight. How, she wondered, could "her" modest, diminutive moss hold its own against this fierce competitor?

When out collecting on the Kickapoo one day, she noticed a snag of grass caught on a stick high above her head, and she realized that the Kickapoo's water level must rise dramatically at times. The river has what hydrologists term a "low capacity for water," meaning it floods quickly after heavy rain. A mild, shallow stream transforms to a raging river spilling its banks in a matter of hours and then receding in short order. Furthermore, liverworts grew only above where she determined the high-water mark to be.

Back at the lab, Kimmerer created her own flood, inundating her mosses and liverworts for twelve, twenty-four, and forty-eight hours. The mosses survived the flood without damage, but the liverworts did not. They turned black and died.

So the mosses' flexibility in dealing with water enabled them to grow in an area subjected to frequent flooding and evade a superior competitor that was not as flexible.

....

The Kickapoo River had other vegetation that drew our eye. On some of the upper reaches of the cliffs grew immense, old hemlocks.

These dramatic conifers with twisted trunks and massive limbs don't grow in Minnesota, and we always appreciate them when paddling in the eastern United States. The hemlocks grew with white pines, which were also very large, several hundred years old at least. Neither Wisconsin nor Minnesota has many old pines remaining. I could only assume the Kickapoo's pines were inaccessible to men armed with axes or saws.

In September, songbirds are on migration, and the surrounding hardwoods seemed filled with twitters and flitting. We saw many phoebes and figured they were migrating in a flock, and also many Spotted Sandpipers, dainty little wading birds that teetered at the river's edge and poked about in the water like tiny herons. There were many birds that we caught only glimpses of, bird-watching being a more subtle sport in the fall than it is in the spring.

Kickapoo is an Algonquin word meaning "He who stands sometimes here, sometimes there." It lyrically describes a river that wanders. Although the river is 126 miles long, it is only 61 miles as the crow flies between its source in Mill Bluff State Park near the town of Camp Douglas and where it empties into the Wisconsin River. This means those 126 river miles are ribboned into a compressed serpentine route.

After four hours of paddling, we wearied of S curves and switchbacks. It did not help our ennui that we had encountered a fair number of downed trees that we needed to maneuver around. Our eleven-mile trip proved about three miles too long. The sun was low in the west when we finally reached La Farge.

Nonetheless, we agreed that the Kickapoo was worth a second visit. We had seen no other canoe parties that afternoon. We would have to carry water if we undertook a multiday trip, but there would be many opportunities to refill the jug. Next time, we would start in the town of Ontario, farther upstream, and paddle to the confluence with the broad Wisconsin River and then on the short distance to the Mississippi.

....

I thought a lot about change and the nature of change after our visit to the Kickapoo River. I realized that persistence is not the same as unchanging. The old river valley has long persisted through time, yet it not unchanging. It frequently floods, causing quite dramatic change. That disturbance ripples through the system, selecting winners and losers in the plant community. Yet because this change is recurrent, a kind of balance is struck. The persistent moss species relies on its flexibility to endure in the face of change; liverworts, on their exuberant ability to grow despite setbacks.

The Kickapoo River's cliffs displayed two different ways to adapt to change. Surely, they have something to say to us.

Urban Adventure

....

THE SUMMER DAY WAS WARM, AND THE SKIES WERE BLUE. We had a Greek guest to entertain, and Minnehaha Creek beckoned. What better way to give a European a peek at behind-the-scenes life in America than put her in a canoe and hand her a paddle? Here was a chance to introduce her to an activity that had given us so much pleasure.

Our guest, a pretty and sociable young woman, age twenty-three, was eager to go. Eleni was the niece of a Minneapolis Greek family we knew. Her English was good and getting better by the day, I suspected, since we had first met her on a trip to Greece last spring. When I arrived to pick her up for the jaunt down Minnehaha Creek, she was dressed in fashionable skintight jeans and a maroon-and-gold crop top with a big gold *M* for Minnesota on the front. A mutual friend had teased her that it was certain we would tip the canoe and get wet; I assured her we would not. She dimpled and said she was very excited for the outing. She added that she thought swimming in a creek, flowing water, was much more sanitary than swimming in a lake. She had not enjoyed the water at her relatives' Wisconsin lake cabin last summer.

I wasn't sure about that reasoning, though oddly enough, it made a kind of sense. However, I told her that no one was going to get wet today. Off we went.

....

Minneapolitans appreciate the beautiful little waterway that winds its way through the southern neighborhoods of the city. City parkland protects its entire length through Minneapolis. Recreational trails run parallel to its banks, heavily used by walkers, runners, cyclists, parents pushing strollers, and owners walking dogs.

Seldom have we encountered heavy traffic on the water, though, and never any canoes. There are kayakers that will occasionally ply it, and children in floats or tubes on a hot July day, but not many.

The creek is not always navigable. The U.S. Geological Survey maintains a gauge at the creek as it runs under Hiawatha Avenue. A flow between 75 and 100 cubic feet per second is considered adequate to carry kayaks and canoes. Less than that, and paddlers will likely be scraping on shallows and hauling their craft over sandbars. More than 100 cubic feet per second, and one might be bargaining for a wild ride, with water moving too fast to effectively maneuver a canoe.

The water level of the creek is controlled by a dam at its source, Gray's Bay of Lake Minnetonka to the west. Lake Minnetonka is maintained at desirable levels either by damming its outflow into the creek or letting its excess go. After it leaves Lake Minnetonka, Minnehaha winds through the suburbs of Minnetonka, St. Louis Park, Hopkins, and Edina before crossing into Minneapolis. We usually put in at West 54th Street in Edina in a residential neighborhood. We have not ventured farther west to canoe the stretch between Edina and the big lake, which is characterized as more marshy and less developed.

....

Eleni and I met up with our paddling companions, Tom and our youngest daughter, Christina, twenty-four, at the West Fifty-fourth Street entry point. Christina had met Eleni only once, but we entrusted our guest to her skill as a paddler. When she was a kid, Christina spent time at an Audubon camp, where she learned her canoe strokes on the Kettle River, just below Hell's Gate. She's proud of her prowess—she's better than I am; I readily admit it. She nonchalantly agreed to man the stern.

The young women put on life vests, and we instructed Eleni in only two things: how to do a forward stroke and to keep her weight in the middle of the canoe. Tom held the craft steady as the women climbed in, then pushed them off, and told them we would catch up in a few minutes. Christina's blond head and Eleni's glossy dark one disappeared into the leafy tunnel of the creek.

When we next encountered them, they were doing battle with a fallen willow whose branches impeded progress downstream. There was a narrow passage through, however, and together the women worked to thread the needle, successfully, with a little English and a lot of laughing.

What was our Greek guest thinking at this point? Was she experiencing the wilds of North America? Were we offering a tamed-down version of an African safari? Was she having fun? I had no idea.

....

Minnehaha Creek's path through the well-to-do suburb of Edina cuts through the backyards of some very lovely homes. Porches, picture windows overlooking the stream, patios, rock gardens adorn every house and yard. We admired graceful sculpture—leggy wading birds, herons I suppose; a rotund Buddha; children captured in bronze. We studied the rooflines of cathedral ceilings, French Country houses with hip roofs, redwood decks running the length of the house, and large brick ramblers hugging the well-manicured lawns.

The creek is hidden in its sojourn through Edina. Everything is under private ownership. There is no public space on this stretch. Years ago, on our first paddle on the creek, we made snide comments about property owners that ran their highly fertilized, emerald-green lawn right down to the water's edge. The living sod carpet curled under the lip of the stream bank.

This summer, however, many and perhaps most property owners had planted buffer strips of attractive vegetation, like purple coneflowers and decorative grasses, and ground cover, like sedum and moss roses. Buffer strips impede lawn runoff from entering the creek. Owners who maintain buffer strips protect the water by safeguarding the shoreline. They demonstrate their neighborliness in caring for the creek's well-being.

The summer had experienced torrential rains in June, causing eroded banks that crumpled from being undercut. Many yards had meshwork and pegs holding it in place to prevent further erosion. Perhaps it was during the alarming downpours that people got religion and stopped mowing to the water's edge.

The major streets in both Edina and Minneapolis cross the creek, and most of the bridges are named, so it is possible for paddlers to keep track of their progress. After scrutinizing Edina's homes and determining which ones we would like to live in and which ones we would not, we passed under France Avenue. The creek wound around to the left, and we passed another landmark, Adath-Yeshurun Cemetery.

The small Jewish cemetery fronts France Avenue, and when one drives by in a car, the eye catches just a glimpse of exotic Hebrew script engraved in granite. Alas, the back view of the burial ground is not much more enlightening. The cemetery is very old and still in use. Later I learned it was set up in 1885 when a Minneapolis congregation established the previous year by Jewish immigrants from Lithuania, Romania, and Russia bought the two acres in what was then undeveloped farmland. The two entities have since split, and the congregation has moved to Minnetonka.

Minnehaha Creek is astonishingly verdant for so urban an existence. Overhanging trees create a leafy passage with every shade of green in a shifting collage of sunlight and shade. The water is surprisingly clear. The creek bottom has gravel and aquatic plants. Pale amber fish skitter away as watercraft approach.

We rounded another bend, and a huge Great Blue Heron took wing, its spindly legs trailing. This could be anywhere, I thought. But that bird stalks fish in the middle of a city.

....

When the canoes passed under the Xerxes Avenue bridge, we entered Minneapolis. Immediately, the creek was flanked by parkway, the houses now far removed, across a boulevard and a street. At this point, Minnehaha Creek becomes public space, a shared responsibility of the residents who see it every day.

After Penn Avenue's bridge, we passed a set of tennis courts, fully occupied on this lovely late-summer day. We could hear the thwock, thwock of tennis balls going back and forth, back and forth. "That's a good use of a floodplain," I commented to Tom. Minneha-ha Creek can rise significantly. Two months ago, in the wake of the heavy rains, stretches of the parkway were mini-lakes—but private yards were not flooded.

Three minutes past the tennis courts, we glimpsed neon-green tennis balls bobbing in the water.

I had hoped, naively, that once we reached Minneapolis's portion of the creek that the going would get smoother, for we continued to encounter downed trees. On one oxbow in Edina, we had gotten out and hauled the canoes across a muddy stretch. Eleni picked up the bow of the girls' canoe and with Christina, trekked it over to the put-in point. Again, I thought, "What is she thinking?" She was a lot stronger than her petite frame would indicate. She kept smiling.

And in the stern, Christina did a marvelous job of keeping forward movement. Usually, the women remained ahead of Tom and me, so they were pondering a way through a tree obstacle before we had a chance to assess it. At one particularly troublesome point, a sturdy cottonwood trunk with only an inch of water running over it, I watched Eleni half stand up to do a little push. Yikes, I thought. A sure way to spill into the water.

But no, they were fine. When their stern reached that point, Christina planted one flip-flop-clad foot on the trunk and shoved. They made it look easy. Eleni beamed at us.

. . . .

There is a charm to confronting problems to solve, real-life puzzles to be worked out in the moment. It's a challenge, and it feels good when you solve it. Human settlement anywhere in the world was based on solving these puzzles. It's a way of dealing with nature. Nature is indifferent to our interests. Through wrestling with it, we advance our endeavors, including our plan to paddle down Minnehaha Creek. I was sure that in the month that Eleni visited her relatives in Minnesota, no one was going to give her a chance to mingle so intimately with nature. So maybe that's why she was smiling. We had not intended the trip to be so hindered by downed trees. "By the end of this," I told Tom, "those girls are either going to love or hate each other."

....

Nicollet Avenue's bridge. Then, the freeway bridge, I-35W. The cars thundered overhead, unaware of the float party beneath them. And now the jets taking off from Minneapolis–St. Paul International Airport roared in the sky, one blue-and-red fantail after another passing overhead. Deafening.

We have been on Minnehaha Creek when the jets were coming in over south Minneapolis to land, instead of taking off. That's the more interesting scenario. It's noisy either way, takeoff or descent, but when they are descending, they are really low, and you get a detailed glimpse of the big machines and can imagine all the passengers, their carry-ons stashed and their trays and seats in upright position, staring down at the green grid of the neighborhoods. When I fly in, I usually look for the lakes, not for the green winding ribbon that is the creek.

What do the animals think about the horrendous noise? I have seen flycatchers cringe at low-flying jets. There's a pair of Cooper's Hawks that live on this stretch of the creek, and a Barred Owl. We have seen Wild Turkeys and white-tailed deer. Do they become desensitized to the racket? Are their delicate bodies wracked with high levels of stress hormones? Our approaching canoes scared up first the larger, female Cooper's Hawk. She crossed the stream and landed in a basswood tree, displaying to us the terminal white band on her tail and its squared-off shape, the definitive identification mark—plus, she was pretty big. We encountered her mate, noticeably smaller, a few minutes later. He stayed with us, alternately flying and perching, fanning his banded tail and not uttering a peep, so we got a good look at him, too.

....

After Cedar Avenue, the creek enters the Hiawatha Golf Course, owned by the city park system. Suddenly, the leafy tunnel was replaced by views of fairways and roughs. Because of the torrential rains and flooding, the course never opened this year. On past trips we have kept our heads down as golfers teed off over the creek; we have shouted out to let them know we were coming through. On this trip, though, the course was quiet. Residential Belted Kingfishers flew up ahead of the canoes, rattling a welcome or a warning, we couldn't tell which.

Then the creek winds through the southern edge of Lake Hiawatha. Hiawatha, once known as Rice Lake, undoubtedly for fine crops of wild rice in the fall, has been worked over by Euro-American settlers. It was dredged in the 1920s to make it a proper lake, renamed, and claimed as parkland. There is a fishing pier at the southeast corner, and fishing must be good in Hiawatha, because there are always anglers with tackle and other gear attending lines.

On this trip, we saw a young couple and a baby stroller. The line had a red-and-white bobber on it. Is there a Minnesotan alive whose heart doesn't skip a beat at the prospect of a bobber suddenly taking a dip, then a second dip, then a complete submersion, as the fish at the other end has decided to commit to the fateful meal?

We waved hello and paddled on, nearing now our destination.

....

Eleni had seen Minnehaha Falls before, and we had been nearly three hours on the water, so when we approached East Thirty-eighth Street, where we had parked our car, we got out and flung out arms eastward. "Minnehaha Falls is just a kilometer away," we told her. Eleni measured distances in kilometers. "Nine miles on the creek?" she had asked at the beginning. "How many kilometers is that?"

Willows sweep the water at our take-out point. Christina beached the canoe, looked at us, and said, "I think that was my toughest time in the stern ever. So many things to go around!"

Eleni hopped out, ran to the dry bag, and fished out her camera. She motioned to Christina to join her by their canoe, and each grabbed a paddle to pose with. She handed Tom the camera, and then the two girls wrapped their arms around each other and smiled big smiles.

Father's Day

THE FOX RIVER, 2014

....

We stood on the banks of the clear flowing river outside of Portage, Wisconsin, and watched the water streaming northward. The town of Portage is situated in south-central Wisconsin, a small community with a big reputation. Its name says it all. Portages are historic links in presettlement North America.

"This is it!" exclaimed Tom, gesturing with his hand. "The famous Fox!" He wasn't being sarcastic. Tom studies maps and reads background information on the rivers we canoe, far more than I do. He knew this river had been crucial to travelers for centuries, and it had long been on our list of rivers to paddle.

Before roads crisscrossed the continent, there were water highways, rivers and lakes traversed by Native Americans and, later, French Canadian voyageurs and exploring expeditions, using the aqueous routes to move from one watershed to another. The Fox River empties into Green Bay on the western shore of Lake Michigan, a stream that upsets our conventional expectation by flowing northward from its source. Waters coming into Lake Michigan head farther eastward to the St. Lawrence River, the Seaway, and the Atlantic.

At the site where we stood, the Fox flows very close to the Wisconsin River, a many-channeled waterway flowing in the opposite direction and draining a large portion of what is now the state of Wisconsin. The Wisconsin River empties into the Mississippi River and from there, into the Gulf of Mexico. A portage between the Fox and the Wisconsin enabled travelers to pass from one major watershed to the other, giving them access to villages and trading posts.

The portage was two miles long, and there is very little elevation difference between the two rivers—just enough to define a watershed.

People think of the Fox River in the twenty-first century as heavily polluted, in a league with some of the nation's Superfund sites. But that is the Lower Fox, the portion of the river leaving Lake Winnebago and receiving waste pouring out of Green Bay's paper mills and other factories. The Upper Fox, the segment of the river upriver from Lake Winnebago, is a lovely little stream, with birdlife and green banks. Here it is possible to conjure in the mind's eye an intact environment with thick forests and clear water. I imagine Kickapoo people living in rounded, thatched wigwams along the fresh, flowing rivers, and voyageurs singing as they paddled birch-bark canoes.

....

It was Father's Day, and we looked forward to an afternoon on the Fox. In the morning, Andy treated his father to brunch. Andy's girlfriend, Katherine, joined us, and we ate our omelets and poured cups of coffee while we discussed the river and our plans for the day.

Then the two men, Tom and Andy, strapped the canoes to the cars. I, the mother, watched as they worked, marveling how alike in form they were—tall, lean, long waisted. Andy had on a supercool hipster fedora. Tom, not so fashionable, wore his faded canvas canoe hat. The June day was sunny, but dark storm clouds piled high on the northwestern horizon, and the forecast had been dire: rain was inevitable, and tornadoes were possible.

Tom and I pondered that sky and thought we should opt for a short paddle, not the longer four-mile trip we had planned over brunch. Even then, we figured we would probably get wet.

Andy, armed with his smartphone and weather radar app from NOAA, was far more sanguine. Neither he nor Katherine brought rain gear. Why the difference? Tom and I had consulted the Weather Underground website and then looked at the sky. The millennials looked at real-time radar maps, which showed the movement of actual storms and *knew* the future. Not for the first time, I thought, the gulf between us and our children is wide.

·······················

As many as twenty-five thousand people lived in the region of the Fox River before European contact. They followed the waterway in the course of a year, visiting, hunting, moving about. The first European to portage from the Fox River to the Wisconsin was a Frenchman, Jean Nicolet, in 1634. The first Europeans to actually paddle down the Wisconsin to the Mississippi River were also French, Father Jacques Marquette and explorer Louis Jolliet, who made the trip in 1673. In fact, we learned from reading a sign at the portage on Father's Day that they took the portage 341 years and 1 day before we did.

Father Marquette kept an account of his travels and in his journal recorded that he was very keen to convert native North Americans to "the mysteries of our holy religion." This confirms the conventional view of the French missionaries who traveled to the New World with exploratory parties. But Marquette was complex. His writings reveal that he was also physically tough, curious, and fearless, as well as conversant in six languages. Wintering at Chequamegon Bay of Lake Superior, he had learned from American Indians of a great river flowing south—so far south that the Illinois Indians did not know where it ended. Marquette thought it was unlikely that such a large river flowed into Virginia—the extent of European knowledge at that time. Talk of the river intrigued him.

Using language we would never employ today, Marquette declared, "If the savages make me a canoe, we shall travel on this river as far as possible." Clearly, the Jesuit priest was looking for adventure.

The Jolliet party left in the spring from a French trading post on Mackinac Island and headed down the west shoreline of Lake Michigan toward Green Bay. The first people it met were the Menominee, who were friendly with the French. The Menominee were alarmed to learn that the "black gown" and his party were destined for the Great River. They considered the Great River "very dangerous, full of frightful monsters who swallow up men and canoes together."

Father Marquette thanked them for their solicitude but said that "the salvation of souls was at stake"—he had to proceed. What did he think about the river monsters? He thought that the French explorers were up to the task of defending themselves against any kind of monster.

At another village, where Mascouten, Miami, and Kickapoo Indians resided, the Jolliet-Marquette party hired two Miami guides to lead them up the Fox River to the Wisconsin River. Marquette had a compass and knew they should travel in a general southwest direction, but he noted that the Fox was fraught with marshes and little lakes and that the river could be obscured by a thick growth of wild rice—they needed natives to lead them to the portage.

The two Miami paddled with the party up the Fox to the portage and helped them carry the canoes and gear over to the banks of the Wisconsin—Marquette referred to it as the Meskousing—and then departed. "Here we leave the waters which flow toward Quebec," Father Marquette wrote, "to follow those which will lead us into strange lands."

Marquette and Jolliet continued their exploration to the Mississippi River and then south, passing the mouth of the Missouri River and then that of the Ohio River. They met new peoples—ones who called themselves the "Illinois," which they understood to mean "the men"—as if the other Native Americans were mere animals. They met the Mitchigameas, who nearly attacked, and the Arkansas, whose chief "was singing quite agreeably" as he approached them, holding out a pipe to smoke. Marquette recorded that the buffalo were "very fierce," often killing men; that the Shawnee at the mouth of the Ohio were "by no means warlike"; and that the Illinois, of all the peoples he had encountered, were the most likely to convert to Christianity.

The party turned around at the mouth of the Arkansas River, 435 miles from the Gulf of Mexico, because they feared encountering Spanish colonists, who they thought were in the region. The next year, Marquette returned to the Illinois peoples to set up a mission but fell ill and died within the year at age thirty-nine.

....

We launched our two canoes into the Fox at the portage. Marquette and Jolliet paddled upstream to reach the Wisconsin River, but we took the easy way and paddled downstream for four miles, forgetting all worries about storms. Though the sky still scowled in the distance, from our low perch on the water, we saw only blue skies overhead. The river may not look as it did when Father Marquette paddled through, but the land is not harnessed to human development either. From Portage north downriver, large, tall stands of cattails lined the waterway. These were great hiding places for birds. Mallards and herons flushed from their recesses as we passed. Small, nervous warblers sang their thin, reedy songs. High overhead, cottonwoods loomed. Some were dead—good places for woodpeckers. Others whispered with flat, clattering leaves. The Fox wore all shades of green in June, from the walls of grassy cattails to the gray greens of a cottonwood canopy.

The Fox is not a popular canoe river, at least not this section. We encountered several great, barely submerged old cottonwoods that extended across its breadth. Tom and I watched Andy and Katherine maneuver their canoe through impossibly narrow passages. They backed up, edged forward, turned the prow ever so slightly, did it again, working as a team, patient with each other. Andy propped his foot on a log for leverage, to push over a particularly shallow spot. Tom and I followed, getting creative with technique. I was sure we would need to get out and guide or carry the canoe through the narrow parts, and I eyed the water nervously for leeches and bottom muck. But Tom is patient and tenacious, too, good with small moves and nimble turns. The downed cottonwood gave us our one challenge of the afternoon.

There was little by way of excitement on the river. No big rocks, no riffles. The greatest thrill came as we approached the end of the paddle. Someone had constructed a minor dam, and water spilled over in a tiny curtain. At lower water levels, this might have meant a portage, but in this wet June, we got momentum going, and the canoes made the drop with ease.

. . . .

The Leaf family paddling together is an appropriate way to observe Father's Day. Tom introduced his own father to canoeing forty years ago, after taking a canoeing course in college. His father had had lots of experience with rowboats, fishing with his father, Tom's grandfather, as a child and later as an avid adult angler. Del took to canoes with enthusiasm and paddled lakes and rivers for years. In fact, his last time in a canoe, in his eighties, was with grandson John. They were bass fishing, and Grandpa's shifting balance problems proved too much for the Old Town. It spilled both Grandpa and John into the water. The tally was two drenched and chastened fishermen and two lost cell phones. Grandpa hung up his paddle after that.

But our children paddle on, introducing boyfriends, girlfriends, classmates, future husbands, and buddies to life on the water. Tom, a paddler, a swimmer, a skater, and a skier, in love with water, can claim that as a father's legacy.

Draining the Ancient Lake

THE RED LAKE RIVER OF
NORTHWESTERN MINNESOTA, 2014

....

ON A LATE-SUMMER MORNING, TOM AND I SURVEY WHAT seems like the flattest landscape we have ever seen. It is a sea of green below a yawning blue sky. It fits the popular conception of a prairie, but most prairies are not this flat. Prairies tend to undulate, rolling with hollows and hillocks that can conceal a person.

No, this land is a level plane, deceptively simple, with little trace of what has occurred here. It is like a platform, like the surface of a lake, and this seeming kinship to water is nearer the truth, since where we stand, in the Red River valley, was once a lake bed of the largest lake North America has ever known, Glacial Lake Agassiz. Prairie vegetation once grew here and bequeathed to the lake bed its fertile soils. Today, it is one of the richest agricultural regions on Earth. Few navigable waterways wind through it. The one we will canoe today is the Red Lake River, the major tributary of the Red River of the North, which forms the Minnesota–North Dakota border.

We have traveled to the far northwestern corner of Minnesota to canoe this river and to immerse ourselves in the atmosphere of an ancient lake bed for a few hours. To arrive at the river, we left the land of lakes and pines, turned right at the town of Gully (population sixty-six), and drove due north, down a hill—a terminal moraine, the end of the ice sheet of the last glacier—and out on to the flats, flanking the Red Lake Indian Reservation until we reached the Neptune Bridge, which crosses the river.

At the bridge, we see that the river is swollen, nearly brimming, and flowing fast. Most of Minnesota had experienced torrential rains the week before. Tom guesses we will have a quick trip today. Our take-out point will be eight miles downstream at the Pennington County Road 3 Bridge, spanning the river.

The landing at the Neptune Bridge is a solid concrete ramp. It will be easy to launch the canoe from there. We get back in the car, and after a quarter mile driving north, we turn left on perfectly straight County Road 3 heading west. The secondary roads in Pennington County are straightforward: east–west or north–south, intersecting at right angles. The flat topography facilitates the grid.

At the County Road 3 Bridge, highway workers are mowing the roadside. I wonder if they are surprised to see a car pull up with a canoe strapped to its roof, two people get out and stash bicycles in the weeds by the river. Later, when we arrive by canoe at this landing, we will leave the boat on the bank, hop on our bikes, and pedal back to where we began the trip to retrieve the car.

We have to be content to lock the bikes together and lay them on the ground. There are several huge cottonwoods nearby, but no saplings, no shrubs to which to lock them. There are no people either—just the two mowers. The expansive view shows a handful of farms, a patchwork of big fields, yellowing wheat and green sugar beets, and a grain elevator, far, far away.

....

Back at the Neptune Bridge landing, I take stock of the river. It is very clear and deep enough that I can't see the bottom. A ragged assortment of nonnative herbs—tansy, reed canary grass—line the banks. A stiff wind tugs at my hair and my pants legs. Normally, I would expect us to battle a headwind while on the water, but on this river, we will sit low enough that we will be protected.

Although farm fields stretch on either side, the banks of the Red Lake River are feathered with a lush growth of small willows, ash, and basswood. Bigger cottonwoods, the mark of a prairie waterway, rise in the distance.

The Red Lake River arises in Lower Red Lake, within the reservation. The two big lakes, Upper and Lower, are remnants of Glacial Lake Agassiz, so in a way, the Red Lake River flows west out of the ancient lake toward its confluence with the Red River of the North. The tribe requires that an American Indian guide accompany paddlers wanting to ply the upper reaches of the river. There is little cultivation within the reservation, and the river emerges from it clear and clean.

As we leave the Neptune Bridge landing, Tom and I begin to see a lot of wildlife. Water attracts birds, and the river offers the only surface water in the area. Fall migration is under way. Restless little songbirds twitter in the willows lining the river. Small flocks of ducks scatter before us on the water—Mallards, Blue-winged Teal, Wood Ducks.

We spend perhaps five minutes mesmerized by a Northern Harrier cruising over a hay field, diving and rising in graceful arcs. The bird seems unbothered by us, though surely it knows we are present. We have never seen a harrier so close—close enough to see the black wingtips, the bold bands on its tail.

As we paddle, we mull over the lay of the land. Since the early days of our marriage, I realized that Tom, an erstwhile geology major, saw different things than I did. He could pick out glacial moraines, kettles, and potholes, where I just saw hills and ponds.

So I have strived to see through geologist eyes too, trying to make sense of a topography and give it a story, to not just take it for granted. Now, I wonder about the Red Lake River. It flows through the flattest land on Earth, but land that is tilted ever so slightly to the west and the north, and then drained by the Red River of the North, which streams into Lake Winnipeg. I think that such a river cutting through a plane would meander in tiny little S curves—and the Red Lake River does that farther downstream. But along this stretch, it is very straight, almost reminiscent of the canals in Flanders, albeit much less manicured. I suspect this segment of the river had been ditched and straightened some time in the past. So much in the valley has been ditched. A topographical map, consulted later online, confirms this suspicion.

We have a meeting to make later in the day, so we can't afford a leisurely paddle. Tom pushes forcefully, wanting to tick off the miles, and with the fast current, the canoe sails through the flatness like a catamaran on a lake. We pass tiny little outlets draining fields, thickets of willow and ash, and an occasional farmhouse, though they are very few. A beaver crosses in front of the canoe. A Great Blue Heron wings and wheels away from the water.

....

What would this land have looked like when a glacier pressed down on it? Glaciers were colossal structures with ice a mile high. I imagine a wall of ice rising up higher than the tallest skyscraper, the aquamarine blueness of big ice as the crystals reflect the color of the sky. From the canoe, I look out over the Red River valley and try to conjure a glacier.

The ice chills the air. At the toe of the glacier, the land harbors scant vegetation. Summers are cool. Winters are snowy. It's a bleak world, dazzling in sunshine, somber in cloud cover.

....

And then, after eons, after an ice age, the mammoth ice sheet begins to pull back. It recedes north, it melts, and suddenly there's a lot of water.

Glacial Lake Agassiz formed between twelve thousand and eight thousand years ago, as the most recent glacier withdrew. Meltwater was dammed by the retreating ice—the weight of the glacier tilted the slope northward. Water pooled to form a lake that covered a large share of what is now Alberta, Manitoba, and western Ontario, about the area of Asia's Black Sea. It may have been the largest body of freshwater ever to exist on Earth. The finger of the lake that is now the Red River valley was actually a small portion of the immense body of water.

The melt and recession took place over thousands of years as the continent experienced warm spells and cooler spells. The lake assumed many different shapes. In Minnesota, there is evidence of four different Lake Agassiz beaches, delineating varying lake levels. These ancient beaches can be discerned by the naked eye—subtle changes in elevation. Geologists also identify them by soil composition—a gravelly substrate as befits a shoreline. The lake bed itself was a gray clay, which can be seen in cliffs farther downstream, at the towns of Red Lake Falls and Huot.

We will not paddle as far as Red Lake Falls today, and will later regret that we did not see the scenic clay cliffs, which are a tourist attraction. Vertical cores taken from the cliffs at Red Lake Falls indicate at least three glacial advances in this area. They contain limestone fragments from the Winnipeg area, and shale from farther west. There are boulders from the Canadian Shield, northeast of the region, on top of the cliffs.

....

Despite the headwind, Tom and I are moving downriver at quite a good clip. The current must be quicker than we had first thought. At noon, Tom suggests we pause for lunch. There's not a good takeout spot. The banks are thickly vegetated with reed canary grass, and there's no way to get a foothold on it, so we decide on a floating trail lunch. I pull out a block of Cotswold Cheddar and a box of Triscuits. We have pears and cookies. It's amazing how even a modest lunch can seem gourmet as a break from wind, water, and physical exertion.

....

When Lake Agassiz drained, a tallgrass prairie established on the lake bed. Because of the flat nature of the land and the clay base, drainage was poor. Tallgrass prairies are noted for their "wet feet." It was a lush grassland and attracted abundant game, elk and bison. These, in turn, drew in the Native Americans. The Dakota first occupied the land, but by the blossoming of the fur trade in the late 1700s, the Ojibwe had moved into the area, having been pushed west by the immigrating Europeans.

The purveyors of the fur trade, the trappers, were French Canadians. Tough, hardy, seemingly impervious to inclement weather, these men were flexible in language and culture. They found compatibility with the native Ojibwe and frequently married Ojibwe women. Their children were conversant in both French and Ojibwe, sometimes formally educated in Montreal, and comfortable in both cultures. They formed the basis of an emerging people, the Métis.

The Métis became what historian Mary Wingerd has termed "cultural brokers" in shaping the relationships between the American Indians and the whites. They acted as interpreters, set up trading posts, and were the drivers of the first long-distance overland trade route in the region, using oxcarts to transport goods to market. The oxcart trails often followed the ancient beaches of Lake Agassiz, natural roadways that were level and well drained. The Red Lake River watershed has several early Métis settlements: Gentilly, St. Hilaire, Huot, and Red Lake Falls.

As a sixth-grader studying Minnesota history, I learned about the New Englanders, followed by the Scandinavians and Germans, who set up Minnesota's government and infrastructure. The Métis, earlier in time than the latter groups, were glossed over, but decades later, I find myself attracted to them for their color and verve.

The Métis were nominally Catholic. The religion preached by Jesuit missionaries became infused with Native beliefs and practices. They were known for their fiddle music and their bright red caps. Métis oxcart trains traveled a diagonal across proto-Minnesota, carrying hides, pelts, and pemmican from the Red River valley to early St. Paul. The creaking of the wheels could be heard from a distance. Early residents of St. Paul were alerted to the approach of the Métis in the fall.

The traces they left on Minnesota are discernible: an old cemetery at Little Canada, on the outskirts of St. Paul (Little Canada, itself a remnant of the Métis presence); St. Genevieve's Catholic Church in Centerville, another Métis overwintering site; the Frogtown neighborhood in St. Paul, where the Métis liked to camp next to a marshy lake. The deep ruts that their oxcarts left in the mud can still be seen in places. The crossing over the Red Lake River at Huot is one such place.

The Métis thought of themselves as neither Canadians nor Americans. Neither did they consider themselves American Indians, though they were allied with the Ojibwe through many marriages.

They lived in villages, they worked small subsistence garden plots, and they hunted buffalo. In 1845, they ran into trouble with the U.S. government when they targeted bison herds that had been promised to the Dakotas. About that time, the Métis settlement of Pembina, on the North Dakota–Minnesota border, boasted of 1,100 people, making it a significant town, second in population only to St. Paul.

....

At the County Road 3 bridge, we haul the canoe out of the river, sidestep the poison ivy growing on the banks, get on our bikes, and head back to the car. The headwind from the west is now a tailwind, pushing the bicycles along. We pass farmers taking down wheat, massive combines that mow the stalks, collect the wheat seeds, and emit clouds of golden dust. We pedal by fields of the signature Red River valley crop, sugar beets, still green. They will be harvested in late October.

Then we make the right-hand turn to the south, pedaling toward the car, and feel that strong west wind push us all over the road. There is scarcely any traffic, but I am happy to reach the landing nonetheless.

....

After retrieving the canoe, we continue our travels west to the tiny hamlet of Huot. The State of Minnesota commemorates a historic treaty that occurred there in 1863 between the United States and the Red Lake and Pembina bands of Ojibwe. It was a traumatic time for the Ojibwe. The year before, the Dakotas, pressed to their limit by hunger and broken promises, had waged war on settlers in southern Minnesota. Many white settlers left the state, and the remaining ones were edgy and made no distinction between American Indian tribes. The Ojibwe, though they played no role in the 1862 battles, felt pressure to come to a resolution with the United States.

The treaty was interpreted by Pierre Bottineau, a Métis; Alexander Ramsey, with accompanying aides, represented the United States; seven chiefs represented the Native Americans. They agreed to turn over ten million acres of what would become fertile farmland for annuity payments of twenty thousand dollars a year for twenty years—a wretched bargain, and one miscast as merely permission to cross American Indian land. One of the Red Lake chiefs, May-dwa-gun-on-ind, opposed the treaty. He was left out of the negotiations.

The meeting place is now a modest park on the banks of the river. Tall cottonwoods shade a grassy lawn. The river's gray clay cliffs are picturesque and look pristine, an ironic contrast to the human deception that occurred on the other side of the river. Treaty negotiators chose the site for its significance as a Métis crossing on the "Woods Trail," friendly territory. The Woods Trail was a trade route from 1844 to the 1870s, which passed through land controlled entirely by the Ojibwe. When Métis oxcarts traveled through the more westerly route along the Red River of the North, they were subjected to Dakota attacks.

Tom and I had read that because of the crossing and its preservation now as a park, wheel ruts are still discernible. Imagine seeing ruts that were 150 years old! I have seen ruts of wagon wheels from the Oregon Trail at Scotts Bluff, Nebraska, and I wanted to see these. We poke around at Huot, trying to reason out where the oxcarts crossed (perhaps that little dip between two hills?), trying to imagine the treaty signing—the Ojibwe bringing sixteen hundred people to the site, far outnumbering the Euro-Americans. The tents, the cooking arrangements, the children and dogs running around. The pomp, the ceremony, and the sad results. The inevitability of it all.

A tangle of jewelweed and cow parsnip grows in a low area where we were told the ruts were. If they could still be seen in the twenty-first century, it would not be until after a frost that killed the vegetation.

. . . .

We leave the Red Lake River sparkling in the late-afternoon sun. A day that began in clear, cool air, as we surveyed the tranquil expanse of the Red River valley, has become warmer and more complicated. I think of several glaciers moving across this land, and of the giant lake that formed when they melted. And when it drained, the fertile prairie that supported abundant wildlife. That great fertility was a cause for strife, as people jockeyed to lay hold of its abundance. The Métis and their oxcarts were a distant memory, the creak of the wooden wheels only a slight echo in history. So much lying beneath the surface of a sea of greenness under a yawning blue sky.

What Is the Good Life?

....

Our social studies teacher scrawled the question in chalk across the blackboard. "What is the good life?" That, he said with a flourish, dotting the question mark, is the next unit.

It was spring of my senior year of high school. Apparently, we had left the serious business of education behind—conjugation of German verbs, tangents and cosines, East Indian literature—and entered the world of "values clarification," the trendy new curriculum of the 1970s. I was OK with that. I had already been accepted into the college of my choice. As our windowless classroom heated up under the May sun, I felt my academic zeal dwindling.

Mr. Johnson went on to say that we would work with a partner on this project and it needed to be presented to the class at the end of the term. I surveyed my options for partners among my classmates. I had taken college-track coursework since tenth grade, but this course, Senior Social Studies, had thrown all the classmates together again. I had not seen some of my fellow seniors for several years.

There was a blond kid, big and crammed into one of those flimsy desks, across the room from me who might be a possible partner. He and I ran in the same social circle, but I didn't know him well. I did know he wasn't a slacker. He would pull his own weight in a project. He would be going to Gustavus Adolphus College with me in the fall. Maybe I should get to know him better.

We agreed to team up. When we discussed the project in class for the first time, it seemed to go well. We agreed: the good life was a fairly quiet one. We wanted to spend time in nature. We wanted to travel. We wanted a happy family and meaningful work. We decided to make a slide show, using photographs from our own childhoods and landscapes of the American countryside. Rural. Idyllic. Serene. He set it to music. We chose tunes from James Taylor, Chicago, and just a bit of edge from Paul Simon as he sang, "Let us be lovers, we'll marry our fortunes together," and went off to look for America.

That blond kid and I did just that, seven years later.

....

Tom and I have risen in the gray light of early morning on an overcast day and are now standing with several others in a pine plantation of gnarled, scrappy jack pines. We have come to the northern part of Michigan's Lower Peninsula to canoe the Au Sable River, but before we do, we are pursuing a quest: we are looking and listening for Kirtland's Warblers.

Kirtland's Warblers are a holy grail for birders. In all the world, the small, colorful birds can be found only in three counties bordering the Au Sable River (and recently in a couple other sites in Upper Michigan and Wisconsin). The population now numbers four thousand birds, up from a low of four hundred in 1970. When the Endangered Species Act was passed in 1973, the warbler was listed as endangered, and the full weight of the U.S. Fish and Wildlife Service was thrown into its protection.

It was known that the bird nested only in young jack pine stands between five and twenty years old. These once grew extensively on northern Michigan's least productive sand plains but required fire to clear out brush and generate young stands. With logging and the suppression of fire, the warblers' habitat dwindled and so did the population.

I knew that Kirtland's Warblers needed young, even-age pines for their breeding grounds, but I had envisioned lush stands of white pines. What we were looking at in the drizzle was not that at all. The six-foot jack pines were twisted and sparse, really unlovely. Equally beleaguered blueberry bushes formed a thin understory beneath the misshapen lower pine boughs. Tawny sand, little pointed pinecones, and last fall's discarded oak leaves filled in the spaces where blueberries did not grow.

We would have driven right by such a stretch of "forest" and called it a regenerating clear-cut, never thinking to look for the warbler in such a barren landscape. But a guide from Michigan Audubon had led us here, to this USFWS plot, to see the bird. Indeed, birders cannot enter the habitat without an escort, and woe to those who might think to use recorded "play-back" songs to lure the bird into view! These are banned. I nervously touched my smartphone, stuffed into my pocket; I had a Kirtland's Warbler song on it and had listened to it for a week beforehand. "Pishing" (calling in a bird by making little noises with your tongue and lips, something I did reflexively when birding) was also a no-no. I made a point to be mindful of my impulses.

We are not at the site for more than ten minutes before I hear a Kirtland's male singing, loud and sweet, a distinctive song. He is not at all shy. Even though it has started to rain, the bird sings from a lower branch, not of a jack pine but of a box elder, the sole deciduous tree in a sea of pines. Later we spy another male caroling at the top of a jack pine, and then from the dead pinnacle of another tree.

Even in gray light, we see it is a beautiful bird. Its breast is a bright yellow, streaked with black; when it faces away from us, its gray back is mottled and well camouflaged. For hours, we walk the sandy road bordering the scrubby pines, listening to the sweet territorial song and taking in a Kirtland's Warbler's world.

The Kirtland's Warbler lived the good life amid the vast stretches of regenerating jack pine forests following the retreat of the last glacier. The young trees of the pine barrens offered it protective lower branches in which to conceal a nest. When the jack pines grew taller and the lower branches died, no longer providing cover, there were other regenerating stands to utilize. The warblers' sizable beaks, not as delicate as some warblers', could handle the blueberries that ripened just when parent birds needed to feed fledglings.

Today, thanks to the Endangered Species Act and a society reluctant to let any species disappear from the face of the earth forever, the warbler continues to enjoy the good life. The good life for any wild species is simply one in which it can reproduce and raise young to maturity. If a species cannot do this one thing, it will cease to exist.

When Tom and I were seventeen and first considered the good life, reproduction was part of the equation. We called it "family life." We were surprisingly clear-eyed about this most fundamental truth. But human beings are so much more complicated than our wild animal cousins. With the human population at 7.2 billion and rapidly expanding, we can't all seek the good life in children. What else might comprise the good life?

....

The Au Sable River flows east out of the town of Grayling, Michigan. Locals pronounce the river "Awsable," much like "usable." Tom and I were happy to learn this. Our French is not good, and we would not have to use it. We decided to begin our trip not on the Au Sable, though, but on a major tributary, the South Branch, which flows past the small community of Roscommon, where we launched.

After we agreed we had fulfilled the quest of a Kirtland's Warbler, we packed the Duluth packs with the needed gear for a three-day trip and loaded our canoe in fine mist around noon at a canoe livery in Roscommon. It is disheartening to begin a trip in the rain. Right from the start you are dealing with raincoats and pants, damp packs and wet life jackets, camp stove, water jug, and anything else that can't be fitted under a protective tarp. As we packed for the Au Sable, I found myself already in a snit, because Tom neglected to tuck the two red-and-white camp chairs under the tarp with the packs. "Why," I hissed, "why bring chairs at all if you can't sit on them because they're wet?"

Beginning a trip with an irritated bowman is worse than beginning a trip in the rain. Tom found room for the chairs, which were only damp, under the tarp, and we shoved off.

The South Branch of the Au Sable River is the less developed of the two, at least above the confluence. Leaving Roscommon, we paddled past houses and cabins for a couple of hours. The river was narrow and intimate and reminded us strongly of Wisconsin's

Brule River, which also flows north through a narrow, vegetated valley, sometimes past high, exposed banks, other times along thickets of alder and willows. It continued to rain, sometimes just a mist and sometimes in earnest. It was a summer rain, fairly warm, and the local residents had told us they were most grateful for it. North-central Michigan had been dry, and a few damp days tamped down the fire danger.

The rain did little to lessen the swarm of biting insects that happily pursued whatever exposed skin was available. Tom had pocketed a small bottle of Muskol containing 100 percent DEET, the heavy artillery in mosquito protection, and after an hour of futilely swatting at the enemy, we gave in and slathered it on.

The mosquitoes were in alliance with blackflies, which swarmed in a grayish cloud about my face. DEET repels them, too, but an hour passed before I realized that the tiny little insects had crawled under my rain pants, under my quick-dries, and up my socks to locate the skin they desired. Somehow, this maneuver seemed more devious than insects ought to be.

After a lunch break on someone's dock, we entered the section of the river famous among fly fishermen everywhere: the Mason Tract. The tract is 279,000 acres of state-owned land that began as a gift from the George Mason family. Mr. Mason was an automobile entrepreneur and an avid angler and hunter. Upon his death, his family donated the land to the Michigan Department of Natural Resources with the stipulation that it never be sold or developed and that it be managed as a permanent game preserve. Private cabins and docks in the preserve were acquired when they went up for sale, and removed. So management of the Mason Tract reversed the trend toward development and created a reconstructed wilderness that seems pristine to paddlers on a river trip.

We thrilled to this section of the river. Tall white pines, some near maximum height at two hundred feet, rose high overhead at intervals. There were boggy sections of black spruce, the dark spires extending upward like spiky hats. The mist in the air muted the colors and contributed to the aura of otherworldliness. Tall, mature trees and untrammeled land are rare on the Lower Peninsula.

People entering the Mason Tract get a sense of the past, of beauty debased and an Eden destroyed, and this enhances their reverence.

At the height of the breeding season, the birds were cacophonous. We racked up a list of more than fifty species in the first four hours on the river, mostly by identifying their songs, since it is impossible to do much with binoculars as a canoe clips along at four miles per hour. There were Tufted Titmice, relatives of chickadees, which are a bit exotic to us, since they are a southern species uncommon in Minnesota. "Peter, peter, peter," they called from thickets. But there were also Winter Wrens, with a drawn-out tinkling chant, and Red-breasted Nuthatches, both of whom inhabit the conifer north woods in Minnesota. It surprised us, too, because the Au Sable River runs at about forty-five degrees latitude, parallel to the Twin Cities, and Minnesotans don't consider the Cities "north." It reinforced our sense that the Michigan forest ecosystem, which superficially looks like Minnesota, is its own entity and more eastern.

One noticeable bird was the American Robin. Birders often disregard robins as overcommon generalists. These Michigan robins were not hanging out in suburban yards but acted like wild birds—flying across the river, calling from thickets or branches in the "pristine" Mason Tract. The robin is the Michigan state bird, a fact I had previously deplored as unimaginative (and privately rooted for the Kirtland's Warbler), but maybe American Robins, too, are more in their natural element farther east, and resort to suburbs and small towns in Minnesota because our more western woods are not "home" enough for them.

Originally, the Mason Tract banned camping within its boundaries for twenty-five years. Even today, campers have only one option within the wilderness area: Canoe Harbor, a state forest campground near the northernmost border of the tract. A gravel road connecting to "civilization" runs past the campground, so anglers often arrive by vehicles pulling campers. Ours was the only canoe. We hauled it out of the river and set up camp twenty feet from the water. The rain had tapered off, leaving a damp woods with abundant mosquitoes. How often have we recalled Lewis and Clark's assessment of June days: "the moskitos were verry troublesome."

But the DEET was still working. We rigged up a tarp to protect the cooking station and table in case the rain returned. It didn't. A pair of fly fishermen, father and son, were casting about near the landing. They told us they used barbless hooks—catch and release. It was all about the thrill of outsmarting a trout. The fishing was better at night, and they expected to return in the dark, after supper.

The anglers were filled with awe at the seemingly untouched beauty of the Mason Tract—true wilderness, they called it. The fly fishermen who come to the Au Sable for its spectacular qualities (the clear, cold water, the several species of trout, the pristine nature of the surrounds) are true adherents to a wilderness experience.

In fact, the Michigan Department of Natural Resources caters to them and this desire. "Sportsmen, slow your pace," a state sign reads at the border of the Mason Tract. "Ahead lies the fabled land of the South Branch. Here generations of fishermen have cast a fly on one of the great trout streams of America." It also manages the wilderness stream for trout. At intervals we had noticed bundles of three or four dead full-size trees, intentionally places with spires pointing downstream. We knew that such structures provided shelter for young trout. A cabin owner told us such placement had been performed by helicopters less than a year ago. The anglers were pleased.

This is the good life, they would tell you: being in nature as God intended it, acting out our prehistoric role of outwitting wily fish but not depleting them, not destroying their habitat, not marring the silence by motors or radios. The good life was Eden; human constructs detract from it.

....

The next morning we emerged from the tent to discover the rain had cleared and a sunny day was in the offing. After a breakfast of oatmeal and coffee, we took down a mostly dry tent, folded a barely damp tarp, broke camp, and left.

Within minutes, we had paddled out of the Mason Tract and soon approached the confluence of the South Branch with the main stream of the Au Sable River. The waterway widened, and cabins appeared with more frequency. But much of the river was bordered by state forest and remained without the mark of human beings.

The cabins seemed to be clustered in a long stretch of buildings, and just when the Au Sable seemed distressingly built up, there was a long stretch of spruce bog or upland woods. Tall white pines continued to sweep the horizon with their magnificent boughs at intervals. Sapsuckers knocked uneven, distinctive drills on dead wood. The hollow chant of a Veery arose from deep in the forest.

We enjoyed the cabins, actually. I had spent childhood summers in what I considered a classic cabin—stone fireplace, pine paneling—on a clear, pine-rimmed lake in central Minnesota, and Tom and I now owned a different summer place. It, too, has a stone fireplace and knotty pine walls, and it is just odd enough with floors that slant, windows mismatched, and mice abounding to make it complete in its quirkiness.

So we kept a running assessment of the retreats we passed. We liked the woodsy ones with rough cedar siding. We liked stone fireplaces, like ours, although ours is terribly inefficient in heating the place; a well-designed wood-burning stove would be much better. There is a disconnect between aesthetics and function in our affinities. We liked porches that allowed people to observe the river, windows overlooking hummingbird feeders, and second floors only if they had actual rooms and were not just the wasted space of a vaulted ceiling.

We deplored nice, grassy yards, particularly if there seemed to be no weeds, lawns that ran to the water's edge, and buildings that seemed too close to the riverbank. "Is there no setback?" we would ask every so often. The answer seemed to be not when these places were built, for most of them seemed fifty years old or older. The lower reaches of the Au Sable, farther east than we were going to paddle, have a federal Wild and Scenic River designation, and along that twenty-three-mile stretch, from the Mio dam to Alcona Pond, the lot size is regulated, and the setback is two hundred feet from the ordinary high-water mark for new buildings.

The cabins varied greatly in style—some craftsman, some solid log homes, some cobbled together like our home cabin. Some would now be classified "midcentury modern"—a very hip commodity these days, with big picture windows and long horizontal lines. Tom mused, "They are all the owner's idea of the good life—or," he added, reflecting further, "as much of the good life as they can afford."

So here we are, I thought, dipping my paddle in and out of the river. Back to the good life. What is the good life?

In the forty-some years since we first pondered that question together, we have made choices toward achieving what we consider the good life. We haven't specifically framed our decisions in that light, but isn't that what everyone does? Within certain constraints (money, time, responsibilities to family, friends, and job) we are crafting our version of the good life day by day.

Do we want to live in the city, the suburbs, the exurbs, a small town? Do we want to spend a significant time in a car every day? Is that a good trade-off for not having close neighbors? How do we want to spend our free time? At concerts and plays, or at ball games and bars? Camping or going to movies? Dinner with friends at home, or being with family?

When we two seventeen-year-olds pondered the good life in Senior Social Studies, we had wanted to travel and to be in nature. Later, when we were first married, we had very little money. We lived on student loans. A canoe trip, a bicycle trip, camping, and hiking were the cheapest vacations possible. Nature is almost always free. But we were unwittingly wise to seek recreation—re-creation—in nature. Thinkers and poets through the ages have recognized the renewal to be found in the earth's greenness. Now that idea is backed up by scientific study. So today, even though we no longer live on loans, we still spend our free hours on rivers and lakes, out in the woods or prairies, in the sunshine, and in snow being re-created. That is part of our good life.

Tom and I were amazed to learn in 1971 when we watched our classmates present their projects that most seventeen-year-olds wanted nice cars and big houses. We didn't consider ourselves hippies in our teens, but we asked ourselves, Weren't cars and houses part of the Establishment? Isn't that considered not cool?

One thing we never considered when we worked on our project

was how our pursuit of the good life might affect others. For one thing, we were still living in an America that seemed to have abundance everywhere. There felt like enough of everything to go around. And we were still self-centered teens, thinking mainly of our own needs and of the need to grow up and become our own authentic selves.

Today I do consider this. Every day I think about how my pursuit of the good life is affecting others. This is an entirely selfish exercise, because the others I think about aren't the poor and the hungry of my own country. I think of my grandchildren, my hypothetical grandchildren, whom I may never have but who in my imagination look inquisitively at me. They ask me, I imagine, what my life was like as a little girl, and I tell them of swimming in clear lakes, of catching sunfish bigger than my dad's hand. I describe our sliding hill and how we would take our sleds on Saturdays in the winter and stay out all morning, or how we skated every night after supper on the skating rink near the grade school, under lights strung on a pole, as the frozen lake nearby cracked and boomed in the cold. And I imagine that they look at me as if I had two heads or maybe six eyes, because none of that—not the swimming lake or the ice or the snow—will mean anything to them.

I am uneasy when we travel to the southern United States and have plans to tour a plantation—sugar plantations outside New Orleans or cotton plantations near Memphis. The owners of these places might have thought they had the good life, but was it really so good if slaves made it all possible? It is hard for me to appreciate the beauty of those houses, to fantasize living there.

I have read of comparisons between the social structure, South and North, which relied on slavery, and today's society, which relies on fossil fuels. It seems a useful comparison, if limited. It helps me understand how people who knew that slavery was egregiously wrong could still perpetuate it, because there is momentum in the system, because to suddenly end the enslavement of people would pull the whole society down. The comparison gives me a little cover as I continue to drive a car fueled by diesel and to heat my house with natural gas, as we grow deeper in understanding that we are creating a hot world for our children and grandchildren, a world that we ourselves wouldn't want to live in.

These were dark thoughts for a sunny day on the Au Sable River. I didn't share them with Tom. We can talk ourselves silly lamenting this, and the conversation degenerates into feelings of smugness. We, of course, Do The Right Thing—and yet, did we not drive eight hundred miles to a river in Michigan, when we have perfectly wonderful rivers to canoe in Minnesota?

Instead, I waved my arm airily and gestured toward a modest, somewhat shabby place and compared it with its too big *Better Homes and Gardens* neighbor and said, "I'd rather live there than in that place!" I learned how rash my declaration was when we passed the ramshackle cabin and saw that the windows were broken and the roof needed repair. Tom seemed to snort from the back of the canoe. "But still," I retorted, "it's the right size."

....

"What Is the Good Life?" might have been a unit in a social studies class in high school forty-three years ago, but it has taken me many years to see it is a question that serves best when it is not answered once and for all but returned to at intervals for renewed pondering.

I have come to see the question as kind of a koan, a Zen riddle that perplexes. "What is the good life?" can be a straightforward question, as we posed it in our youth and sought to answer it. Now, in midlife, we see it is unanswerable, as least in a forthright way. There are no boundaries to the question. Asking it will take you far. You will wander in trying to answer it.

Perhaps it can be stated a different way: "What? is the good life." This statement implies it is always good to question, that asking is more satisfying, ultimately, than answers, that a life that does not question is not a true life. Certainly, I agree with that. I grew up with adults who did not question or did not question enough, and I decided early that I did not want to live that way.

These two statements are restless. The askers never are at peace with known truths. Their minds roam unceasingly. Here is a statement that comes to rest: "What is: the good life." Never wanting more, never striving for more, never trying to accumulate stuff. Surely those seventeen-year-olds in Mr. Johnson's classroom, at least two of them, saw even then the glimmer of wisdom when it is asked this way.

The veracity of this statement is especially obvious when sitting in a canoe, making your way across sparkling blue water, with everything you will need for the night and the next morning stowed in Duluth packs wedged between thwarts. One's needs and desires are bounded by what is, and surely it is good, beauty, and grandeur apparent at every hand.

Acknowledgments

A TIP OF THE PADDLE FIRST TO THE LATE VIC GUSTAFSON, physical education instructor at Gustavus Adolphus College for nearly four decades. A pioneer in outdoor education before the endeavor even had a label, he taught canoeing and camping courses (for credit) at the college and awarded me a passing grade on the final test in my canoeing class even when I got wind bound on the far side of St. Peter's sewage treatment pond.

I owe much to my wonderful writing group, the core of which has been together eighteen years. We meet every other week to critique each other's work. The writers' discerning eyes have read every essay in this book, and their insights made the pieces stronger, richer, and clearer. Past and present members include Judy Helgen, Patti Isaacs, Gayla Marty, Paula Moyer, and Susan Narayan.

I am grateful to Erik Anderson, my editor at the University of Minnesota Press. His initial enthusiasm for the essays encouraged me to continue. As I completed the manuscript, his sense that something was still missing pressed me to make crucial connections that shaped the book in a surprising and satisfying way.

Thank you to my four children, Andy, Katie, John, and Christina Leaf. Once again I have mined their childhoods as fodder for my pen. They acquiesce to the exposure with humor and grace. A tip of the paddle (but not the canoe) to them, too.

Above all, I am indebted to my husband, Tom Leaf. With imagination and initiative, he plans every trip, organizes outfitters (if we need them) and maps, carries the canoe on portages, and navigates on white water. He can still flip a sixty-five-pound canoe, and he still wants me in the bow. Thanks, partner.

Sue Leaf is the author of *The Bullhead Queen: A Year on Pioneer Lake* (Minnesota, 2009); *A Love Affair with Birds: The Life of Thomas Sadler Roberts* (Minnesota, 2013); and *Potato City: Nature, History, and Community in the Age of Sprawl*. Trained as a zoologist, she writes on environmental topics, especially those close to her Minnesota home. She and her husband, Tom, have paddled the waters of North America together for forty years.